Policy Studies Institute
(The European Centre for Political Studies)

PARTNERS AND RIVALS IN WESTERN EUROPE: BRITAIN, FRANCE AND GERMANY

List of Contributors

Nicholas Bayne, formerly British Ambassador to Zaire, is now the British Permanent Representative to the OECD in Paris.

Caroline Bray is a former Research Fellow, European Centre for Political Studies and PSI.

David Gladstone is British Consul-General in Marseilles. In 1982—83 he was a Visiting Lecturer at the Civil Service College and a Senior Visiting Fellow at the European Centre for Political Studies.

Christopher Layton, formerly Director for Technology Policy in the EEC Commission, is the Editor of *New Democrat*.

Roger Morgan is Head of the European Centre for Political Studies.

Geoffrey Shepherd is Director of the Sussex European Research Centre at the University of Sussex.

Helen Wallace is a Research Fellow at the Royal Institute of International Affairs.

William Wallace is Director of Studies and Deputy Director of the Royal Institute of International Affairs.

Policy Studies Institute
(The European Centre for Political Studies)

Partners and Rivals in Western Europe: Britain, France and Germany

Edited by
Roger Morgan
Head of the European Centre for Political Studies
and
Caroline Bray
Former Research Fellow, European Centre for Political Studies

Gower

Published by

Gower Publishing Company Limited,
Gower House,
Croft Road,
Aldershot,
Hants GU11 3HR,
England.

Gower Publishing Company,
Old Post Road,
Brookfield,
Vermont 05036,
USA.

87-7911

British Library Cataloguing in Publication Data

Partners and Rivals in Western Europe : Britain, France and Germany.
  1. Europe——Foreign relations——1945—
  I. Morgan, Roger, *1932—*   II. Bray, Caroline
  III. European Centre for Political Studies
  327'.094   D1058

ISBN: 0 566 00938 8

Printed in Great Britain by
Blackmore Press, Shaftesbury, Dorset

Contents

List of Abbreviations

AFVG	Advanced Variable Geometry Aircraft
BDI	Bundesverband der deutschen Industrie
BILD	Bureau International de Liaison et de Documentation
CAP	Common Agricultural Policy
CBI	Confederation of British Industry
CDU	Christian Democratic Union
CEPT	European Committee on Posts and Telecommunications
CERN	Centre Européen de la Recherche Nucléaire
CETS	Committee of the European Telecommunications Services
CGT	Confédération Générale du Travail
CIEC	Conference on International Economic Cooperation
CIRAC	Centre d'Information et de Recherche sur l'Allemagne Contemporaine
COI	Central Office of Information
CNPF	Conseil National du Patronat Français
CNRS	Conseil National de la Recherche Scientifique
COPA	Comité des Organisations Professionnelles Agricoles
CSCE	Conference on Security and Cooperation in Europe
CSU	Christian Science Union
DGB	Deutscher Gewerkschaftsbund
ECS	European Communications Satellite
EC	European Community
ECSC	European Coal and Steel Community
EFTA	European Free Trade Association
ELDO	European Launcher Development Organisation

viii

EMS	European Monetary System
EMU	Economic and Monetary Union (of the EEC)
ENA	Ecole Nationale d'Administration
EPC	European Political Cooperation
ERDF	European Regional Development Fund
ESA	European Space Agency
ESPRIT	European Strategic Programme for Information Technology
ESRO	European Space Research Organisation
ETUC	European Trades Union Confederation
EUTELSAT	European Telecommunications Satellite
FAR	Force d'Action Rapide
FDP	Free Democratic Party
FIAT	Fabbricazione Italiana Automobili de Torino
GATT	General Agreement on Tariffs and Trade
IEA	International Energy Agency
ISDN	Integrated Services Digital Network
MARECS	Marine European Communications Satellite
MFA	Multi-Fibre Arrangement
MLF	Multilateral (nuclear) Force
MRCA	Multi-Role Combat Aircraft
MRG	Mouvement des Radicaux de Gauche
MRP	Mouvement Républicain Populaire
MTU	Motoren- und Turbinen Union
NATO	North Atlantic Treaty Organisation
NEC	National Executive Committee (of Labour Party)
OTS	Orbital Telecommunications Satellite
PAD	Pädagogischer Austauschdienst
PT	Postes et Télécommunications (formerly PTT = Postes Télégraphe Téléphone)
RACE	Research and Development in Advanced Communication Technologies in Europe
RPR	Rassemblement pour la République
SDP	Social Democratic Party

SGCI	Secrétariat-Général du Comité Interministeriel pour les Questions de Coopération Economique Européenne
SPD	Social Democratic Party of Germany
TNF	Theatre Nuclear Forces
TUC	Trades Union Congress
UDF	Union pour la Démocratie Française
UNICE	Union of Industries of the European Community
VLSI	Very Large Scale Integration
WEU	Western European Union

Preface
Roger Morgan

Observers of Western Europe have tended to regard it as axiomatic, at least since Britain's entry to the Community in 1973, that the relations between France, Britain and the Federal Republic of Germany are critical for the future of Europe. It is generally accepted that only if these three states are able to coordinate their policies can the European Community move towards closer unity, industrially, economically or politically; only if the three can adopt common positions on defence and security problems, as well as international economic issues can Western Europe hope to exercise any influence on the United States; and only if the three work together can Western Europe carry out the long-expressed aspiration of making a 'European voice' heard in world affairs.

Even though proponents of such cooperation between London, Paris and Bonn are usually scrupulous in rejecting any notion of a *directoire* for Europe, and careful to stress that trilateral action must be developed with tact and discretion so as not to offend the rest of the Community, there is a pervasive consciousness that the *lignes de force* in Western European affairs run between these three capitals. If there are strains or failures of communication, between any two of them, not only the triangle, but wider structures too, will be weakened.

This means that what we have to consider are three bilateral relationships — the Franco-German, the Anglo-German, and the Franco-British — each of which requires careful examination in its own right. The main questions to be answered in assessing whether each of these bilateral relationships is on the whole 'effective', or 'cooperative', 'good' or 'bad', include the following: How successfully do the two states in question cooperate in handling the problems they must handle together? How easily (and how successfully) do they embark together on joint ventures they do not really 'have' to undertake? How much trust or mistrust prevails, at the influential levels of government, administration, and society, between one country and the other?

When the three bilateral relationships are considered in these terms, it is obvious that each of them has many unique features and a distinctive quality or 'flavour' of its own. The Franco-German relationship in today's Europe is characterised by intensive and highly structured communication, provided for in the Elysée Treaty of 1963; it is also marked by a powerful and durable political determination, extending from the highest levels downwards, to overcome conflicts and to make Franco-German interdependence and cooperation — economic, diplomatic, strategic and cultural — into a permanent reality in an uncertain world. The Anglo-German relationship, in contrast, seems to proceed in a generally cooperative way with a considerably less formal structure of intergovernmental transactions: the British and West German governments appear to be committed to common objectives, at least in the fields of NATO defence and (up to a point) economic and industrial policies, even though their views on the policies and the future of the European Community diverge fairly widely. Finally, the relationship between London and Paris often seems to be marked by the age-old rivalry between two of the longest-established and proudest nation states in Europe: despite frequent high-level declarations of agreement (often justified) on many points, and despite good working relationships between important sections of the British and French governmental machines, there remains an overall impression of a degree of Anglo-French tension or even rivalry, which sometimes takes the form of competition for the goodwill of Germany.

In view of the idiosyncracies of each bilateral relationship as briefly sketched here, it is not surprising that most practitioners concerned with these issues, and the overwhelming majority of scholarly or other outside commentators, should have concentrated on only one relationship out of the three, and not attempted any comparative assessment. Each of the three relationships has been the subject of a very extensive flow of publications. This is particularly true of the Franco-German relationship, partly because of the commitment of the two governments to stimulate its fullest possible discussion, exploration, and public cultivation, but Anglo-German and Franco-British relations have also been fairly copiously studied. However, virtually no scholarly attention has been given to the *comparative* study of these three phenomena, nor to the further question of what kind of triangle they may add up to, either in the present or in the future.

If one reason for this neglect is the evident uniqueness of each bilateral relationship, which makes its study a matter for specialists, a further reason is the uncertainty (both of practitioners and of observers) about what, in the end, actually determines the character of each bilateral relationship.

In the Franco-German case, for instance, there have been a variety of explanations of exactly how and why the 'hereditary enemies' of earlier years have achieved such a cooperative relationship since the 1960s. Observers from other countries — including Britain which has at times felt excluded from an intimate partnership, and occasionally even threatened by it, especially on EC issues — have sometimes argued that the key to the striking reconciliation of France and Germany lies in the

1963 Treaty itself, with its elaborate provisions for conflict resolution by continuous consultation. Another explanation has been that the top political leaders of the two countries have understood each other particularly well, and that cooperation at lower levels has really flowed — treaty or no treaty — from their manifest commitment to bilateral cooperation. (This view was particularly associated with the long period, from 1974 to 1981, when President Giscard d'Estaing and Chancellor Helmut Schmidt held office: as a highly-placed British observer put it, commenting on a Franco-German exchange rate conflict in 1983, 'Giscard and Schmidt would have found a way to handle this'.) A third explanation is that significant elements in French and German society, after 1945, felt an overriding need to replace the horrible conflicts of the past by making Franco-German cooperation the basis of a new and better Europe. Lastly, a fourth and less idealistic theory is that 'states will be states' and that, quite irrespective of Treaty commitments, individual leaders, or shifts in public sentiment, France and Germany have been brought together by the hard facts of common interests: economic, political, and strategic.

It seemed to us that the only way to test these various explanations for the apparent effectiveness of the Franco-German relationship — and indeed, to form a serious judgement on how effective it has actually been — was to examine it from a number of angles, at the same time systematically comparing it with the other subjects of our enquiry, the Anglo-German and Franco-British relationships.

We have tried, starting with the relevant phenomena *within* each of the three countries — the salient features of the national economies, administrative traditions, and political systems — to proceed to a systematic comparison of the relationships *between* the countries, analysing the main elements of these relationships one by one.

This approach has dictated the structure of the book. After an introductory essay by William Wallace, the next Chapter places the present in context by surveying the development of relations between Britain, France, and Germany in the four decades since 1945 (an essential part of the background, not only because the situations and relationships of today and tomorrow often repeat those of yesterday, in varying degrees, but also because in these emotive questions so-called 'lessons of history' very often condition the attitudes and actions of political decision-makers — a point considered further in Chapter 4).

It is clear that the facts of economics, as well as the legacy of history, exercise a strong influence on relations between the three countries. Chapter 3 examines those aspects of the national economies of France, Britain and Germany which affect their mutual relations. On some of the central issues of economic philosophy, the three countries appear to be fairly sharply divided: Germany is firmly committed to a market economy (despite some elements of interventionist industrial policies, particularly at *Land* level); France believes in a larger degree of state intervention (even under Giscard, and even through the less strictly socialist phase of Mitterrand's presidency from 1984 onwards); and Britain under Mrs Thatcher pursues a more 'liberal' economic policy than even the Federal Republic, combined with a strong commitment to monetarism. As Dr Shepherd shows, however, these differences in economic doctrine mask a substantial degree of de facto convergence between the policies of economic management in the three countries: in terms of their influence on the propensity of the three to cooperate in economic policy, the differences of doctrine are less important than the objective degrees of interdependence between the three economies. In particular, the very high level of economic transactions between France and Germany — in terms both of trade and of investment — provides a strong impulse for bilateral cooperation, both in commercial and in monetary policy: it is no accident that the European Monetary System (as Chapter 9 shows in more detail) was established through Franco-German cooperation, from which Britain held back.

Chapter 4 examines a further factor which influences the possible scope for intergovernmental cooperation, namely the images and opinions which the people of each country have of the others. How do the 'lessons of history' play a part in shaping the perceptions of the French, the Germans and the British — perceptions both of each other and of their nation's historical identity? What images of the other countries are portrayed, assumed, or reinforced by the way the media report on current news? And what effects do historically conditioned stereotypes, media images and other sources have in influencing the readiness of the three nations to trust each other, as measured by a selection of opinion polls? As the evidence in this chapter indicates, a two-way process is at work: each national public's view of the other countries is influenced by the current and long-term state of diplomatic and other- high-level relations, as well as vice versa. When relations at governmental level are good, the public image of the nation concerned tends to be positive. However, governments are aware of the need to take account of public opinion, both in their own country and in their partner countries, for instance, in deciding what kind of stance in an international negotiation is likely to be politically advantageous or diplomatically effective. Thus they pay attention — more or less effectively — to opinion-formers within and outside the media.

This consideration leads to the range of governmental activities surveyed in Chapter 5, the attempt to win support and understanding in one's partner countries by promoting a favourable image of one's own. Cultural relations, as a dimension of external policy, have been pursued particularly actively in the Franco-German relationship (the traditional French emphasis on this branch of diplomacy coinciding with the Federal Republic's wish to promote a positive image of the new Germany), but similar activities also play an important part, as the chapter shows, in France's and Germany's relations with Britain.

The next three chapters deal with various aspects of the management of relations between the three capitals. Chapter 6 considers a critical dimension of this management process, namely the differing patterns of recruitment, training and professional role of the three countries' civil servants. Its starting-point is one which has been expressed by Robert Putnam: 'the norms and behaviour of Europe's senior civil servants reflect the type of education to which they have been exposed — the proud technocrat from the French *grandes écoles*, the relaxed humanists from Oxbridge, the formalistic, cautious lawyers of the traditional German *Juristenmonopol*'.[1] What do these differences of administrative culture or bureaucratic ethos amount to, and how do they affect the negotiation of agreements, and the general handling of relations, between the three capitals? David Gladstone's conclusion is that the officials of France and Germany, because of similarities between the two countries in training, constitutional norms, and administrative practice, find a basis for cooperation with each other more easily than with their British counterparts.

Is the same natural alignment between Paris and Bonn also true more generally of the national political élite — including ministers, parliamentarians, and leading figures in powerful interest groups — within which the national administrative cadres are (in varying ways) situated? Chapter 7, which considers this question, concludes that on the whole, within a very complex and differentiated pattern, the two national élites with the easiest communication are those of Germany and Britain. Despite some striking cases of Franco-German intimacy at the highest level (between de Gaulle and Adenauer, or Giscard and Schmidt), and the ministerial and administrative communication that has flowed from them, Franco-German contact at the parliamentary or party political level has not been an important motor of cooperation. Again, the relations between Britain and France, from the level of heads of government through those of ministers, parliamentarians, party organisations and interest groups, have been handicapped by a number of obstacles, including linguistic barriers, different social habits, and a historical legacy of mistrust and even rivalry between the two countries. It is thus the relationship between the political élites of Britain and Germany which appears the most cooperative and open. This relationship has been aided by common approaches to many policy issues (including, in particular, defence), by the existence of effective channels of non-governmental communication (notably the annual Königswinter Conferences), and by the active participation of British and German parliamentarians, businessmen, journalists and others in a variety of 'Atlanticist' (and usually American-led) discussion fora from which the French élites have substantially kept themselves apart.

Chapter 8, taking into account the factors analysed so far, focuses on the precise ways in which the three governments conduct their relations with each other. How far does the volume of political and administrative resources invested in the Franco-German partnership make it a 'special relationship'? How far is it the procedures laid down in the Franco-German Treaty of Cooperation which give this relationship its particular intimacy? And how effectively do the Coordinators for Franco-German Relations, or the corresponding officials (with less formal status) now responsible for overseeing Franco-British and Anglo-German relations, influence what happens? These questions are answered, with reference to some of the important issues that have required intergovernmental handling between the three capitals, and the strengths and weaknesses of each arrangement are assessed.

After this consideration, in the first half of the book, of the domestic factors affecting the relationships, and of the channels available for non-governmental communication or for the management of official intergovernmental relations, the remaining chapters are devoted to specific areas of policy.

Chapter 9, which considers the performances of France, Britain and Germany as members of the European Community, assesses how far the intimate Franco-German partnership at the heart of the European integration process has been complemented by a corresponding British dialogue with either Germany or France. In broad terms, dialogue of comparable intensity has failed to develop in either case, partly because of Britain's domestic hesitations about Community membership, the long-running issue of Britain's budget contribution, and Britain's reluctance to join the EMS. If the Fontainebleau agreement of June 1984 provides a lasting settlement at least to the budget issue, the prospects for a better balanced triangular relationship will be more substantial.

Chapter 10 examines the roles of the three countries in the debate on international economic management, and in particular the degree of coordination of their respective policies towards the annual Western economic summits of the last ten years. Again the picture is one of fairly close Franco-German coordination particularly during the Giscard—Schmidt period which saw the first six of the annual summits (during a period when the British prime ministership was held by three successive incumbents). The author, who writes from intimate involvement as an official in international economic diplomacy, gives as his personal opinion that British policy should come closer to the Franco-German preference for more institutionalised consultative arrangements.

Chapter 11 turns to a different aspect of the economic relationships between the three countries: their mutual dealings in the field of high technology. Writing from his experience as a former European Commission official with responsibility for dealing from Brussels with all three governments, Christopher Layton confirms the judgement given in Chapter 3 that their ostensible differences in economic philosophy are not as important in practice as they seem. They are not the major reasons for failure of London, Paris and Bonn to cooperate more closely in the high technology area. In the aerospace sector, British hesitations, and Rolls Royce's preference for American partners, were serious handicaps to European cooperation, although the current prospects for the 150-seater A320 Airbus, planned with trilateral support at last, are good. In the vital sector of information technology, progress in Anglo-Franco-German cooperation has again been beset by hesitations and rivalries, so that Europe has had great difficulty in standing up to American and Japanese domination of the market. In computers, Europe has been decisively overtaken, and the same is likely to happen in telecommunications unless current national attitudes change. In space technology, finally, early divisions between the three European countries — with Britain again more interested in working with American than with European partners — were to some extent made good by cooperative work through the European Space Agency. Satellite TV technology, however, has opened up new divisions between Britain, on the one hand, and France and Germany on the other. These case studies illustrate the difficulties, but also the necessity, of European cooperation, led by London, Paris and Bonn, if Europe is to have a future in high technology.

The last two chapters of the book deal with the interrelated issues of foreign policy and defence. As Chapter 12 shows by surveying the foreign policies of the three countries over the last twenty years, divergences between the three have become progressively less marked, and the consultative systems for managing potential problems have become progressively more effective. In this respect, the Paris—Bonn relationship has again developed in a more sophisticated way than either of the others, having worked out means for reconciling very divergent national policies (towards the USA or East—West relations, for instance), over a long period of intense bilateral consultations. The Anglo-French and Anglo-German consultative systems, however, have in recent years become more effective too, particularly as a result of Britain's membership of the Community and the associated Political Cooperation system; and the convergence of French, British, and German interests in an increasingly unstable world environment has also promoted cooperation along all three sides of the triangle.

The same factors, as Chapter 13 shows, have been at work in the area of defence policy. Here, as in international affairs generally, the relationships between the three countries have been profoundly affected by the actions and policies of outside powers, notably of course the two superpowers. This chapter underlines the critical role of Germany in European security, and the varying attitudes towards defence of France and Britain. 'Security policy' means different things to the geopolitically exposed Federal Republic and to the two nuclear powers of Western Europe (both still more engaged in non-European commitments than Bonn, although this is changing). Closer Western European cooperation in defence, as in economic policy (and indeed in military production, which links the two), depends essentially on London, Paris and Bonn, and the prospects for this cooperation, with the three bilateral dialogues merging into one, are currently not unhopeful. The aim of the study as a whole, with its sequence of analyses of the London—Bonn—Paris triangle from many different angles (each one of which, we have become very aware, would merit an entire book to itself), is to place the reader in a position to judge the strengths and weaknesses of each bilateral relationship, the reasons why they are what they are, and the prospects and problems of making this whole triangle into a stable foundation for a more united Europe.

Our attempt to explore the topic, and to indicate some policy options, was made possible by a financial grant to the European Centre for Political Studies from the Leverhulme Trust, which is most gratefully acknowledged. The research team are also indebted to a number of politicians, officials and other experts in all three of the countries concerned, who have answered our questions, raised questions of their own, and helped us in one way or another with our research.

We have benefited from the chance of discussing our work, as it progressed, at a number of useful seminars: a meeting convened by the Universities Association for Contemporary European Studies at Reading University; a seminar for senior officials at the Civil Service College in Sunningdale; and a discussion with a group of experts at the Franco-German Institute in Ludwigsburg.

Particular thanks are due to Dr Robert Picht, not only for arranging the last-mentioned discussion at the Institute which he directs, but also for his friendly interest in the whole project and for reading and commenting on the draft manuscript. Professors Geoffrey Goodwin (London) and Alfred Grosser (Paris) were also kind enough to read and comment on the manuscript as a whole, and individual chapters were the subject of useful comments by Peter Holmes, John Pinder, Anne Stephens, Henrik Uterwedde and several government officials who have to be thanked anonymously. No-one but the authors of individual chapters, of course, is responsible for the views or conclusions they contain.

Thanks are also due to Margaret Cornell, for editing the manuscript in her usual rigorous way, to Sandra Jeddy for typing and retyping large parts of it, and to Amanda Trafford for her many contributions to the success of the whole enterprise. Finally, as well as thanking all the authors for their parts in a complicated collective operation, I should like to pay particular tribute to Caroline Bray for all her work in collecting material, chasing both references and witnesses, and contributing to the book in many ways besides writing the two chapters that appear under her name.

Roger Morgan
1985

Notes

1. R.D. Putnam, *The Comparative Study of Political Elites* (Englewood Cliffs, New Jersey, Prentice Hall, 1976), p. 95.

1 Introduction: the Shaping of Close Relationships
William Wallace

During the course of the 1970s the relationship between Paris and Bonn came to be seen as different in quality and intensity from other bilateral relations between West European states. Within the multilateral frameworks of the European Community and the Atlantic Alliance, the Franco-German relationship represented an exclusive and privileged partnership, compared only to the Anglo-American 'special relationship' of the post-war years. The British government, having at last succeeded in entering the European Community in 1973, failed to establish as close or as politically charged a relationship either with Paris or with Bonn. In the late 1970s British officials and ministers were given to expressions of bafflement and frustration at the difficulties they faced in breaking into the 'Paris—Bonn axis', either in Paris or in Bonn.

The aim of this study is to examine this triangle of bilateral relations; to ask in what ways the Franco-German relationship *was* closer than the relationship of either with Britain during this period; and to consider how far the pattern of relations observed reflected long- or short-term factors, or political, economic or security interests. Even after the signature of the Elysée Treaty between France and Germany in 1963, it had not been universally self-evident that the Franco-German link had become intrinsically closer than that which either country had with its other major partners; nor that the relationship was necessarily proof against serious differences on policy or shifts in the international environment. The German government opposed the French withdrawal from the integrated NATO structure in 1966, just as it had opposed the French government during the quarrel on the structure and financing of the EEC the previous year. On this, as on a range of Community issues, the EEC member states regularly split 5—1 (not 4—2) with Germany or the Netherlands leading the opposition to French proposals. When Britain renewed its application to join the European Community in 1967, the German government again offered its support, against French resistance. The French government's uncertainty about committing itself fully to the link with Bonn was reflected both in the ill-fated de Gaulle—Soames conversations of early 1969, and in the more successful and potentially more far-reaching consultations between Heath and Pompidou in 1971—72. In all three capitals — and elsewhere within Western Europe — there were expectations that British entry would create a triangular relationship, a potential *directoire*. Why were those expectations unfulfilled? Should we look to underlying geopolitical, historical and cultural factors to explain the asymmetrical relations between these three interdependent neighbours? Or to less permanent economic, industrial and security concerns? Or to such short-term factors as political leadership, élite contacts and personal commitments and assumptions?

Bilateral relations are shaped partly by long-term continuities and partly by immediate actions and concerns. The geographical relationship between these three neighbouring countries has condemned them to close relations which follow patterns and issues recognisable over centuries: France's concern for its weak and undefined northern frontier; English concern to keep open its access to continental trade. The Franco-German relationship is fundamentally between northern France and southern Germany, focusing around the Rhine and its French and German tributaries. The Anglo-German relationship remains most intense between eastern England and northern Germany, focusing around the North Sea ports and their long-established trade. Hanoverians and Brunswickers fought among the British regiments at Waterloo; regiments from Württemberg and the Palatinate marched with Napoleon to Moscow. Britain's island position has given its leaders a certain detachment from the continent, a certain wariness about 'the continental commitment'.[1] For France and Germany, detachment is impossible: the necessities of continental politics, the proponents of Franco-German cooperation argue, allow no third choice between hostility and active partnership.[2]

Geopolitical theorists have derived from such observations an almost determinist view of history, in which little influence remains for the actions of governments and the initiatives of statesmen. Yet any study of European history since the Second World War must call into play the impact of personality and political leadership, either as a great exception, in the interpretation which some have given to de Gaulle, or as a continuing factor shaping and reshaping the constraints under which governments operate as they interact. Adenauer and de Gaulle, Heath and Pompidou, Giscard and Schmidt, stand out as examples of personal ties between heads of government which altered the configuration of relations; other less successful personal links, with their suspicions and misunderstandings, altered prevailing patterns for the worse. The constraints under which such leaders operate derive from the domestic political consensus, from the prevailing assumptions of their national media and the prevailing images and stereotypes — among the élite and the wider public — of their partner countries and their governments, as well as from established patterns of trade and industrial collaboration and the assumptions which underpin them. Short-term and longer-term factors interact, as deliberate political action reshapes prevailing images for better or for worse, as negotiations on defence or industrial collaboration are successfully concluded or break down. But political systems are maintained by the inertia of established assumptions, which can only be reshaped — revolutions and wars excepted — by cumulative action and experience over extended periods of time. Throughout this study we shall therefore be concerned to disentangle, where we can, the transitory and the permanent, the short-term impact and the long-term trend: to ask how far each relationship in the early 1980s has been shaped and set by the experiences of the last 30 years and more, or remains open to rapid redirection by voluntary action and political decision.

The cautious social scientist will shy away from such concepts as national stereotypes. They are unavoidably imprecise and extraordinarily difficult to measure. Yet perceptions — and misperceptions — are accepted to be a vital factor in international relations; and perceptions necessarily rest upon operating assumptions, general images and expectations of behaviour in relating to other groups. The press finds it convenient and necessary to refer to 'French attitudes' or 'German reactions', generalising about patterns of behaviour. So too do officials, ministers, even prime ministers in their discussions and documents.

Such images and stereotypes form part of the conventional wisdom of each country's political culture, passed on from one generation to another and from the élite to the wider public through the teaching and interpretation of history, through reinforcing experience and through the constant repetition of standard phrases and descriptions. But they are not immutable. Divergent experience will modify attitudes and expectations; so too will deliberate attempts to alter them by political rhetoric and action. The formative assumptions of adolescence and early adulthood differ from one age cohort to another, as a generation rises to positions of influence for whom the First World War is history and the Second World War something about which their parents told them. The seven years of intensive Franco-German collaboration overseen by Giscard d'Estaing and Helmut Schmidt may well successfully have modified expectations about cooperation and commitment within both governments, thus leaving behind a 'different reality' from that which they inherited. Continuing British ambivalence about the 'European commitment' on the other hand may have served to reinforce existing assumptions within the French and German élites about British behaviour, feeding back into the British debate as a perception of coolness towards Britain which, in the absence of evidence or action to the contrary, further reinforces that ambivalence.

Any study of intergovernmental relations must begin by considering what are the basic dimensions of each relationship. What is the key to a bilateral partnership: political relations between the two governments, or between the wider political élites; economic relations, competitive or complementary; convergent or divergent interests in defence and security; or some particular combination of these three? What is fundamental and what marginal in building a sense of mutual commitment? The Marxian historian, and the political pragmatist, will incline to dismiss the rhetoric of political speeches and the atmosphere engendered by informal meetings as part of the superstructure of real politics which must be built upon the firm foundations of economic and security interests. Yet, as the following chapters will argue, it is by no means self-evident that French and German interests in economic or security matters were easily compatible, or more often compatible than British and German interests, for example. The success of the Franco-German relationship over the past 20 years is a record of determination to accommodate divergent interests through positive political action, to explain or to tolerate differences and to minimise their impact; not a simple record of convergence in economic, industrial, political or security interests and outlooks.

Relations among governments and political systems are conducted at a large number of different levels, from the symbolic exchanges of heads of state to the petty transactions of junior officials and the routine exchanges of news reports, parliamentary delegations, even school parties and language teachers. The intensity of interaction among the highest levels of state and government has markedly increased within Western Europe during the last two decades, both bilaterally and multilaterally. The Elysée Treaty of 1963 instituted the first regular bilateral summit, between Paris and Bonn, to be joined in the course of the 1970s by similar bilateral summits between Britain and both France and Germany, and later extended by all three to include Italian heads of government in this developing bilateral network. Heads of government and senior ministers of the three governments were also meeting by the end of the 1970s in three European Councils per year; in the annual 'Western' economic summits, initiated on the proposal of Giscard d'Estaing in 1975; in less regularly calendared NATO summits, and in occasional *ad hoc* summit meetings such as the four-power gathering in Guadeloupe in December 1978 and the restricted 'North— South' summit of heads of government at Cancun in October 1981.

Partly as a consequence of such high-level gatherings, but more importantly as a consequence of intergovernmental business to be transacted within the European Communities and within NATO, ministers and officials — from senior to junior, in multi-layered relationships — became caught up in a close and complex network of contacts. When heads of government meet, their agenda represents the digested consultations of some hundreds of officials and ministers, and their assumptions and expectations are filtered through the presentation of the issues in their national media and the preconceptions of their parties and political élites. In turn, their conclusions, their agreements or their failure to agree, are absorbed into the working assumptions of their national administrations and filtered back into the press and the political debate. We therefore have to examine the different layers of these intricate relationships and their interaction – even if we forego any hope of demonstrating a clear or verifiable pattern of causality between one layer and another.

Historical interpretation can never be entirely scientific. One cannot *prove* that a sequence of developments necessarily led to the consequences observed, however carefully the circumstantial evidence is marshalled. So with this study: we do not claim to be able to establish conclusive answers, least of all within the confines of a single volume. Our more modest aims are to suggest where the answers to such questions may lie, to test the soundness of the conventional wisdom, and so to provoke a more vigorous debate.

Most comparable previous studies have focused on a single bilateral relationship, or on a wider balance among powers within a wider system. We are examining the development of particularly intense bilateral relations between the three leading West European countries, set in the context of the increasing intensity of intergovernmental contacts among all West European governments, societies and economies, and – more widely, though less intensively – among the advanced industrial democracies as a whole. As will become clear in the chapters which follow, the London–Paris–Bonn triangle is not equilateral: it represents, rather, a tangle of multiple asymmetries, with distinctive patterns in different dimensions and distinctive densities from pole to pole.

In spite of the expectations aroused in the early 1970s, the triangle has not yet become as firmly fixed as the three bilateral relationships. There have been trilateral meetings from time to time, some of which still continue under differing criteria of visibility or secrecy. But there is little sign of an emerging European *directoire*. A triangular relationship, some participants would argue, is intrinsically more difficult to manage than a bilateral link: two's company, three's a crowd. The politics of these three relationships might thus be envisaged as one of competitive partnership, with recurring possibilities for shifting the balance. Thus British governments have swung from Paris to Bonn and back in their search for a reliable European interlocutor; thus Pompidou in 1970–72, and perhaps potentially Mitterrand in 1981–82, looked to a closer relationship with Britain to counterbalance a less secure or mutually confident relationship with Bonn.

To an extent the three countries have been pushed closer together in the early 1980s by changing external circumstances. In the 1960s and 1970s the United States remained for Britain – and to a lesser extent for Germany – the alternative key partner, while French governments flirted with the attractions of *la troisième voie*, clinging to the idea of a special relationship with Moscow and a special role in the Third World. Within a narrower perspective it is possible to argue that France and Germany were pushed together by the unavailability of

Britain as an alternative partner and by their mutual need for partners in a situation of economic and political vulnerabilities.

The external environment has changed, however, cumulatively but qualitatively, over the last five to ten years. United States administrations preoccupied with the Caribbean and the Pacific as well as with their strategic relationship with the USSR have paid declining attention to the interests of Britain or Federal Germany. The Soviet Union has lost interest in political flirtation with France, while becoming increasingly interested in political relations with West Germany. The shifting balance of forces in the Arab—Israeli conflict has encouraged a convergence of views among these three governments, and a divergence of views between the three and the US Administration. The impact of Japanese and American competition in the advanced industries has been felt in Germany as well as in Britain and in France. Bilateral links, and triangular relations, are necessarily affected by the interventions and reactions of other parties. For each of these three governments, its relationship with the other two has been among the most important dimensions of its external relations. But for none of them have these links been sufficiently dominant for other ties to be neglected or ignored. The changing impact of American policy must therefore be of repeated concern throughout this volume and so, less frequently, must be the policies and actions of the other member governments of the European Community, of the Soviet Union and its East European allies, and of Japan.

Any study of particular relationships involves a degree of abstraction from the complex interdependencies of international politics. The contexts within which these three close partners played out their policies are examined in the chapters which follow: the European Community and the interventions of its other member governments; the Atlantic Alliance and its subordinate groupings; the East—West relationship within Europe; the institutional structure of international economic management. But these are not our main focus. They form for our purposes the background to the intense interactions between three countries which have come to regard themselves as the key to the stability and future development of Western Europe, and which are regarded in similar terms by their other partners.

Notes

1. *See* M. Howard, *The Continental Commitment* (Harmondsworth, Penguin Books, 1974).
2. R. Picht (ed.), *Das Bündnis im Bündnis, Deutsch—Französische Beziehungen im internationalen Spannungsfeld* (Berlin, Severin and Siedler, 1982).

2 The Historical Background 1955-85
Roger Morgan

This book is mainly concerned with issues of the present, and it also looks to the future. However, very few contemporary issues can be understood without some knowledge of their historical background, and any realistic attempt to assess what is likely to happen, or to say what *should* happen, in the future needs to take account of the past as well. The purpose of this chapter is to describe the historical developments which have led to the situation of the 1980s, so that the issues and problems analysed in the ensuing chapters can be seen in their historical context.

The survey which follows attempts to provide sufficient information on the historical developments of the last 30 years to allow the reader to assess the significance and weight of the arguments on specific issues which will be presented in the remaining chapters of the book. The reader who is mainly interested in the present situation and its likely future evolution will not want to be told in detail why France and Germany signed a Treaty of Cooperation in 1963, or what was the specific international constellation which brought the Federal Republic into NATO in 1955, or the United Kingdom into the European Community in 1973. However, the fact that these things happened, and the significance which different parties attached to them at the time and since are, in reality, important elements of the contemporary situation.

As well as providing a purely factual survey of events, this chapter will try to give a sense of the overall evolution of each bilateral relationship, and of the development of the whole London–Paris–Bonn 'triangle' and its international context, through the successive phases of the story since the 1950s. The interpretation offered here, although necessarily brief and impressionistic, should allow the reader not only to become aware of what has actually happened in the past and why things have become as they are, but also to appreciate what is new and what is *déjà vu* in the issues and situations we face in the present and may meet in the future.[1]

The survey begins in the mid-1950s. The year 1955 marked the starting-point of the development of relations between the United Kingdom, France and the Federal Republic of Germany as we know them today: namely, the Federal Republic's accession to NATO and the Conference of Messina which began the process leading to the Treaty of Rome, introducing a pattern of relations between the three countries of which some aspects have remained unchanged. Developments *before* 1955 have, of course, continued to exert an influence (not least in the attitudes and perceptions of decision-makers and others), but the important turning-point was in or about that year. The period from 1955 to the mid-1980s in fact falls into three distinct sections which will be discussed in turn. The first runs from 1955 until 1963, the year of the Franco-German Treaty of Cooperation and of de Gaulle's rejection of the first British attempt to join the European Community; the second runs from 1963 to 1974, the year when Heath, Pompidou and Brandt were replaced by Wilson, Giscard d'Estaing and Schmidt, and when the European economy turned from growth into recession; and the third runs from 1974 to the present.

1955—63

Heads of government
FRG: Adenauer.
France: Mendès-France, 1954—55; Edgar Faure, 1955—56; Mollet, 1956—57; Bourgès-Manoury, 1957; Gaillard, 1957—58; Pflimlin, 1958; de Gaulle from 1958.
UK: Churchill, 1951—55; Eden, 1955—57; Macmillan, 1957—63.

In many ways, the contemporary relationship between Britain, France, and the Federal Republic begins in 1955. In international law, this was the year in which the Federal Republic was accepted as an equal partner with Britain and France; Germany regained a degree of sovereignty, saw the end of the Occupation Statute, and became a member of the Western European Union and NATO. In economic terms, 1955 saw Germany's 'economic miracle' in full swing and a national economy which was moving from desperately poor beginnings towards comparability with that of France and of Britain. Politically, 1955 was the year when Britain and France came to terms with the idea of West Germany as sovereign and rearmed, and as having rights as well as obligations: in exchange for Germany's promised contribution to Western defence, Britain and France pledged themselves to back Germany's national aspiration for political reunification. In Britain's case, this pledge was accompanied by a further commitment, under the Western European Union Treaty, to keep a specified number of divisions in Germany for 50 years, the duration of the treaty. This commitment — quite without precedent in the entire history of Britain's relations with the continent — marked a realisation that Britain's future security was inextricably tied up with that of the continent, and also implied a degree of political commitment too.

Meanwhile, France and Germany were developing their own mutual commitment of economic integration. The European Coal and Steel Community (ECSC), established in 1952, had succeeded in keeping the idea of European integration alive while the more grandiose schemes for a European Defence Community and an associated European Political Community rose (1950–53) and fell (1954). The next stage of attempts at European integration began with the Conference of Messina (June 1955) when the six member states of the ECSC took the first steps towards the Treaty of Rome (March 1957), which led to the European Economic Community's inauguration in January 1958. France and the Federal Republic played central roles in this process: Britain, which had boycotted the ECSC and which withdrew its representative from the working meetings which followed the Messina Conference, did not.

The late 1950s were thus a period in which a new pattern of relations in Western Europe was taking shape and settling down. France and Germany were deepening their economic interdependence and the political intimacy which accompanied and, in part, caused it. Britain and Germany were developing an increasingly harmonious relationship, embedded in their joint membership of NATO. Between France and Britain (both by now embarked on the process of being nuclear-armed powers) there were differences of perspective, which were accentuated by the experience of the Suez crisis of 1956.

On the *Franco-German* side of this complex also, a certain tension resulted from the fact that Germany relied heavily on American protection, while France resented the policy of the United States (in Indo-China up to 1954, in North Africa in 1955–62, and in NATO affairs throughout the whole period) as being uncooperative or domineering. This Franco-German difference of course reflected the fact that Germany's concerns were almost entirely European, while France was in the throes of decolonisation and the process of post-colonial redefinition of relations in the outside world. The scope for friction with the United States, in France's worldwide range of action, was obviously greater than in the European theatre which concerned Germany.

Having accepted German rearmament with great reluctance, France during this period worked with Germany, Britain and the other Western allies in the framework of the NATO command structures established in the early 1950s. One episode in the history of Franco-German military discussions, which was to find echoes in later years, occurred almost at the end of the Fourth Republic: in 1957–58, during the prime ministership of Félix Gaillard, Adenauer and his Defence Minister Franz-Josef Strauss held substantial discussions with their French counterparts about the possibility of Franco-German cooperation on nuclear weapons, with France providing the warheads and Germany taking the lead in rocket research. Discussion of this politically unrealistic project was ended by the terminal crisis of the Fourth Republic, and, under de Gaulle, Franco-German cooperation took a different form.

Once France was freed from its costly military commitment in Algeria (July 1962), de Gaulle felt able to build actively on his well cultivated relationship with Adenauer (cemented by the latter's largely unjustified apprehensions of possible softness both in Washington and in London during the Berlin crisis of 1958—62) and to draw Germany into the Treaty of Cooperation signed at the Elysée Palace on 22 January 1963. (The year 1962 had also seen the rejection of de Gaulle's proposal for a European political secretariat separate from the institutions of the European Community — the 'Fouchet Plan' — and the immensely successful visits to France by Adenauer and to Germany by de Gaulle.) The Elysée Treaty committed the two governments to regular consultation in all major areas of policy and to regular twice-yearly meetings at summit level, as well as intensive consultations between the two national bureaucracies, designed to ensure that cooperation was maintained even when administrations changed.

A difference of perspective between Paris and Bonn was, however, apparent when the Bundestag, rightly sensing that de Gaulle wished to detach Germany from its close alliance with the United States, refused to ratify the Treaty until it had been amplified by a preamble reaffirming the priority of Germany's commitment to the Atlantic Alliance (June 1963): this profoundly contradicted the original purpose of the Treaty. There was also some German reluctance to support de Gaulle's veto of British membership of the European Community (imposed in the month the Franco-German Treaty was signed), although Adenauer's government ultimately went along with de Gaulle's policy.

The *Franco-British* relationship, which reached an open crisis on this question in January 1963, had meanwhile traversed other difficulties too. Britain's refusal in the early 1950s to join the European Defence Community continued to be resented in France, and this British rejection of a commitment to the continent helped to cement France's direct *rapprochement* with Germany.

A graver crisis in Anglo-French relations occurred in 1956—57 with the failure of the two countries' joint military operation against the Suez Canal. While Britain retrospectively blamed France for instigating this abortive expedition (planned by France and Israel with considerable British collusion, and designed partly to preserve France's position in North Africa), France bitterly resented Britain's readiness to abandon the campaign, under American pressure, before Egypt had been defeated. After the Suez failure, while Britain under Macmillan reacted by working energetically to re-establish good relations with the United States, France in contrast strove to achieve greater independence from the USA, in part by developing the European Community in partnership with Germany. France also resented Britain's collaboration with the United States in offering Anglo-American 'good offices' in resolving a French conflict with Tunisia (the bombing of Sakhiet), which arose early in 1958 from the Algerian war.

These contrasting perspectives set the scene for an acute deterioration in Franco-British relations in the following years, when Britain reversed its previous policy of indifference to the European Community and applied in 1961 to join it. One of the decisive issues was again that of relations with the United States. In late 1962 de Gaulle, confident that he could lead Germany and the rest of Europe into a position of independence from America, appeared to be under the impression that Macmillan had agreed (at a critical meeting at Rambouillet in October) to collaborate with France rather than America on nuclear defence. Two months later, the Nassau Agreement confirmed the priority given by London to the Anglo-American relationship in defence questions, and this helped to provoke de Gaulle's veto on Britain's E C membership in January 1963. As a result, the quality of the Anglo-French political relationship was seriously damaged.

The *Anglo-German* relationship, on the other hand, had proceeded smoothly and cooperatively during the same period, but without great political intimacy. Adenauer had little personal sympathy with the British, who had not only removed him from the Mayorship of Cologne in 1946 but, more importantly, were not part of his Europe in the way that the Italians were under de Gasperi and his successors, or the French under Schuman, Mollet or de Gaulle; Britain was also much less important to him than the United States. None the less, Anglo-German cooperation within the framework of NATO was satisfactory, and economic relations between the two countries also developed as the West German economy grew.

The Berlin crisis which was provoked by Khrushchev's ultimatum of November 1958, and intensified by the building of the Berlin Wall in August 1961, led to some difficult moments in Anglo-German relations (as well as a cementing of Franco-German ones): from 1959, the British election year, until 1962 when the Berlin issue led to a memorable clash in Adenauer's relations with President Kennedy, British policy gave the impression of readiness to compromise with Soviet demands on Berlin in a way which Adenauer found very alarming. Indeed, throughout the whole period from 1955 to 1963, when Britain under Eden and Macmillan appeared ready to consider concessions to the Soviet Union while Germany insisted rigidly on a tough position both on Berlin and on non-recognition of the GDR, there was a permanent undercurrent of tension in Anglo-German relations.

This tension contributed to the crisis in which Adenauer acquiesced in de Gaulle's veto of Britain's membership of the European Community. Indeed, the events of January 1963, when de Gaulle signed the Treaty of Cooperation with Germany, vetoed Britain's Community membership (with little opposition from Bonn), and issued a challenge to the American 'grand design' for the Atlantic Alliance (a point which *did* provoke considerable German reservation), forced the relationships between the West European countries into a new pattern which was to prove fairly durable.

1963—74

Heads of government
FRG: Adenauer, —1965; Erhard, 1965—66; Kiesinger, 1966—69;
Brandt, 1969—74.
France: de Gaulle —1969; Pompidou, 1969—74.
UK: Douglas-Home, 1963—64; Wilson, 1964—70; Heath, 1970—74.

In the aftermath of de Gaulle's challenge of 1963 both to his European
partners and to Europe's American ally, Western Europe continued to
be dominated by a sense that France was setting the pace of events.
Fortified by his close relationship with Germany (despite the German
misgivings outlined above), the French President continued to impose
his will on European and NATO developments. He compromised the
progress of the six-nation European Community by his 'empty chair'
boycott of Community institutions in 1965—66, which was ended in
January 1966 by the so-called 'Luxembourg compromise', giving member states the right to veto Community decisions. He then threw NATO
into confusion by his announcement that the alliance's headquarters
must move from Paris (it moved to Brussels in 1967), and that France
was withdrawing from the integrated military command. He further
proclaimed France's mission of freeing Europe from the 'double hegemony' of the two superpowers, and illustrated this by well publicised
visits to Moscow in 1966 and to Romania in 1968 (the latter visit interrupted by the student revolts in France which heralded the end of de
Gaulle's ascendancy and his resignation in April 1969).

To the irritation of Washington and the alarm of Bonn, in this period
France thus took over in a more grandiose form the international role
which Britain had occasionally assumed under Churchill and Macmillan
during the 1950s: that of the would-be mediator between East and
West. Before the 1960s were out, however, Bonn itself had assumed
this role, and the *Ostpolitik* pursued by Brandt (a policy of 'small steps'
while Brandt was Foreign Minister under Kiesinger in 1966—69) accelerated under his chancellorship to the negotiation of treaties with
Warsaw, Moscow and East Berlin in 1969—72.

By this time — 'the era of negotiations', as President Nixon called it
— the improvement of East—West relations had been adopted as a
general goal of the Western Alliance, which endorsed the Harmel
Report of 1967 including détente as well as deterrence in NATO's
goals. The 'internal' affairs of Western Europe were also in a sense
tidied up, when negotiations for British entry to the EEC were renewed
in 1970 (after a further French veto in 1967) and led Britain into
membership in January 1973.

The *Franco-German* relationship was at the heart of these developments. As long as Adenauer remained in office, broad German support
for French policies could be relied on (though not without some

reservations on Adenauer's part), and even after he reluctantly retired in 1965 (complying with a condition laid down by the Free Democratic Party for joining his last coalition in 1963), the habits and mechanisms of consultation resulting from the 1963 treaty ensured at least a degree of continuity. It is true that Adenauer's successor Erhard deviated from the Gaullist idea of a 'European Europe' with which Adenauer had shown much sympathy. In 1963–64 he negotiated actively with the United States on a multilateral nuclear force (MLF), which some elements in the Kennedy Administration promoted in order to strengthen West Germany's links with NATO. However, these 'Atlanticist' leanings on Erhard's part were counteracted by the pressure of the so-called 'German Gaullists' in his own party (including ex-Chancellor Adenauer and ex-Defence Minister Strauss); by the fact that the Johnson Administration withdrew the whole idea of the MLF at the end of 1964; and ultimately also by the financial crisis (linked with the issue of offset costs for American troops in Germany) which led to the downfall of the Erhard government the following year. In defence matters, Germany's relationship with the United States was thus not reinforced as it might have been by the MLF, but, on the other hand, the relationship with France was not developed either.

In Germany's 'grand coalition' government of 1966–69, there were several ministers who attached great importance to good relations with France — including Chancellor Kiesinger and Franz-Josef Strauss, who re-entered the cabinet as Finance Minister. But the Social Democratic ministers, led by Brandt (the Vice-Chancellor and Foreign Minister), gave priority to the new aim of establishing a dialogue with Germany's Eastern neighbours, at the same time as maintaining close contact with the United States on such sensitive issues as the Nuclear Non-Proliferation Treaty currently being negotiated with the Soviet Union.

Although Franco-German relations had been active under Kiesinger and de Gaulle, an even more active phase began when they were replaced by Brandt and Pompidou in 1969. The combination of growing German economic predominance and a more active German policy towards the East led to French concern about how the power of Germany could be contained and channelled into Western purposes. (Indeed, the personal relationship between Brandt and Pompidou was not one of mutual confidence.) The establishment of the EC's Economic and Monetary Union (EMU) in 1973 was one response to this situation (though the weakness of the franc forced it to leave the EMU currency 'snake' in 1974); France's readiness to admit the UK to the Community — confirmed when Pompidou and Heath met in May 1971 — was another.

The *Anglo-French* part of the European complex took some time to recover from the débâcle of January 1963. The Labour Party's return to power in 1964 removed any thoughts of an early resumption of British attempts to enter the EC, and it was only in 1966 that the

Wilson Government took renewed soundings in the European capitals, which were cut short by the further French veto in 1967. Further tension was created by the 'Soames affair' in early 1969, when de Gaulle's private overtures to the British Ambassador in Paris appeared to have been clumsily revealed to Bonn. By 1970—71, however, when de Gaulle and Wilson had been replaced by Pompidou and Heath, Britain and France appeared to be much more closely aligned. Even in their respective internal situations, despite many problems arising from the different position of agriculture in the national economies and such political contrasts as the presence of a large Communist Party in France, it really appeared that the two nations were becoming a good deal more compatible.

In the direct bilateral relationship, despite some disagreement about the precise financial terms of Britain's entry into the European Community, there were many examples of successful cooperation in advanced technology and other branches of industry (the negative aspects of the Concorde aircraft venture were not then as apparent as they later became), and the two governments were able to reach agreement on such important matters as policy towards the world monetary system, which had sharply divided them in the 1960s. Within the framework of the Community and the Atlantic Alliance, the French and British governments of this time were much closer to each other than their predecessors. Heath's strong commitment to European unity included the view that Britain and France should work together to reduce Europe's dependence on the nuclear protection of the United States (he spoke of the French and British nuclear deterrents being 'held in trust' for a future united Europe which would one day have its own defence policy). At the same time the Pompidou government had clearly modified some of the more extreme anti-American elements in de Gaulle's foreign policy. In world affairs generally, despite some continuing Franco-British divergences resulting from different historical experiences and from the differing nature of the two countries' links with other parts of the world, there were fewer conflicts than before: in the new framework of European political cooperation, France and Britain appeared to approach such problems as the Middle East conflict or the future of Southern Africa in a broadly similar fashion.

Thus, at the time when Heath, Pompidou and Brandt took the lead in laying down the ambitious programme for the 1980s which the European Community's Paris summit of October 1972 adopted, there was good reason to think that a close partnership between Paris and London, comparable to that between Paris and Bonn, would form a central element of an increasingly united Community.

Some strains arose in *Anglo-German* relations in the mid-1960s because of the Labour government's tentative revival of the idea that Britain should act as a diplomatic mediator between East and West. At the same time, however, there was increased cooperation on a range of technical projects, especially in aerospace.

London and Bonn saw fairly closely eye-to-eye during the prelude to the renewed negotiations on Britain's EC membership which started in 1970. Britain's decision in 1968–69 to withdraw from a military presence East of Suez was seen in Germany as a sign of firmer commitment to Europe: it meant, for one thing, that the British Army of the Rhine and the British garrison in West Berlin could be maintained at their full strength – at least until they were depleted by the needs of Ulster. This Anglo-German understanding on military matters – which was not shared to such an extent by France – was the product of a close relationship developed over the previous decade in the defence and foreign policy fields through cooperation in the Bonn Group (on Berlin and Germany) and in NATO and, from 1968, the NATO Eurogroup, of which France was not a member. The British government was the more easily able to support Bonn's *Ostpolitik* as a positive move to ease East–West tensions, because it was clear about West Germany's firm anchorage in the Western Alliance. London and Bonn had already developed effective links, as joint leaders in the NATO Eurogroup (where their Defence Ministers Healey and Schmidt cooperated very closely), and in collaboration in a variety of bilateral and multilateral contexts, particularly in the defence field, which continued into the 1970s.

The British government hoped to obtain strong German support for its renewed application to join the European Community, since Paris under de Gaulle's leadership was unhelpful on this score. In addition, the experience of Bonn's refusal to revalue the Deutsche Mark at London's request in 1968 had revealed the need for Britain to cooperate more closely with the strongest economy in Europe rather than try to exert pressure from a distance. At the EC summit meeting at The Hague in December 1969 Brandt unequivocally pledged German support for British membership, arguing that enlargement of the Community was a prerequisite for its further development.

In 1969–70 the relations between the two left-centre administrations – the SPD/FDP government and the British Labour government – were particularly close; Brandt's personal popularity in Britain (demonstrated on a visit to London in March 1970, when he and Wilson claimed 'complete identity of views') was a further important factor. On European issues, however, Brandt was of course closer to Heath than to Wilson, and this became clear when detailed negotiations on British entry to the EC began after the Conservative election victory of June 1970. Although Heath dedicated his and his government's major diplomatic effort to obtaining French approval for British entry, the backing of West Germany, which remained staunch, was crucial to success.

There were nevertheless misunderstandings both in London and in Bonn about what British membership would bring. The Germans hoped that Britain as a Community member would act as a political counterweight to France (in a sense, a mirror-image of Pompidou's hope of using Britain's weight to help counteract that of Germany), and they also expected that British parliamentary traditions would contribute to the strengthening of the democratic control of the Community. On the British side, part of the reason for turning to Europe was the hope of recovering a leadership role which was no longer attainable outside Europe; but in some circles there was a misapprehension that German support for Britain's role as a counterweight to France implied acceptance of British leadership.

Both these sets of expectations were to be disappointed. As British Community membership began, British and German interests appeared similar on agricultural policy, where both were keen in principle to avoid inflationary price rises, but Bonn's policy on the CAP was influenced by the German farm lobby and opposed the placing of limits on agricultural prices. Then conflicts arose over the Regional Development Fund, as the size of the gulf became apparent between what Britain, for one, expected West Germany to contribute and what the West Germans were prepared to pay to help redistribute wealth to the less developed regions of the Community. London failed to see the need for a switch of diplomatic efforts on this issue from Paris to Bonn. By 1974 a pattern began to be set whereby Germany felt it was, as Schmidt put it, 'Europe's paymaster' and Britain, disappointed with the economic results of its membership, was forced to adopt the role of *demandeur* on policies from which it could hope to recoup benefit. The 1974 oil price rise exacerbated these problems, and imposed a correspondingly greater strain on Anglo-German relations.

1974—85

Heads of government
FRG: Schmidt, 1974—82; Kohl, 1982— .
France: Giscard d'Estaing, 1974—81; Mitterrand, 1981— .
UK: Wilson, 1974—76; Callaghan, 1976—79; Thatcher, 1979— .

For a number of reasons, the year 1974 marked a turning-point in relations among Western European countries. The political leadership in all three major countries changed hands: Heath was replaced by Wilson after the British election of February; Brandt resigned and handed over to Schmidt in May; and Pompidou was replaced by Giscard d'Estaing, also in May. This meant that the three leaders who had presided over Britain's entry into the Community in January 1973, and who had led their countries through the period of Brandt's *Ostpolitik*, the Quadripartite Agreement on Berlin, and the evolution of post-Gaullist France towards a more 'Atlanticist' orientation, were all replaced almost simultaneously.

Of these changes, the one with the most immediate impact on relations within the London—Paris—Bonn triangle was probably the replacement of Heath by Wilson. The new Labour government was pledged to 'renegotiate' the terms on which Britain had joined the EC, and if dissatisfied to take the country out again. Within weeks of the February election, Wilson's Foreign Secretary Callaghan was presenting his Community colleagues with an outline of Britain's budgetary demands, and these dominated the agenda of intra-Community debates for some months to come.

The striking *rapprochement* of the new French and German leaders was partly due to their shared reluctance to accept Britain's demands (though Giscard and Schmidt, who had worked together as Finance Ministers, agreed on many other points as well). Before the year was out, the problems of making progress in the EC had led the Paris summit (in December) to establish the European Council, a formal thrice-yearly conference of the Community's national leaders. The deliberations of this body, partly because of Britain's attitude under both Labour and Conservative governments, came to be dominated by a Franco-German consensus which other member states were under strong pressure to follow.

The year 1974 saw changes not only in political leadership in the national capitals, but also in the international economy. The 1973 Yom Kippur War unleashed a fourfold increase in energy costs, which helped to precipitate serious recession and growing unemployment throughout the world economy by 1974. The major European governments failed to act together in dealing with the United States at the Washington Conference of February 1974: this conference produced the International Energy Agency, but France — amid some acrimony — refused to join it. London, Paris and Bonn were also soon involved in a series of annual Western economic summits, which were the most obvious symbol of the attempts at collective measures for economic recovery. In addition Britain, France and Germany were soon to play leading parts in the 'North—South dialogue' between industrialised countries and raw material producers, which reached its climax in the Paris Conference on International Economic Cooperation in 1975—77.

At about the same time, the efforts at East—West détente, undertaken during the 'era of negotiations' in the early 1970s, reached their culmination in the Helsinki Declaration of August 1975. They then entered a period of disillusion, as the expected benefits of détente failed to materialise (except for improved relations between East and West Germany), and as US—Soviet tension began to rise again as a result of conflicts in Angola and elsewhere.

In this situation of disputes within Western Europe and threats to prosperity and stability from without, the relationship that developed most effectively within the Western European triangle was that between *Paris and Bonn*. Giscard d'Estaing and Helmut Schmidt were able to develop their close working relationship into an intensive partnership partly because of the obvious pressure of external events and partly because of the preoccupation of British governments from Wilson to Thatcher with Britain's financial relationship with the EC and its budget.

At the regular Franco-German summits, and in continuous personal dialogue (pursued in frequent meetings and by telephone), the two leaders promoted intensified cooperation between their countries, in economic, EC and diplomatic (including international security) affairs. After Raymond Barre succeeded Jacques Chirac as Prime Minister in August 1976, French economic policy moved towards the market economy approach of the Federal Republic and, at the Franco-German summit of February 1977, the two leaders agreed on closer coordination of economic policies through regular meetings of their respective Ministers of Economics and Finance, as well as central bank governors. This coordination in economic policy was a factor in making the Franco-German partnership the driving force in the European Monetary System, established in 1979 and joined by all the EC's member states except the UK.

In other aspects of EC affairs, Franco-German agreement also ensured that the first direct election to the European Parliament took place (although only in 1979, not in 1978 as first agreed), and that Greece entered the Community in 1981.

In foreign and security affairs the French and German leaders generally adopted common positions on East–West relations (for instance in their declaration on Afghanistan in February 1980). On the Polish question, however, there were divergences in approach with Paris being concerned at the generally mild German response to the imposition of martial law, and Bonn being surprised by Giscard's hastily arranged meeting with Brezhnev in Warsaw.

The partnership between Giscard and Schmidt terminated in May 1981 when Giscard was replaced by Mitterrand. The intergovernmental mechanisms of the Franco-German treaty evidently played an important role, both in this French transition and in the German transition in October 1982 when Schmidt lost his parliamentary majority and was replaced by Helmut Kohl. In both cases the new leaders promptly proclaimed the high priority they attached to Franco-German relations. In the period of uncertainty between Schmidt's fall and the election of March 1983 which confirmed Kohl in office, there was strong French concern at the risk of a left-wing coalition government which would fail to implement NATO's policy on missile-stationing. President Mitterrand's personal intervention in the election campaign, warning against such a development, appears to have been influential.

In general, cooperation between a Socialist French President and a right-wing German Chancellor has been fairly close. The period has seen divergences in economic policy, with revaluations of the Deutsche Mark reflecting the relative strength of the German economy, and a growing deficit in France's trade balance with Germany. However, these issues have been managed without great difficulty. The period since 1982 has also seen a much-publicised attempt to develop Franco-German co-operation in defence and security policy, developing an aspect of joint endeavour which had remained underdeveloped ever since the signature of the Treaty 20 years earlier. The balance sheet of this decade of Franco-German relations was thus a positive one, with the close mutual understanding established by Schmidt and Giscard largely surviving their departures from office.

In *Anglo-German* relations, the inescapable factor influencing the contacts between leaders and governments was the economic dominance of the FRG in nearly every respect. Whereas the French chose to emulate Bonn as far as possible, British Labour governments under Wilson and then Callaghan were reluctant to follow German liberal market economic precepts which seemed to conflict with socialist plans for Britain. To the extent that by early 1976 British efforts were concentrated on overcoming inflation, they met with Schmidt's approval, but his exhortations (to all his Community partners) to follow the successful German model aroused resentment, particularly when this appeared to be the precondition for German disbursements for Community social and welfare policies which would favour Britain.

Fear of economic subordination to Germany had featured in some anti-EC arguments before Britain joined the Community. As the German economy was seen to develop so much more satisfactorily than the British, despite the impact of world inflation and recession, anti-German resentment added to growing Labour Party dissatisfaction with the capacity of the European Community to address the problems of unemployment. Relations between the two governments were not helped by Callaghan's frequent prompting of Schmidt to reflate the German economy in order to lead the West out of recession, revealing a British underestimation of German fears of inflation. Only a modest reflationary package was introduced by Bonn in 1978.

Just as Britain was disappointed by lack of German cooperation on economic matters, so Germany was disappointed in British ideas about European integration. As a leading German politician (Richard von Weizsäcker) said at the Königswinter Conference of 1978, Britain seemed to behave less like a member of the Community than like a third party negotiating with it, and even when the arguments of the British were understandable, their style of approach was wrong.

Britain was widely blamed in the Federal Republic for the year's delay (to June 1979) in the holding of direct elections to the European Parliament. Moreover, hopes of the British parliamentary tradition strengthening the formation of a future European Union were disappointed when, for instance, Callaghan agreed with Giscard d'Estaing in 1978 that the European Parliament should have no new powers conferred on it after direct elections. As Paris and Bonn worked together in 1978—79 to create the European Monetary System, London — after some initial secret involvement — appeared to concentrate on domestic concerns.

Much of this un-European behaviour was dictated by the strongly anti-Market faction in the Labour Party, and the small government majority. The Labour Party's National Executive Committee vote in 1978 to re-examine — yet again — Britain's terms of membership, aroused concern in Bonn, which was not allayed by the Party Conference vote reaffirming Britain's commitment. It was seen as an indication that British divisions over the Community would continue into the 1980s.

Schmidt nevertheless probably understood quite well the problems facing Callaghan, with whom, despite differences on economic priorities, he apparently had excellent personal relations and with whom he shared a right-wing social-democratic outlook. They were backed by close cooperation between their governments in the fields of defence and foreign policy, in the development of European Political Cooperation following on the negotiations in the Conference on Security and Cooperation in Europe, and in British support of Western rights in Berlin. In 1976 Schmidt urged the development of closer consultations between Callaghan, Giscard d'Estaing and himself in the interests of the running of the Community. In 1977 their relationship flourished as a result of Callaghan's assistance in dealing with the hijackers of a Lufthansa plane to Mogadishu: at their 1977 summit meeting the long-running irritant of British Rhine Army costs was removed by German agreement to offset costs caused by exchange-rate fluctuations. The fact that British views of Germany were far from negative was confirmed by an opinion poll of 1978 which showed that the British now felt the same level of friendship for Germans as for Americans, and saw West Germany as Britain's closest friend in Europe.

Since 1979, under a Conservative government, London's policies have certainly been closer to those of Bonn than were Labour's, and — aided by North Sea oil — have shown signs of greater success in overcoming inflation (though not unemployment). But Mrs Thatcher's stand on the Community budget repayments and CAP reform (both of which entailed some cost to the Federal Republic) has reinforced German doubts about Britain's European commitment. Even so, Bonn gave strong diplomatic and economic support to London during the Falklands crisis of 1982. The transition from Schmidt to Kohl later in 1982, and the election victories of both Kohl and Thatcher the following year, left Bonn and London with strongly based centre-right governments, which have been able to maintain close agreement on many bilateral and East—West issues (notably that of missile deployment) but are further from agreement on EC matters, as the European Council in Athens in December 1983 confirmed. It was not until the Fontainebleau meeting of the European Council in June 1984 that the EC's budgetary problems appeared to find a solution.

When the two governments undertook a systematic review of Anglo-German relations in 1983–84, its conclusion was that the relationship both at governmental and non-governmental levels was generally effective and cooperative. The appointment early in 1985 of part-time coordinators for Anglo-German relations both in London and in Bonn (a retired Ambassador in each case) was intended to advertise the good condition of these relations, rather than to indicate that major improvements were necessary or possible.

The economic troubles of the 1970s also affected *Franco-British* relations, but here there were some special factors at work. Quite apart from the issue of the Community budget, there were, after 1974, some problems of personal communication between the two leaders. In contrast to the far-reaching international perspectives which Heath and Pompidou had shared, and which Giscard d'Estaing to some extent continued, Wilson's attention was focused mainly on Britain's internal problems (including the divisions of his party and his extremely small parliamentary majority), and it was not a complete exaggeration when Michel Jobert, the French Foreign Minister in 1973–74, contrasted Heath, 'a man of the Rhine', with Wilson, 'a man of the Scilly Islands'.

Despite these differences, however, and despite the attempts by Wilson and his Foreign Minister Callaghan to revive London's 'special relationship' with Washington (partly perhaps to counter the increasingly close partnership between Paris and Bonn), the British and French governments settled down to the task of working together in the framework of a loosely organised European Community to solve their many common problems.

Any hopes of a big improvement in Franco-British relations when the Conservatives returned to power in 1979 were to be rapidly disappointed. The personal relationship between Mrs Thatcher and President Giscard d'Estaing was very cool, and there appeared to be little 'meeting of minds' between them. Mrs Thatcher's determined campaign to improve Britain's EC budgetary position dominated several meetings of the European Council and lesser Community fora during 1979–80. Even though one of the countries most affected by her demands was the Federal Republic (which returned in 1981 to its previous position of being the biggest contributor or 'paymaster' of the Community as a result of the acceptance of part of the Thatcher demands), it can be argued that the main conflict to result from this situation was between London and Paris. France did in fact accept a compromise in the spring of 1980, when a provisional solution was reached. However, the continuing negotiations within the Community on the implementation of the 'Mandate of 30 May' — the Council's instruction that the principles of the Community budget should be reconsidered in an attempt to reach a permanent solution — were marked by continuing divergence between the British and French points of view. These arguments continued during 1981, 1982 and

1983, when the Athens summit saw an evident clash between Mitterrand and Thatcher.

The change of government in France in 1981 indeed might have been expected to compromise relations between Paris and London yet again, since the pronouncedly left-wing policies of President Mitterrand and the Mauroy government were in sharp contrast to the ultra-conservative monetarist policies of the Thatcher regime. It was therefore a matter of some surprise, as well as general relief, that Mrs Thatcher and the new French President appeared to develop a good working relationship almost from their first contact. After a friendly reference to Britain in his inaugural press conference and a number of brief meetings with Mrs Thatcher during the summer of 1981, President Mitterrand made his first formal visit to London in September of that year. It was apparent even before the discussions, and it was confirmed as they took place, that the two leaders were finding a good basis for successful cooperation, and that this was shared by their respective ministerial teams.

According to the communiqué issued after the meeting, the two leaders had a useful discussion of the problems facing the European Community. Even though there were obviously considerable differences between Mrs Thatcher's continued insistence that Britain should receive reimbursement from the Community, and the view of President Mitterrand and his ministers that the Community should launch a large-scale attack on unemployment by a programme of job creation, it was a hopeful sign that the two leaders were able to discuss these problems in a friendly and cooperative spirit. Agreement was also reached to revive the old question of a cross-Channel tunnel, on which new studies were to be made (an agreement to proceed with some form of 'fixed link' was reached early in 1985). The two leaders also agreed to pursue joint activities in a number of other areas: the development of a fast-breeder nuclear reactor; increased cooperation in the fields of computers, telecommunications, and aircraft engines; and the intensification of Anglo-French cooperation on the European airbus project.

Progress on these projects in 1981—84 was inevitably overshadowed by the continuing conflict over the EC budget but, with the resolution of this conflict in 1984, there was strong evidence that Britain and France were making serious efforts to develop common interests and to maintain a good working relationship. One sign of this was their agreement to set up a more formal administrative structure for the supervision of their bilateral relations: this structure, introduced in 1982—83, while less elaborate than the Franco-German mechanism flowing from the Elysée Treaty, symbolises top-level political will to maximise Franco-British cooperation.

Events in May 1985 gave an illuminating vignette of some of the essential features of relations between the three capitals. After a well publicised disagreement at the Bonn economic summit, when France sharply disagreed with Britain and West Germany over the timing for new international trade talks, there were characteristic reactions on all three sides of the Paris—Bonn—London triangle. Between Paris and Bonn there was much public agitation about the urgent need for a Kohl—Mitterrand summit to demonstrate the healing of this lamentable breach (in a Franco-German partnership which both the governments saw as vital, but in need of constant cultivation). Between Bonn and London, the Kohl—Thatcher working meeting of 18—19 May followed its usual course of low-key discussion of practical issues (including some quite difficult ones such as the Strategic Defence Initiative, EC grain prices, and the prospects for European Union), without attracting much media attention at all. And between London and Paris, the impression prevailed that both governments were agreeing to differ — notably on the trade talks issue, but also on the question of European Union and many others — and that the Franco-British relationship, while predictable and relatively stable, was not marked by any great cordiality or any great wish to intensify communication or cooperation.

Notes

Further accounts will be found in the historical works listed in the Bibliography. See in particular Alfred Grosser, *The Western Alliance* (London, Macmillan, 1978); Roger Morgan, *West European Politics since 1945* (London, Batsford, 1973); and *The United States and West Germany* (Oxford, Oxford University Press, 1974). The more specialised works, journals and periodicals contain more details on specific episodes.

3 A Comparison of the Three Economies
Geoffrey Shepherd

Introduction

This chapter sets out some of the salient characteristics of the three economies — their structure, recent development and policy priorities. The principal objective is not to look at actual or potential economic bilateralism, but to ascertain the common and contrasting, converging and diverging characteristics of the economies as a basis for considering what kind of bilateral relationships may be likely or feasible.

Economic bilateralism in a narrow sense, as practised for example in Eastern Europe, is not considered here. The basis of the Western economic system since the Second World War has been multilateralism — the observation of a set of non-discriminatory rules which allow trade and payments to flow freely among nations without the need for these to be bilaterally balanced. The European Community in many ways reproduces the rules of the broader international system. Indeed, while this regional arrangement allows some discrimination against non-members (notably in agriculture), it permits even less discrimination among members than the broader international system.

Multilateralism — in both its international and regional variants — is credited with having played an important role in the 'golden age' of Western economic expansion — the quarter-century to 1973. The principle is still sufficiently widely regarded that, although it has come under severe strain, it has not yet given way under the recessionary pressures that have built up since 1973.

Thus political bilateralism does not have its obvious counterpart in economic bilateralism. None the less, two important forms of economic bilateralism can be observed in Western Europe. In the first place, Western European countries cooperate on specific projects — in aerospace, energy and, increasingly, information technology, for instance. (Some aspects of this cooperation are covered in Chapter 11.) In the second place — and in fact more importantly — multilateral economic systems are created, managed, or modified through essentially political processes in which individual powerful countries, and coalitions of these (and individual people) play leading roles. Clearly, the current international debates on reflation, protection and international debt, and the EC debates on the budget, the Common Agricultural Policy and internal and external protectionism come into this area. Such economic diplomacy often has a strongly bilateral character which is influenced by the economic and policy systems that are the subject of this chapter.

In fact, the Federal Republic of Germany, France and Britain occupy a particular position where some forms of economic bilateralism have special attractions. First, their size, their economic power and, indeed, their illustrious history put them in a unique position in the Western world. Individually, they have aspirations as world economic powers, yet they do not have the resources — particularly the large domestic markets enjoyed by the US and Japan — to fulfil this role properly. On the other hand, they are not small enough — unlike the Benelux and Scandinavian countries — to take their role in a multilateral system as given. Thus the small giants of Western Europe are tempted by a mixture of going it alone — as exemplified in industrial policies to foster 'national champions' in 'key' industrial sectors — and of looking for strength within a European grouping. This European route has often been pursued through bilateralism, the most potent example being the Franco-German axis which has been at the centre of the West European integration movement since the Schuman Plan of 1950.

The next section of this chapter makes a broad comparison of the structure of the three economies: their economic endowment; their recent performance; and their position in the international economy (with particular reference to bilateral exchange links). The third section broadly characterises the differences in economic systems and policies between the three countries, especially those affecting industrial performance. Some conclusions are drawn in the final section.

Economic structures

Endowments and the structure of economic activity

The three countries have populations of similar size, a similarly modest endowment in raw materials, and similarly high endowments in industrial and service skills. As a result, real domestic product, both on a total and on a per capita basis, is broadly similar for the three countries, with Germany leading and Britain lagging behind (see Table 3.1).

In the quarter-century following the Second World War all three countries were able to catch up technologically with existing US standards. France and Germany in particular had in many ways drawn level by the 1970s, but during this decade the United States re-emerged as a clear leader in the newest technologies, particularly information technology, while Japan was able to overtake Europe and catch up with the US in many areas. The three European countries now share a strong perception of a national and a Western European lag in high technology, although this is selective as between different sectors.

Table 3.1 Miscellaneous economic indicators

		Germany	France	UK
1. Gross Domestic Product in current US $ bn at purchasing power parity[1]	1970	222.9	174.7	182.2
	1980	583.3	491.5	433.0
2. Population (millions)	1970	60.7	50.8	55.5
	1980	61.6	53.7	56.0
3. Gross Domestic Product per capita in current US $ at purchasing power parity[1]	1970	3,674	3,441	3,282
	1980	9,435	9,150	7,730
4. Gross fixed investment as per cent of GDP	1961–70 average	24.9	22.9	18.1
	1971–80 average	22.3	22.9	18.6
5. Enrolment ratio in higher education (per cent)[2]	1960	6	10	9
	1979	26	25	20
6. Output per man-hour in manufacturing (in 1973 US $ at purchasing power parity)	1973	6,230	5,260	3,280
	1981	8,550	7,310	3,910

Notes:
1. Purchasing power parity exchange rates provide estimated corrections for different price levels in different countries (GDP is at market prices).
2. Number enrolled as percentage of population aged 20–24.

Sources:
Items 1, 2 and 3: OECD, *National Accounts of OECD Countries*, Paris, annual.
Item 4: Commission of the European Communities, *European Economy*, no.18, November 1983, Brussels, Table 14 of Statistical Appendix.
Item 5: World Bank, *World Development Report 1983*, Washington DC, 1983.
Item 6: A.D. Roy, 'Labour Productivity in 1980: an International Comparison', *National Institute Economic Review*, London, August 1982.

Table 3.2 Distribution of GDP by kind of economic activity, 1960, 1970 and 1980

	Agriculture %	Mining %	Manufacturing %	Other %	Total %
Germany					
1960	6	3	40	51	100
1970	3	1	41	54	100
1980	2	1	36	61	100
France					
1960	9	-	37	-	100
1970	7	1	31	61	100
1980	4	1	29	66	100
Britain					
1960	4	3	35	58	100
1970	3	1	31	64	100
1980	2	7	27	64	100

Source: Own estimates, based on national statistics and OECD, *National Accounts of OECD Countries*, various issues.

Table 3.3 Distribution of employment by kind of economic activity, 1960, 1970 and 1980

	Agriculture %	Mining %	Manufacturing %	Other %	Total %
Germany					
1960	14	3	37	46	100
1970	9	1	40	50	100
1980	6	1	35	58	100
France					
1960	22	2	28	48	100
1970	14	1	28	57	100
1980	9	1	26	64	100
Britain					
1960	4	3	38	55	100
1970	3	2	35	60	100
1980	2	1	27	70	100

Source: Own estimates based on OECD, *Labour Force Statistics*, Paris, various issues, and International Labour Office, *Yearbook of Labour Statistics*, Geneva, various issues.

Table 3.4 Ratio of trade to GDP by product group, 1960, 1970 and 1980 (%)

		Food, beverages and tobacco	Basic materials	Fuels	Manufactures	Sub-total goods[1]	Services	Total
Germany								
Exports	1960	0.3	0.5	1.0	14.6	16.6	0.9	17.5
	1970	0.6	0.5	0.6	16.9	18.9	0.9	19.8
	1980	1.1	0.6	0.9	20.4	23.5	2.1	25.6
Imports	1960	3.5	3.8	1.2	6.3	14.8	0.5	15.3
	1970	2.7	2.2	1.5	9.6	16.5	0.9	17.4
	1980	2.5	1.9	5.1	12.7	23.0	1.8	24.8
Net exports	1960	− 3.2	− 3.3	− 0.2	+ 8.3	+ 1.8	+ 0.4	+ 2.2
	1970	− 2.1	− 1.7	− 0.9	+ 7.3	+ 2.4	–	+ 2.4
	1980	− 1.4	− 1.3	− 4.2	+ 7.7	+ 0.5	+ 0.3	+ 0.8
France								
Exports	1960	1.6	1.0	0.5	8.9	12.0	1.9	13.9
	1970	2.0	0.7	0.3	9.8	12.9	2.4	15.3
	1980	2.6	0.7	0.7	12.9	17.1	3.9	21.0
Imports	1960	2.2	2.7	1.9	4.2	11.0	0.3	11.3
	1970	1.8	1.6	1.7	8.7	13.8	1.2	15.0
	1980	1.9	1.3	5.5	11.7	20.6	2.4	23.0

Net exports 1960	− 0.6	− 1.7	− 1.4	+ 4.7	+ 1.0	+ 1.6	+ 2.6
1970	+ 0.2	− 0.9	− 1.4	+ 1.1	− 0.9	+ 1.2	+ 0.3
1980	+ 0.7	− 0.6	− 4.8	+ 1.2	− 3.5	+ 1.5	− 2.0
Britain							
Exports 1960	0.8	0.8	0.5	12.9	15.3	5.1	20.4
1970	1.0	0.5	0.4	13.3	15.7	6.9	22.6
1980	1.5	0.7	2.9	16.0	21.7	5.0	26.7
Imports 1960	6.4	4.4	2.0	6.0	18.8	2.8	21.6
1970	4.0	2.7	1.9	9.2	18.1	3.6	21.7
1980	2.8	1.8	3.1	14.2	22.7	2.0	24.7
Net exports 1960	− 5.6	− 3.6	− 1.5	+ 6.9	− 3.5	+ 2.3	− 1.2
1970	− 3.0	− 2.2	− 1.5	+ 4.1	− 2.4	+ 3.3	+ 0.9
1980	− 1.3	− 1.1	− 0.2	+ 1.8	− 1.0	+ 3.0	+ 2.0

Note:
1. Includes small amounts of miscellaneous goods not elsewhere classified.

Sources:
Calculated from: Commission of the European Communities, *European Economy*, no.18, November 1983, Brussels, Tables 26 and 30 of Statistical Appendix; and United Nations, *Commodity Trade Statistics Series D*, New York, various issues.

countries show broad similarities in the evolution and
output (Table 3.2) and the distribution of employment
here has been a consistent, often rapid, decline in the
culture in economic activity. This was particularly impor-
sing labour for urban activities in Germany and France in
nd 1960s, but less so for Britain which has long had a small
and a ___ nt agricultural sector. In spite of agriculture's decline, all
three countries have been improving their level of agricultural self-
sufficiency in the last two decades, largely as a result of the CAP (see
Table 3.4). The share of manufacturing in economic activity generally
declined in the 1960s and 1970s. With few significant energy resources
beyond coal, the three countries have tended to have large import bills
for oil, which became critical factors after the oil price rises of 1973–
74. Shortly after 1973, of course, Britain began to build up its own
production of North Sea oil, to the point where it became a net export-
er at the beginning of the 1980s and can look forward to oil self-
sufficiency up to the end of the decade. Finally, the three countries
have all experienced a shift of economic activity into the service sector.

In spite of the broad similarities, there are a number of differences
in the structure of economic activity with an obvious bearing on the
extent of common interests between the three countries. Britain has the
least problems as regards energy. On the other hand — and not unconnected with the effect of energy self-sufficiency on the exchange
rate — it faces substantial problems in an internationally uncompetitive
manufacturing sector which has substantially declined in absolute terms
since 1979. Other notable, though less important, British structural
characteristics are the speed with which its trade balance in food has
improved and also its traditional strength in service exports (see Table
3.4). Germany retains a very large and highly competitive manufacturing sector in spite of a relatively rapid decline in that sector's share of
GDP in the 1970s. France still retains the largest agricultural sector and
the largest energy deficit, equivalent to 5 per cent of GDP in 1980
(compared with 4 per cent for Germany; see Table 3.4). Finally,
France's manufacturing sector is significantly smaller than that of
Germany.

It would at first seem paradoxical that France, with population and
productivity levels approaching those of Germany, should have so much
smaller a manufacturing sector than Germany. Part of the explanation
resides in Germany's far stronger trade surplus in manufactures (Table
3.4). Lack of information about the relative price levels in the two
countries makes an accurate comparison of the size of the two manufacturing sectors difficult, but it would seem that the real output of
German manufacturing is at least 60 per cent, and possibly over 100 per
cent, higher than that of France (and two to three times higher than
that of Britain). France's energy deficit and this apparent industrial
weakness *vis-à-vis* Germany are important elements in its perceptions of
its economic objectives.

Economic performance

There are evident similarities in economic performance among the three countries, particularly if we adopt a long-term historical perspective. All three economies participated in the post-Second World War acceleration of economic growth and the achievement of full employment and reasonable levels of internal and external stability. All three participated in the post-1973 misery of lower growth, higher unemployment and higher inflation.

But even the long-term trends reveal important differences. Over the very long period Germany appears to have exhibited a consistently higher rate of real GDP growth than most other industrialised countries, and Britain a consistently lower rate (see Table 3.5). France, on the other hand, experienced a low rate before the Second World War and a high rate after. Moreover, its post-war growth appears to have accelerated relative to that of Germany. This has meant convergence of the French on the German economy in terms of size and, indeed, since 1975 both economies appear to have grown at very similar rates (see Figure 3.1). On the other hand, Britain, ever since it was overtaken in per capita GDP terms by the other two economies (around 1960 by Germany and later in the 1960s by France), has suffered from a growing divergence in terms of GDP.

In others aspects of macroeconomic performance, this Franco-German convergence has been less evident in the period since 1973. In the decade ending with 1983, while Germany's rate of inflation averaged 4 per cent per annum, the French rate averaged 11 per cent, closer to Britain's 14 per cent (see Figure 3.2). However, in the most recent period, the British rate of inflation has rapidly been falling towards that of Germany. Since the middle of the 1970s Britain and France have also clearly had higher rates of unemployment than Germany, yet the rapid rise of the German unemployment rate since 1980 has again meant convergence (Figure 3.3). Finally, the instability of the exchange-rate regime since the beginning of the 1970s, combined with different rates of inflation in different countries (which did not always offset exchange-rate changes), has meant a particular instability in the international cost relativities of the three countries. Monetary cooperation between Germany and France, particularly in the context of the European Monetary System since 1978, has to an extent dampened down some of these problems. Britain, on the other hand, has faced a very unstable environment, with, for instance, its unit labour costs relative to other countries rising by 50 per cent in the period 1977 to 1981 (see Figure 3.4).

Bilateral exchanges

Historically France and Germany have had a higher share of their total trade with Europe and with each other than has Britain, whose trade was dominated for much of the twentieth century by imperial/

Table 3.5 GDP growth rates *(Average % per annum)*

	1870–1913	1922–37	1953–61	1961–73	1973–79	1979–83
France	1.6	1.8	4.9	5.6	3.0	0.7
Germany	2.8	3.2	7.2	4.5	2.4	0.4
Britain	1.9	2.4	2.9	3.1	1.3	–
OECD Europe	2.0	2.5	4.9	4.7	2.4	0.4[1]

Notes:
1. EC–10 only.

Sources:
1870–1979: Andrea Boltho (ed.), *The European Economy: Growth and Crisis* (Oxford University Press, 1982). Tables 1.1 and 1.6.
1979–83: Calculated from Commission of the European Communities, *European Economy*, no.18, November 1983, Brussels, Table 8 of Statistical Appendix.

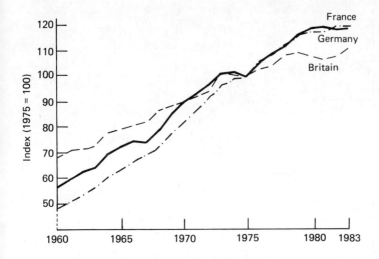

Source:
Based on Commission of the European Communities, *European Economy*, no.18, November 1983, Table 8 of Statistical Appendix (figures for 1983 are estimated).

Figure 3.1 GDP at 1975 market prices, 1960–83

Commonwealth ties. A strong intensification of Franco-German trade ties occurred with the integration process in the 1960s (Table 3.6). As a late relinquisher of empire and a late member of the EC, Britain did not experience a significant growth in its bilateral links with the other two countries until the 1970s. Despite their very fast growth since Britain joined the EC, these links have still not reached the intensity of the Franco-German links.

France and Germany are each other's most important trade partners. In fact, Germany dominates French trade more than vice versa (the Netherlands is almost as important a trade partner of the Germans as France). Indeed, 18 per cent of France's 1982 imports came from Germany. This is the single most important case of trade 'dependence' among the four large countries of the EC (although Denmark, Belgium and the Netherlands are all more 'dependent' on Germany than is France).[1] On the other hand, for neither France nor Germany was Britain more than third or fourth trade partner. Britain's major partner is still the United States, while Germany comes second, and France and the Netherlands are in third place.

Germany has long dominated EC trade as both major source and destination. In the bilateral network of relationships, France's 'dependence' on Germany, and particularly its bilateral trade deficit which has

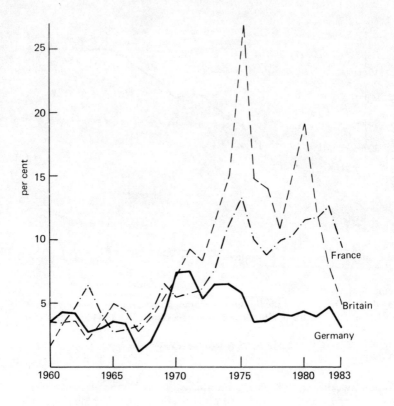

Note:
1. GDP deflator.

Source:
Ibid., Table 17 of Statistical Appendix (figures for 1983 are estimated).

Figure 3.2   Annual rates of inflation, 1960–83[1]

grown in the 1960s and 1970s (and was equal to 3 per cent of French imports in 1982), has become a source of great concern. This French concern about a phenomenon that is not normally the stuff of high politics cannot be separated from the general history of Franco-German relations in the years before 1950, but does the deficit have an economic significance?

In one sense France's worry can be justified on macroeconomic grounds, inasmuch as the volume of trade is large relative both to total trade and to GDP. In consequence, the overall balance of trade can be significantly affected by divergence in the two exchange rates or by

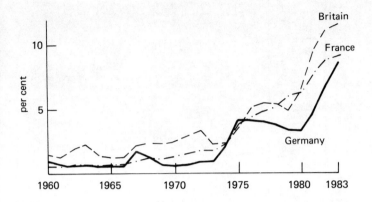

Source:
Ibid., Table 3 of Statistical Appendix (figures for 1983 are estimated).

Figure 3.3 Unemployment (as percentage of civilian labour force), 1960–83

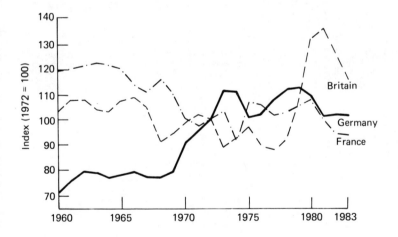

Source:
Ibid., Table 25 of Statistical Appendix (figures for 1983 are estimated).

Figure 3.4 Relative unit labour costs in a common currency in manufacturing, 1960–83

Table 3.6 Importance of bilateral flows of merchandise trade, 1960, 1970 and 1980

	Share in total trade (per cent)			Share of trade in GNP (per cent)		
	1960	1970	1980	1960	1970	1980
Germany						
Imports from France	9.0	12.7	10.7	1.3	2.0	2.5
Exports to France	8.7	12.4	13.3	1.4	2.3	3.1
Imports from Britain	4.1	3.8	6.6	0.7	0.6	1.5
Exports to Britain	4.4	3.5	6.5	0.7	0.7	1.5
Total Imports	100.0	100.0	100.0	14.4	16.1	22.3
Total Exports	100.0	100.0	100.0	16.2	18.4	23.3
France						
Imports from Germany	15.7	22.2	16.2	1.7	2.9	3.3
Exports to Germany	13.7	20.8	16.0	1.6	2.5	2.7
Imports from Britain	3.6	4.5	5.4	0.4	0.6	1.2
Exports to Britain	5.0	4.0	7.0	0.6	0.5	1.2
Total Imports	100.0	100.0	100.0	10.5	13.0	20.5
Total Exports	100.0	100.0	100.0	11.5	12.2	16.9

Britain

Imports from Germany	3.9	5.9	11.1	0.7	1.0	2.5
Exports to Germany	4.5	6.0	10.5	0.6	0.9	2.3
Imports from France	2.8	3.9	7.7	0.5	0.7	1.7
Exports to France	2.4	4.1	7.6	0.3	0.6	1.6
Total Imports	100.0	100.0	100.0	17.7	17.5	22.5
Total Exports	100.0	100.0	100.0	13.4	15.6	21.8

Source:
United Nations, *Commodity Trade Statistics Series D*, New York, various issues.

differences that develop in macroeconomic policy between the two countries (for instance, the French reflation of 1981 sucking in imports concurrently with Germany's deflationary policy which served to discourage French exports). On the other hand, in a world where trade is cleared multilaterally, there is no reason why bilateral flows should need to be balanced.

It seems that part of the cause of French concern has to do with the perception of German industrial strength that we have already mentioned. Indeed, a key feature of this bilateral exchange has been Germany's enduring trade surplus in engineering goods. Yet an examination of the commodity structure of the French bilateral deficit in the 1970s clearly indicates that France has been able to maintain a relatively stable bilateral deficit in this product group (improving on a deteriorating performance in the 1960s in fact). The major single cause of the deterioration of France's bilateral balance in the 1970s appears to have been a fall in its export surplus on agricultural products and on intermediate manufactures. Moreover, if France's deteriorating trade balance with Germany is put into the context of an overall trade balance that was deteriorating even faster in the 1960s and 1970s, it becomes difficult to see how the issue of the Franco-German bilateral trade balance can be represented as one reflecting a long-term *deterioration* in France's capacity to compete with Germany in 'core' industrial activities. It remains, however, that this apparently permanent deficit stands as a symptom of France's continuing industrial weakness (particularly in what are considered to be the 'key' engineering and capital goods sectors), not only *vis-à-vis* Germany, but also among the industrialised countries more generally.

Economic and industrial systems compared

All three economies can be characterised as mixed economies operating in a relatively open international environment. They possess a set of attributes that clearly identifies them in a Western European mould. Among these attributes are:

- the dominance of private ownership and capitalism in most productive activities;
- none the less, a large government role in macroeconomic management, in the provision of public goods and services (particularly health, education and utilities), a broadly progressive fiscal system underpinning a substantial social security system and, increasingly, an active microeconomic management (i.e. industrial policy);
- the organisation of a large part of the labour force into active and influential unions;
- an unprecedentedly high level of openness to the international economy, especially as regards exchange within Western Europe.

The common features of the Western European national economic systems, together with the broad similarities in endowments enjoyed by Germany, France and Britain, provide a potent basis of common

interests among the three countries. It is on this basis that t]
ments of Western European economic integration have be(
achievements that can perhaps too easily be underestir
purpose of this section is to see how large are the variations betwcc..
the three countries, around the common theme of the mixed Western
European economy.

Germany[2]

Germany's post-war economic recovery was driven above all by the idea
of national rehabilitation through economic success and the perception
of the importance of monetary stability for the wellbeing of the economy. The decisive economic reforms of 1948 in favour of a stable
currency and a socially responsible competitive market system (the
'social market economy') laid the basis for the particular characteristics
of Germany's economic system that have persisted until today. In the
1950s German economic recovery was based on rapid export-led
growth under favourable labour market conditions (an abundant supply
of skilled German labour — much of it refugee — and the pronounced
lag in wages behind productivity). Technologically, Germany was able
to resume the exploitation of a long-standing skill base, and, in resum-
ing its strong position in world industrial markets, it was quick to recognise the importance of international competitive capacity as post-war
international trade was liberalised.

Once full employment had been regained by the beginning of the
1960s, Germany began to be preoccupied by the deepening of business
cycles and the acceleration of inflation. As the Social Democrats (SPD)
came to share power (with the Christian Democrats (CDU) in 1966,
then with the minority Free Democrats (FDP) in 1969), the Federal
Republic adopted for the first time a policy of Keynesian demand
management, as well as a more interventionist approach to industrial
policy. This reflected a strong government commitment to social and
redistributive goals and a comparative de-emphasis on stability. It also
meant a decline in the consensus that had been built around earlier
success. Inflation was to increase, however, at the end of the 1960s as a
result of exploding wage demands and increasing international inflation.
This inflation was brought under control with the floating of the
Deutsche Mark in 1973 (which brought to an end some 10 to 15 years
of an undervalued currency) and the recourse to more orthodox monetary and fiscal controls in the same year. However, the coincidence of
this strongly deflationary policy with the first oil price rise threw the
German economy into its sharpest post-war recession. This early medicine — compared to France and Britain — meant an early break in inflationary expectations in Germany; indeed, German inflation has been
significantly lower since 1976 than in the first half of the 1970s (see
Figure 3.2, page 34).

Germany's revaluation — involving something like a one-third increase in its relative industrial production costs compressed into the period 1969 to 1973 (see Figure 3.4, page 35) — has put substantial pressure on its manufacturing sector. None the less, up to the second oil shock of 1979, German economic recovery was comparatively successful. The three years of virtual economic stagnation since the second oil shock have, however, deepened the country's sense of self-doubt. In particular, public awareness of its lagging position in the newest technologies — and of the Japanese challenge — seems to be quite recent.

The current economic debate in Germany is between those who argue that the country's main problem lies in its incomplete ability so far to adjust to the skill upgrading required by revaluation (as the consequence of some loss of general flexibility in the economy), those — often in the same camp — who argue that excessive wages have eaten into profitability and undermined the potential to invest, and those in an opposing camp who stress demand deficiency. Successive federal governments have, broadly, been influenced by the first two arguments and have stuck to a conservative policy on reflation and introduced some elements of a 'supply-side' policy to stimulate innovation and structural adjustment. While there is some split within the SPD on these arguments, it must nevertheless be concluded that even today Germany's consensus on the importance of monetary stability has held better than in most other OECD countries.

For all its commitment to the market, Germany has not eschewed industrial policy. Already in the 1950s — and long before Britain — the federal government was able to direct industrial investment through tax incentives (in a situation where marginal tax rates were very high), through Marshall Aid investment and through control of the capital market. As Germany started to reconstruct its own armed forces, so the government began to develop a strong science and technology policy. It appears that this government role of tutelage in high technology has continued to be accepted by economists of many hues in Germany. A growing perception of the American technological challenge, as well as the arrival of the SPD in government, led to a more permissive view of concentration in the 1960s and to a substantial growth in industrial subsidies, particularly for the regions and for high technology. This growth was somewhat *ad hoc*, although there was some attempt by the Federal Ministry of Economics to set rules: for instance, sectors, not firms, should be aided; aid should be temporary; and aid should run in the direction of the market. In this process, Germany was to catch up on average R and D spending elsewhere in Europe, while there was a gradual switch in R and D policy towards the funding of private projects, often in larger firms. This latter tendency grew apace in the 1970s. On the other hand, the 'importance of competition' policy was re-established in the 1970s (although often with a bias against foreign investment). In general, German industrial policy has been dominated by the importance of regional development aid (particularly as the *Land* governments are as important with regard to industrial subsidies as the federal government) and by the generally non-discriminatory nature of policies as among firms. Germany has certainly had more of an interventionist industrial policy than its free-trade rhetoric might suggest, yet, in comparison with Britain and France, the hallmark of this policy has been its mildness and its non-discriminatory nature.

In such a relatively non-interventionist environment, it is tempting to ascribe at least part of Germany's past success in growth and adjustment to an otherwise very favourable business environment, although sorting out cause and effect between a macroeconomic policy with relative emphasis on stability, a relatively light industrial policy, and favourable institutional factors is very dangerous. First, it is plausible to argue that Germany may have started off in the best of post-war worlds, inheriting substantial industrial strengths and a world market orientation from its previous half-century of economic history, but with the destruction and discrediting of the major political and economic institutions of the inter-war period. In particular, Germany's post-war economy seems to have drawn advantage from political and economic decentralisation, the forging of a consensus around a well enunciated economic system, and a fundamental reform of labour-market institutions.

Economic management, particularly fiscal management, is divided between the federal and *Land* authorities. Germany's central bank (the Deutsche Bundesbank) is independent of the federal government and holds constitutional responsibility for monetary stability. The features of economic decentralisation have limited the scope for any federal government in pursuing an activist micro or macroeconomic policy. Economic and political decentralisation appears to have led to a more even regional spread of industrial activity in Germany and to have sustained the forces of competition, if only through regional rivalries.

Economic consensus in Germany has several origins. The apparent success of the social market economy provided an early cement to a consensus on Germany's economic system. In addition, proportional representation appears to have helped to coalesce economic policies around the centre: the Federal Republic has been ruled by a coalition for most of its existence. Labour-market institutions have also helped to create consensus (see below). In addition, the quality of the public debate on economic issues is noticeably higher in Germany than in Britain or France. Academic expertise plays an important part in this debate — indeed, there has been a legislative basis for expert economic advice since the 1960s — but beyond this lies a relatively well-informed public. Although consensus has been dented since the end of the 1960s by inflation, unemployment, arguments about the distribution of income, and a loss of German economic self-confidence, it still has much strength relative to other countries. Consensus seems to be based on openness — for instance, public debate and industrial democracy — but this has another side: of the three countries, Germany is the one where, in the 1970s, public interest groups were most effective in challenging the government. The faltering of the country's civil nuclear power strategy is perhaps the best example of this.

The post-war reform of Germany's labour-market institutions created a unitary structure composed of a small number of strong industry-based unions. It also introduced substantial mechanisms for co-determination at firm level. This reform has helped to create a disciplined and hierarchical wage-bargaining system which still appears to be the least inflation-prone among the three countries. The German labour movement has also been strongly committed to cooperating in technical change at the industry and firm level. Labour-market conditions and labour-market cooperation have inevitably worsened in the 1970s: both unemployment and labour protection legislation have helped make German labour considerably more inflexible and relations have become more confrontational (most recently, for instance, on the issue of shortening the working week).

Much has been written on the institutional links within industry and the way Germany's industry in a sense manages its own intervention. The role of the large banks, with a substantial control in the equity of the larger firms, and of the trade associations as decentralised information disseminators or quasi-planners has been given some prominence.[3] There is a danger in exaggerating the role of the banks, despite their contribution in organising rescue operations for larger firms in trouble, for instance AEG. This is akin to a defensive industrial policy (like Britain's nationalisation of British Leyland), but with the very obvious sanction of a commercial profitability criterion. Quite apart from the banks, there is none the less a certain 'cement' within industry: for instance, the interchange of firms of all sizes with public research institutions is notable, while the process of setting technical standards — involving the cooperation of government, firms and research institutions — often appears to be an effective conduit for the spread of information. If such institutional ties are important, they none the less operate in a competitive climate that appears to be stronger in Germany than in France or Britain by virtue of the very size of Germany's industrial sector, its regional decentralisation, and the relative mildness of federal government industrial policy.

France[4]

Until the mid-1980s, France appeared never to have properly debated — let alone achieved — the consensus on an economic system that is thought to be part of the explanation of Germany's post-war success. Indeed, such are the divisions in French society — between left and right, big and small business, town and city, and so on — that the French economy has been run on an authoritarian and partly corporatist basis (and certainly less 'democratically' than in Germany). Yet France's post-war economic growth has matched that of Germany, surpassing it notably in the 15 years to 1975; it has also been a good deal less cyclical since 1960.

Where Germany's long-term emphasis has been on economic stability (in the belief that stability provides the best conditions for growth), France's emphasis has been on a pronounced form of national economic ambition: economic modernisation and catching-up with the economic leaders to restore the country's economic and political position in the world. In the period up to 1958 economic planning seems to have been partly a device for raising expectations. It forged a consensus in favour of an economic growth that would mitigate social tensions. Up to 1958 growth occurred within a relatively closed economy (embracing not only France, but also the Franc Zone) where markets functioned a good deal more imperfectly than in Britain or Germany and where inflation, not a prime topic of policy concern, was rapid.

The year 1958 — the beginning of the Fifth Republic, the joining of the EEC, the undertaking of a large devaluation — represented a profound break, moving France towards a European market vocation and a more liberal form of economic organisation. Moreover, from 1963 onwards as the growth effects of the 1958 devaluation wore off, postwar France was subjected for the first time, through Finance Minister Giscard d'Estaing's Stabilisation Plan, to greater financial orthodoxy. Subject to a clearer market and monetary discipline, economic growth accelerated in the 1960s.

The social unrest of 1968 helped to induce a shift to a more permissive macroeconomic policy, closely paralleling events in Germany, and heralded a period of growth with rising, though not yet chronic, inflation that was to last until 1973. Without Germany's strong deflation of 1973, and at the cost of a rapid rise in inflation, France was able to weather the first oil shock — in terms of GDP growth at least — far better than Germany or Britain. Only in 1976 did the government draw up a plan to tackle inflation; in fact, the success of macroeconomic policy to fight inflation at this time appears to have been limited. More important was the institution of a heavy dose of 'supply-side' intervention entailing further liberalisation of the domestic market (through price control), accompanied by substantial sectoral intervention, including a massive shift to an export promotion policy. The new socialist government of 1981 tried to reflate the French economy through orthodox Keynesianism, but in a situation of a worldwide recession. The consequent acceleration in inflation led to a substantial balance-of-payments crisis and three devaluations between October 1981 and March 1983. There was a gradual belt-tightening, with the eventual introduction of a strong austerity package in the spring of 1983, followed by further strong measures in 1984—85.

With the nationalisations of key firms in the late 1940s and the planning of the 1950s, France was the earliest of the three countries to pursue an activist industrial policy. This activism was largely overturned by the comparative liberalism of the decade following 1958. In the 1960s, however, an industrial policy more consistent with a market economy began to re-emerge. With the same perception as in Germany of the challenge of international markets (particularly the 'American challenge'), the government embarked on a 'structural' policy putting substantial emphasis on helping the development of large, powerful firms. In the 1960s tax incentives were used to encourage the concentration process. Government funds and procurement policies were additionally used to encourage selected firms to develop as 'national champions' to spearhead France's ability to compete in world markets (particularly in nuclear energy, aviation and electronics — similar areas to those promoted in Germany). Public investment in telecommunications and nuclear energy was to become an important sustaining factor in French economic activity in the 1970s.

The re-launching of a more active industrial policy by the Barre government in 1976 consisted principally in price de-control on the one hand and a strengthening of structural policies on the other. The latter policy direction, representing an important step in state 'mercantilism', entailed a large growth in export credits related to big firms and big projects. The apparent permanence of public emphasis on large firms and large projects has meant a neglect of the small- and medium-sized sector.

The centrepiece of socialist industrial strategy after 1981 was the nationalisation of leading French firms. In many ways it can be seen as the logical consequence of previous industrial policies (indeed, several publicly-owned firms had been engaged in 'silent nationalisations', acquiring private companies, since 1979). The second instrument of the socialist industrial strategy was greater protection, although it is a matter of debate to what extent this policy has been carried out. At first, the emphasis was on the 'reconquest of the domestic market' but as its EC partners complained, and as France discovered a stronger European vocation, protectionist intentions were switched from the national to the European level.

The post-war economic and industrial rehabilitation of France has been a remarkable feat, even though it has not caught up with its neighbours in every respect. Most commentators would accord an activist industrial policy (including public procurement policy) a part of the credit for this. France's record in intervention, however, is at best patchy, if we look at the outcome of individual public efforts to engineer industrial change. But, even if the government did not always get it right, strong, often authoritarian, government does appear to have helped to create a climate of confidence and a capacity for *relatively* effective intervention. Some of the conditions favouring such an authoritarian economic system are as follows:

— the creation after the Second World War of a reformed, strong, motivated and technically competent civil service;
— the existence of a strong central government since the beginning of the Fifth Republic and, until 1981, a split and weak opposition;
— the legitimacy conferred on an interventionist government by French tradition (notably, not the case in Britain);
— the relative weakness of private industry after the war and the capacity this gave to government to enter into a relationship of tutelage, and develop corporate relations, with chosen larger firms (a process supported by the substantial movement of senior civil servants between government and industry);
— a divided and weak union movement.

Even after some years of socialist government the precise effect on this authoritarian form of organisation is still not clear. The signs, however, are more of continuity than of change.

Britain[5]

After the Second World War there was less impulse in Britain than in France or Germany for a break with the past, indeed less sense of the need for rapid economic growth. The dominant emphasis, built on memories of the 1930s, was on redistribution and full employment. After the Labour government's initial enthusiasm for nationalisation and planning, a consensus around Keynesian demand management in the context of a liberal economic order was formed. This consensus was strengthened by the rapid achievement of a low rate of unemployment and by a growth rate in the 1950s that was high by historical standards. Yet this growth was low by European standards and punctuated by the 'stop-go' cycle as reflation of the economy led to inflation, balance-of-payments crises, and subsequent deflation. The cycle was intensified by the vulnerability of sterling — then an important reserve currency — to international speculation.

As the 1960s developed, a far greater perception emerged of the British economy's failure to grow as fast as those of many other countries and its consequently faltering position in the world economy. But there was no clear consensus on what should be done about this and the period up to 1974 was characterised by a variety of experiments that do not appear to have reversed the relative decline. These included two expansionary 'dashes for growth' (in 1963 and 1973), an abortive experiment with planning in the mid-1960s (cut short by macroeconomic exigencies), incomes policies, a devaluation in 1967, and a brief (1970—72) flirtation with a more *laissez-faire* approach.

Britain was very severely hit by the first oil shock. A subsequent fall in output was combined, as a result of reflationary policies in 1973 and other inflationary tendencies (such as virtual wage indexation), with an extremely steep rise in inflation from 1973 to 1975 (see Figure 3.2, page 34). Inflation thus became the dominant policy issue (even more than unemployment, the balance of payments, or competitiveness).

After sharply reducing inflation with an incomes policy, from 1976 to 1979 the Labour government attempted to introduce a stricter control of the money supply. This was effective at first, but was then hit by the collapse of the government's incomes policy in 1978. This period also saw the reorientation of industrial policy in a more interventionist direction.

The Conservative government of 1979 introduced a far more stringent form of monetary control, together with its own brand of supply-side policy consisting of rolling back government (privatisation and so on). The monetary policy was associated with a dramatic reduction in inflation (from around 20 per cent in 1980 to under 5 per cent in 1983) and an equally dramatic recession from 1979 to 1982. The severity of events since 1973 has led to a substantial undermining of any economic consensus that might have existed. Most of the debate is between the monetarists, who view inflation as the prime problem, and those who view growth as the main problem and advocate reflation with a degree of trade protection.

It is not unfair to characterise British policy towards industry as one of oscillation, most notably on the issue of nationalisation. But there is also a more concealed stability, in the growth of regional incentives and the strengthening of the competitive climate through competition policy *per se*, and the opening of the market (particularly since the late 1960s) to international competition. Regional incentives became so widespread that their effectiveness as the tool of a directive industrial policy (and even their effectiveness in promoting investment) may be doubted. However, the strengthening of the competitive climate — largely consisting of the reduction in restrictive practices among firms, the tariff liberalisations of the Kennedy Round in the late 1960s and British membership of the EC from 1973 — has fundamentally changed the business environment in Britain, although it has been partly offset by the growth of protection in certain sectors.

The nationalisations and the embryonic planning of the first post-war Labour administration appear to have been a false start in industrial policy. A more activist industrial policy showed itself in several experiments of the 1960s: indicative planning, the encouragement of mergers (through the Industrial Reconstruction Corporation), sectoral programmes (in aircraft, shipbuilding, computers and machine tools, for instance) and the development of a more coherent science and technology policy. This trend was temporarily interrupted by the *laissez-faire* approach of the Conservative government in 1970, yet this same government introduced one of the most comprehensive post-war instruments of industrial policy in its 1972 Industry Act.

The second Wilson Labour government gave a new impulse to industrial policy with its 1975 Industry Act, which created the National Enterprise Board; this was intended to be a major instrument of state capitalism, but only partly fulfilled this role as it was soon to become mainly a support for 'lame ducks' (such as British Leyland). At the same time, the government's industrial strategy represented an important new form of planning — or at the very least cooperation/ corporatism — at the decentralised, sectoral level. There was a rash of sectoral aid schemes, for instance encouraging microelectronics and their applications. On balance, however, it must be said that successive governments have drifted somewhat helplessly towards increasing involvement in the rescue of 'lame ducks'. Simultaneously, there has clearly been a learning process at work, in both offensive (for example, high technology) and defensive ('lame duck') intervention. There is now some prospect of government disengagement from the latter commitment but, in spite of its professed *laissez-faire* philosophy, the present government has retained a substantial emphasis on support for high technology. As in France, there have been clear continuities in industrial policy (more so than in macroeconomic policy).

Britain's poor relative economic and industrial performance is long standing. In the light of this, its poor macroeconomic performance can be seen to be as much an effect as a cause of poor microeconomic performance. It is perhaps particularly dangerous to try to disentangle cause and effect as between poor microeconomic performance and some of the apparently disadvantageous features of the British business environment. Some of these features can be subsumed under two headings: mechanisms of coordination and attitudes to the future.

The relative failure of coordinating mechanisms within British industry is apparent in many respects. These failures occur as much *within* the broad categories of 'industry', 'labour' and 'government', as between them. For instance, British companies appear to have faced a particular problem in consummating mergers and takeovers: firms might grow large yet take a long time to perform better than the sum of their constituent parts. The difficulties may partly originate in problems of labour relations, but they also appear to reflect problems of authority and cooperation within the managerial hierarchy of the firm. Similarly, the structure of British unions has, unlike that in Germany, encouraged interunion and interoccupational rivalry over pay and resulted in competitive wage bargaining which can have an inflationary impact. At the microeconomic level, the existence of interunion rivalry and craft demarcations within plants has created particular difficulties in the introduction of new technologies. There are many ways in which the British system of labour relations does exhibit flexibility, but there is a generally aggressive and confrontational nature to the relationship between strong employers and strong unions which is the legacy of history. Generally — and again a product of a long history — government–industry relations, if not exactly confrontational, have not been close. They have perhaps been no more distant than in Germany, but this factor, together with dominant political traditions concerning the role of the state, does undermine the feasibility of any activist industrial policy *à la française*.

A further persistent element in Britain's adjustment difficulties seems to be a relative lack of concern about, and resources devoted to, future industrial competitiveness, and the strategies needed to achieve this. There is overwhelming, if anecdotal, evidence to this effect. For instance, a frequently voiced complaint about Britain's highly developed equities market is that public companies are constantly forced to give preference to short-term profitability over longer-term strategy. The short-term view is also seen in attitudes towards education and training and in the often inferior social status − again a historical legacy − of business and the applied sciences. It all adds up to a general British conservatism in the face of change. This conservatism may have been reinforced by a long period of political stability − unlike Germany and France, Britain has not known recent military defeat − in which relative economic decline has never become unbearable.[6] In this respect, Britain may now be at a turning point: the decades of the 1960s and 1970s can be seen as involving a decisive turning away from reliance on protected Commonwealth markets towards the more briskly competitive environment of Western Europe (and the OECD countries more generally). Thus, the 'new realism' that has been much remarked on in British industry in recent years may not be solely the product of the particular economic disasters that have befallen the country since the recession of 1979.

A comparison of industrial policies
A comparison of the three countries' industrial policies − including trade policies − is particularly relevant for two reasons. First, the prospects for cooperation, either bilaterally or within the framework of the European Community, are the subject of much discussion. Second, industrial goods are the dominant item of international exchange and this helps to explain why industrial and trade policy comes so high on the international agenda.

There are obvious common elements in the development and characteristics of industrial policy in Germany, France and Britain. The present family of industrial policies − somewhat *ad hoc*, eclectic, but designed essentially as an adjunct to properly functioning markets − originates most importantly in initiatives of the mid- to late 1960s. They appear to have been a response to increasing international competition and, perhaps to a lesser extent, a supply-side response to an emerging perception of macroeconomic problems. In the mid-1970s industrial policy was given further impetus by the worsening of macroeconomic problems in the wake of the first oil shock and by further increases in the pressure of international competition. To judge from the (fragmentary) data on expenditure on industrial subsidies, it appears that industrial policy has grown in importance since the 1960s, and again since the mid-1970s, while levels of expenditure in the three different countries are not wildly different (ranging, according to our estimate, between 2 and 6 per cent of manufacturing value added, with France and then Germany being towards the bottom of this scale, and Britain towards the top).[7]

By and large the three governments have tended to promote the same 'strategic' sectors and defend the same problem sectors, with aerospace, electronics and nuclear energy in the first group, and coal, shipbuilding, textiles and steel (and increasingly cars) in the second. The former, more offensive, variant of industrial policy has used subsidies and procurement and concentrated its largesse on a relatively small number of firms. The latter, defensive, variant has used both subsidies and extensive trade protection.

Beyond these similarities, industrial policy in each of the three countries has its own marked characteristics. German industrial policy is the least *structural* (in the sense of supporting specific size structures of industry, specific firms or specific strategies) and the most *environmental* (that is, setting general environments in which firms, sectors or industries operate). It is true that German structural subsidies concentrate, as elsewhere, on a limited number of large firms but, with the exception of substantial subsidies to coalmining, sectoral and R and D support, they do not loom large in the totality of German subsidies which are very much dominated by regional aid. (The *Land* governments, as well as the federal government, are increasingly active in structural policies for industry.) By the same token, Germany is that country of the three which has most successfully resisted pressures for protection, although, of course, it also uses non-tariff protection. Some say that the federal government can afford to use the rhetoric of free trade when it knows that the *Land* governments will pick up many of its 'lame duck' firms and the Commission at Brussels many of its 'lame duck' sectors. Germany's export interests are so large and widespread that it can be expected to maintain its championship of free trade, although it is just conceivable that it may be willing to compromise to a small extent on protectionism external to the EC ('Euro-protectionism') in order to maintain internal free trade.

French industrial policy is, of course, characterised by firm-specific state 'engineering', that is, the promotion of specific national champions through protection, procurement, subsidies and, most recently, nationalisation. Its relative emphasis in subsidies is both on sectoral aid (to national champions) and on a large export subsidy programme (since about 1975). It is difficult to provide any scientific substantiation to the claim that France protects more than other EC countries: since the 1960s, trade has grown in relation to production at least as fast as in other countries. In the early 1980s, however, balance-of-payments crises turned French thoughts more strongly than ever to the possibilities of selective protection, although this tendency appeared to be checked in 1984–85.

The development of British industrial policy bears some resemblance to that of the French, although it has been less systematic and effective. On the surface at least, it appears to have been less capable of influencing major firms (the British government having less effective power than the French government and the firms being stronger). This has even encouraged the government to become an investor in its own right (in the production of standard semiconductors, for instance). There are some indications that the level of industrial subsidisation in Britain is notably higher than in France or Germany; the covering of losses of 'lame duck' nationalised industries has played a large role in this. Nontariff protection in Britain has also grown. Even though protection does not fit so easily into the post-war British economic tradition, the country's industrial problems make it the ripest candidate for growing protection in the Community (with a correspondingly lesser interest than France or Germany in keeping the internal market of the Community open). Britain has also become — at first somewhat accidentally, but increasingly as a matter of policy — the main springboard for Japanese investment in Europe, although such investment is so far largely confined to motor cars and electronics. This has brought it into substantial conflict with the French government, which has viewed British practice as a factor potentially undermining a common European industrial approach (although the French government is now growing less averse to joint ventures with Japan).

The bases for common interests
This final section will briefly recapitulate what appear, from the foregoing review, to be salient points of convergence and divergence among the three countries.

On the *endowment and structure* of the three economies, Britain's achievement of oil self-sufficiency drives a potential wedge between its interests on the one hand and those of Germany and France on the other, but this could equally well be viewed as the basis for the bargaining of mutual benefits. Beyond this, the similar economic structures of the three countries, and the similar technological threat that they perceive from the US and Japan in the newest technologies, could provide for some convergence of views. Governments may be encouraged to seek bilateral and European deals — as in the case of ESPRIT in electronics, for example — but bilateral government-to-government cooperation has not yet proved important or very efficient (with some partial exceptions such as military aircraft and space). So far at least, the technology lag appears to have encouraged a new round of competitive national subsidisation, and the forging of bilateral links with US or Japanese firms, rather than to have encouraged the pooling of efforts among weak European countries and firms. There is evidence that German firms find it particularly easy to cooperate with US or Japanese partners.

The most substantial bilateral axis which exists among the three

Table 3.7 Share of major partners in trade and investment around 1980

	Trade, 1980		Stock of foreign investment, around 1978—80	
	Imports	Exports	Inward	Outward
Germany				
France	11	13	6	11
Britain	7	6	8	4
Other EC	29	28	17	21
US	8	6	41	21
Other	45	47	27	43
Total	100	100	100	100
France				
Germany	16	16		7
Britain	5	7		8
Other EC	24	28		17
US	8	4		14
Other	47	45		53
Total	100	100		100
Britain				
Germany	11	11	2	8
France	8	8	5	4
Other EC	22	25	12	12
US	12	10	60	20
Other	47	46	22	57
Total	100	100	100	100

Sources:

Trade: United Nations, *Commodity Trade Statistics Series D*, New York, various issues.

Investment: Germany: Deutsche Bundesbank, *Monthly Report*, vol.34, no.8, August 1982 (end-1980 stock of investment);
France: *Journal Officiel*, no.3, 25 February 1981, 'Les Investissements Français à l'Etranger et les Investissements Etrangers en France', Table 14 (cumulative value of investment flows, 1973—78);
Britain: *British Business*, 27 February 1981, pp. 425—7 (end-1978 book value of net assets in all industries except oil, banking and insurance).

countries — as measured by the institutionalisation of economic policy dialogue and the level of transactions — is clearly the one between France and Germany (see Table 3.7). Above all, this reflects many decades of political rivalry, followed by the close cooperation of the post-war years, and culminating in the Franco-German initiative to establish the EMS. Even now, this relationship is undoubtedly fostered in part by the French obsession with German economic strength. In addition, the two economies have been growing at comparable rates since the war (with France converging on Germany). If historical legacy and economic convergence are thus the mainstays of bilateralism, this would help explain Britain's peripheral role relative to France and Germany up until now.

This chapter has stressed important differences between the three countries in terms of their national *business environments and societal objectives*, which have done much to form, and influence the directions of, macro and microeconomic policy. Germany's *Leitmotiv* has consisted of stability, consensus and vigorous competition, and France's of growth and authoritarianism. On the other hand, Britain's has been redistribution in a market system that nevertheless lacked the effectiveness of the German system for several historical and social reasons. However, is there not a danger of exaggerating these differences? All three countries have functioned since the war as open, mixed economies. Membership of the European Community has probably moved them even closer together.

There is no clear evidence, however, that a strong consensus exists on *macroeconomic management*. The three countries certainly face similar economic challenges and currently have adopted broadly similar restrictive policies, but Germany has the greatest internal consensus on conservatism in such policies, while in France and Britain in particular a substantial domestic split appears to be developing on the choice of appropriate policy. Under these circumstances, much will depend on the outcome of elections.

Finally, we have seen that there are elements of both convergence and divergence in *industrial policy*. Britain and France resemble each other in style, perhaps, while Germany and France resemble each other in effectiveness. Moreover, the indications are that it is Germany and France which are the more serious about conducting industrial policy within a European framework.

Notes

1. Commission of the European Communities, *European Economy*, no.18 (Brussels, November 1983), Tables 35 and 36 of Statistical Appendix.
2. The discussion of Germany is particularly based on Ernst-Jürgen Horn, *Management of Industrial Change in Germany*, Sussex European Papers, no.13 (Brighton, Sussex European Research Centre, 1982); Klaus Heinrich Hemmings, 'West Germany' in Andrea Klaus-Werner Schatz and Frank Wolter, *International Trade, Employment and Structural Adjustment: the Case Study*

of the *Federal Republic of Germany*, World Employment Programme Research Working Papers (Geneva, International Labour Office, 1982).

3. For an argument along these lines see in particular Andrew Shonfield, *Modern Capitalism: the Changing Balance of Public and Private Power* (Oxford, Oxford University Press, 1965).

4. The discussion is largely based on Patrick Messerlin, *Managing Industrial Change in France*, mimeo (Brighton, Sussex European Research Centre, 1983); and Christian Santtee, 'France' in Andrea Boltho (ed.), *The European Economy: Growth and Crisis* (Oxford, Oxford University Press, 1982).

5. See Margaret Sharp, Geoffrey Shepherd and David Marsden, *Structural Adjustment in the United Kingdom Manufacturing Industry*, World Employment Programme Research Working Papers (Geneva, International Labour Office, 1983); and Michael Surrey, 'United Kingdom' in Boltho, op.cit.

6. See Marcus Olsen, *The Rise and Decline of Nations* (London, Yale University Press, 1982) for a considered argument of how periods of continuity create organisations of common interest that resist economic change.

7. Our estimate is based on figures provided by Schatz and Wolter, op.cit.; Messerlin, op.cit.; and Sharp, Shepherd and Marsden, op.cit.

4 National Images, the Media and Public Opinion
Caroline Bray

Introduction

The 'images' which people develop of another country are complex sets of ideas and associations from a variety of sources and change over time. From childhood on, in the family and at school, impressions are built up, most vividly from travel and direct contact, but more continually from school books, adult comment, the press, radio, television and films. Even as an adult, the individual continues to react to fresh information on the basis of the 'facts' he or she 'knows' already; this applies to impressions of first visits abroad as well as to study. Furthermore, one's image of another country is closely determined by the image one has of one's own country. This holds true for political élites and decision-makers, as well as for the general public.

One vital source of national 'self-images' and images of others is the consciousness of national history. As Alfred Grosser puts it:

Adult French people of today have been marked by the history teaching they received in primary school as 'History of France' . . . French nationalism and the French sense of a mission cannot be explained without this . . .[1]

The stereotyped images of other peoples which a society holds, images derived from its own history and that of others, are often perpetuated for decades, through books, the media and other channels. It goes without saying that deep-seated images of this kind often condition reactions to current events.

This chapter discusses first the kind of historical images of each other which educated French, German and British people may hold. The next section of the chapter discusses the way the media in each of the three countries tend to present the other two, and their common dealings in the European Community, and what are the most common elements of their public images in political and economic terms. Third, trends in public opinion attitudes towards each other in the three countries are illustrated, and the connection between these attitudes and the media images is explored. Finally, some conclusions are drawn about the kind and degree of influence upon élites in the three countries which may result both from media-inspired images and from public opinion trends.

The 'lessons of history' and the images of today[2]

This section will attempt to isolate and assess one of the many factors which influence the attitudes of the German, French and British publics and decision-makers to each other. When a meeting takes place between, say, the German Chancellor and the British Prime Minister, or between a French and a German civil servant, or between a French and a British parliamentarian, their approach to the encounter will obviously be influenced by a variety of factors, including the nature of the occasion and the agenda, the wider implications of the transaction, and the general political or other convictions of each of the participants.

However, one of the important factors — particularly for interlocutors who have not had considerable experience of their partner's country — will be a conception of the other country's behaviour based on some sense of the 'lessons' of historical experience.[3]

The content and effect of any individual's historical perceptions are by definition subjective and individual, but it is worth attempting a summary (itself perforce subjective) of the kind of historical images which appear likely to be at work in influencing attitudes towards each other in the three countries we are considering.

What follows is a sketch of the kind of 'lessons of history' which a British decision-maker or other educated member of the public in the 1980s may 'know' about the Germans and the French; what his or her French counterpart may 'know' about the Germans and British; and what the German counterpart may 'know' about the other two.

A *British* view of *Germany* would start with highly negative images of twentieth-century history, especially the two World Wars, but would probably not contain very clear ideas about anything prior to 1900. (Bismarck might be vaguely perceived as the Iron Chancellor — and possibly even as the originator of social insurance policies copied by the British before 1914 — but this is about all. It is hardly realised in Britain that the Prussians played any part in the defeat of Napoleon at the battle of Waterloo and it is doubtful whether the image would include any notion of what it meant that the Hanoverian kings of the eighteenth century came from Hanover.) The images of the two World Wars would be very clear — both experiences made deep and lasting marks on the British national consciousness, leaving a negative stereotype of Germany as aggressive and militaristic — but they would not be entirely negative: many British would regard the Germans as 'worthy enemies', and such figures as Baron von Richthofen or Field Marshal Rommel have acquired almost the status of heroes.

The British image of Germany after 1945 is one of a prosperous country — prosperous to a point which sometimes provokes envy and irritation. This may be partly because British awareness of Germany's nineteenth-century technical advance was slow to develop. The explanations for this post-war prosperity which were current a few years ago — namely that West Germany received proportionately too high a share of

Marshall Aid, and made no contribution to Western defence — have now given way, probably, to admiration for Germany's higher productivity (based on traditional German virtues of discipline and hard work), but an element of irritation remains. More generally, a Briton's view of the FRG's international role might include the idea that it tended to block possible East—West détente moves under Adenauer, and that it may have gone too far in the other direction under Brandt (although the *Ostpolitik* was welcomed by all British political parties). In any case Adenauer, Brandt and Schmidt will all have left a generally positive image, at least for a reasonably well-informed British observer.

The *British* view of *France* is more complex than the view of Germany partly because the combination of cultural closeness and political enmity between the two countries goes back so much further. Even though few Britons today would seriously regard the Norman Conquest of 1066 as a French invasion, the Hundred Years' War and the wars against Louis XIV and Napoleon, bound up with the British national self-image, have left clear traces, as have colonial contests in India, North America and Africa. As well as the images of Parisian frivolity and decadence in the nineteenth century, many older British people retain an image of France as Europe's cultural leader and the arbiter of taste. Despite the Entente Cordiale, France has seemed to most British an unreliable ally: the French army mutinies of 1917, the collapse of 1940, de Gaulle's wartime intransigence, and the failure of the Anglo-French attack on Suez have left traces in British military minds. The political instability of the Third Republic, leading to the collapse of 1940 (seen as an internal collapse totally unconnected with British policy) is a further part of the British picture. The image of the Fourth Republic is similar to that of the Third; and even though President de Gaulle is still given credit for the restoration of stability and prosperity in France, his intransigent opposition to Britain's perceived interests (entry into the European Community, Atlantic solidarity, or the integrity of Canada) have left him a controversial and unsympathetic figure in many British minds.

The *French* image of what the *Germans* have meant historically still includes the concept of the 'hereditary enemy', the country against which French unity was completed in the Thirty Years' War and which created its own *Reich* in opposition to France in 1871. At the same time, Germany was culturally admired and provided a fitting foil to France's own cultural achievements, but its superior economic and demographic strength has long been seen as a threat. A recurrent theme in the French picture of Germany is *'les incertitudes allemandes'*. The war of 1914 is now seen as only partly *Germany's* responsibility, but the Third Reich tends to be regarded less as an aberration from Germany's general evolution than as a natural development from some aspects of it. The German occupation after 1940, although essentially an appalling memory for the French, will also recall, for some, memories of human contacts between individual French and German people that were cooperative and even pleasant: for occupiers and occupied, there are memories of a shared response to a situation for which few of them felt personally responsible. Partly because of uncertainty over German reunification aims, one aspect of Germany's interwar history which has left strong traces in France is the kind of *Ostpolitik* represented by Rapallo or by the Hitler–Stalin pact of 1939: the image of Germany slipping out of the Western system into an anti-Western understanding with the Soviet Union remains strong. Memories of Briand's failure to create European Union with Stresemann, and its perceived consequences, have contributed to the French idea that cooperation with Germany's leaders, from Adenauer to Kohl, is the only way forward for France. Even stronger in the early post-war period was the determination never again to allow German industry to support German military power. Despite years of peace the inexorable rise of the FRG to economic dominance has frequently evoked historical images of German domination. The negative image of Germany as a soulless, materialist, and ultra-conservative society (at the same time Americanised in the sense of being arch-capitalist and culturally decadent) — the image depicted by some French intellectuals at the time of the Schleyer affair — is also present in some French minds, but seems less influential than the image (as expressed, for instance, in the Kohl/ Mitterrand communiqué at Verdun in 1984) of the country which history has made into France's principal partner.

The *French* idea of the *British* is shaped by memories of centuries of warfare, including not only battles for French territory but also a number of wars where Britain led continental coalitions against France. *'Perfide Albion'* is seen as a power which has often brought disaster to France, usually by a combination of force and deceit, as in the burning of Joan of Arc, the humiliation of Captain Marchand at Fashoda in 1898, or the callous sinking of the French fleet at Mers-el-Kébir in 1940. England is also seen as an incurably hypocritical country, as evidenced by its self-proclamation of liberal tolerance, contrasting with its systematic 'persecution' of Catholics until at least the nineteenth century, not to mention its ruthless oppression and exploitation of Ireland. In international affairs, *'perfide Albion'* is seen as an unreliable partner, as indicated by its behaviour before 1914 and again in the 1930s, its abandonment of France in 1940, and its resistance to the idea of European unity after 1945. In this last connection, the country which for so long insisted on giving priority to its non-European connections, and which tried to put a brake on institutional developments on the continent, is still seen as an unreliable member of the European system. Monnet's idea that the British are better at accepting facts than ideas is widespread in France: Britain's late 'conversion' to Europeanism by 1960 is seen as a reluctant acceptance of the inevitable.

The *German* view of the *French* tends to ignore historical evidence of much cooperation (for instance French support for Prussia against Austria), and to see France as the 'hereditary enemy', the opponent of

German unity through the centuries. France is historically seen as the enemy which has constantly tried to encircle Germany in a ring of alliances and at times to detach Alsace-Lorraine, the Saar and even the Rhineland. The collapse of France in 1940 tends to be seen as a result of the country's internal decadence, and France's claim to be one of the victors of 1945 to be greeted with derision. On the other hand, the fact that Germans and French have a common interest in maintaining a selective picture of the wartime years was for several decades after 1945 a powerful antidote to excessive memories of enmity: the barriers to fuller discussion of the two countries' respective roles have been breached only since the late 1970s, with television films and documentaries such as *Holocaust* or *Le Chagrin et la Pitié*. The French in the post-war period would be seen in Germany as hard bargainers in the process of European unification, but as essential partners in the process of Germany's post-war economic and moral rehabilitation. From Robert Schuman to de Gaulle and his successors, French leaders are mainly seen as reliable friends of Germany, and de Gaulle is sometimes given the credit not only for supporting Bonn more staunchly than Kennedy and Macmillan in the Berlin crisis of 1958—62, but also for being the only Western leader since the war to propose any imaginative solutions for the problem of Germany's division. The German image of Adenauer's generally good relations with de Gaulle, and perhaps also of Schmidt's good relations with Giscard d'Estaing, confirm a general sense that France and Germany — despite, or because of, what are perceived as their centuries of enmity — are linked together in a 'community of fate', a *Schicksalsgemeinschaft*, which it well behoves modern-day French and Germans to develop positively.

The *German* view of the *British* is different. To be sure, there has not been the centuries-long history of warfare, but there have been enough occasions when Britain was one of Germany's enemies, despite Protestant royal links from the sixteenth century (Anne of Cleves) to the Hanoverians (Queen Victoria) and the Battenburgs. Even though Britain *did* fight both in 1914 and in 1939, the uncertainty of this — Bethmann-Hollweg's uncertainty about Grey, Hitler's uncertainty about Chamberlain — seems to have left an image of British policy as *unberechenbar*, 'unpredictable'. As for Britain after 1945, there was a country which was, to be sure, an enlightened occupying power, and reliable on the whole in its support for German interests (including the freedom of West Berlin and even, in theory, reunification), but somehow distant from European concerns at the same time. Britain's attention seemed constantly distracted to non-European issues such as Suez, Rhodesia, or the Falklands. The long British indifference or even opposition to the attempts at West European integration, the hesitations of Britain's approach to Community membership, and the turbulence in its behaviour as a member, have confirmed this image of *Unberechenbarkeit*.

In conclusion, the importance of historical 'scratches on our minds', of the kind outlined here, will inevitably be open to controversy: *'chacun sa verité'* will apply, not only in drawing the 'lessons of the past', but also in judging their influence in the present and the future. The French navy will probably never forget Mers-el-Kébir, but this did not prevent strong naval cooperation during the Falklands war in 1982, and it is mostly unlikely to inhibit Anglo-French cooperation in aerospace. The German picture of Britain as less committed than France to the development of the European Community appears fairly durable, but it does not in practice affect discussions between Bonn and London on a range of other issues, notably those of defence and East—West relations.

Perhaps two general conclusions may be drawn. Firstly, the sense of history, and its role in our present-day relationships, appears to be *very* strong in the relevant French minds, *quite* strong in German minds, and fairly weak in British minds. Secondly (and connected either as cause or as effect with this), German and French decision-makers often appear to act as if they had a degree of shared consciousness, a *Schicksals-gemeinschaft* imposed on them by history as well as geography, and by shared legal and philosophical traditions, which creates a political will to overcome differences and try to work together; the British appear to be excluded (in part self-excluded) from this particular dimension of relations among the three nations.

The media as a source of country images

One way in which the 'lessons of history' may become part of a current image or stereotype of another country in political or economic terms, is when 'memories' are revived by news of fresh events. The chief source of current information about a foreign country is often the media, whether quality press and broadcasting or popular mass media. The journalistic profession thus become the key communicators of information about 'abroad', along with their own stereotyped views. In the quality press they may both reflect and help to mould opinion among decision-makers as well as the general public. Some of the resulting media images are examined below.

Negative German stereotypes have appeared in the French media in response to political events. Anything which suggests right-wing authoritarianism — the existence of the *Berufsverbot* and then the terrorist incidents and official reaction to them — have nourished fear of German totalitarianism. West German anti-communism and the American—German relationship evoked the theme of 'German—American domination in Europe' among (predominantly left-wing) journalists and politicians. In 1977 several anti-German articles published in *Le Monde* provoked a spate of media polemics.[4] On the other hand, the Bonn government's mild reaction after the imposition of martial law in Poland in December 1981 aroused accusations of a pro-Soviet line, and the German peace movement inspired French media fears of a 'new Rapallo', a neutralist deal with the East. In 1983, the long debate about the stationing of medium-range ballistic missiles evoked similar stereotyped reactions. However, since 1983 and the settlement of these issues, French coverage of German affairs has broadened in range and quality of presentation. The above negative images apart, West German politics have for more than a decade provided a model of a stable democracy which French commentators previously found in Great Britain.[5]

Studies of the French and German media highlight the discrepancies between the volume and quality of German coverage of France, and the less extensive French coverage of Germany, especially on television. Concern used to be expressed at the volume of French television coverage devoted to themes of the last war. Since the late 1970s such coverage has diminished and the German image has begun to alter as French producers and historians have examined more deeply France's own wartime activities.[6]

The economic images of Germany in the French press (little such information appears on television) have been contradictory, reflecting differences of political perspective. Fears of German economic domination in some quarters were paralleled in others from the mid-1970s by eulogistic references to the German economic model. The French trade deficits and currency crises of the early 1980s revived the spectre of German economic and industrial imperialism.[7] A more balanced view of German policy became current in the wake of the mid-1983 adjustments by the Mitterrand government, and in the light of Bonn's own difficulties with trade recession.

In both countries, regular coverage of the bilateral relationship and meetings of leaders counterbalances one-sided criticisms. The French press was said by an editor of the news agency, Agence France Presse, to have a 'businesslike' interest in anything planned by the Germans which it sees as affecting France directly, especially in the economic sphere. 'In times of crisis the whole country is aware of how vital to France is the Franco-German alliance. This is not based on sentiment; the French simply feel the Germans are more important to them and are able to help them.' This is not the case with Britain: 'the French take British friendship for granted' but feel it is less useful.[8]

The first thing to note on turning to the German media is that, although their coverage of France is very copious, its quality does not always aid understanding between the two countries. Partly because of the record of the Third and Fourth Republics, France is widely presented as politically, economically and socially unstable. In contrast to a Federal Republic grown conscious of its own international responsibilities, France appears as a country in continual crisis, unable to solve its own problems. Increasingly through the 1970s, the major emphasis in German articles was on the internal political problems of France, a 'blocked' society, but these were judged by German values and criteria.

French communism and nationalism remain little understood by the Germans, because little attempt is made to explain them in their historical or social context.[9] Criticism of the Mitterrand government has been more outspoken, defining the gulf between accepted German economic policy norms and the French interventionist tradition carried to its logical socialist conclusions. However, moderation of the earlier line has somewhat allayed German fears of French instability and unreliability. The anti-French tone of the weekly *Der Spiegel* has moderated since 1983 as have economic strictures by the weighty *Frankfurter Allgemeine Zeitung.*

Although German television frequently tries to present analysis of French events, there has been a relative drop over the last five years in the overall level of broadcast and printed foreign news coverage, reflecting a rising preoccupation with domestic problems. The German media also help to perpetuate many clichés about France as the land of wine, cheese and perfume (assisted by the advertising industry). President Walter Scheel in 1977 criticised the press for too often ignoring positive aspects of French trade and industry, science and technology.[10]

Germany's television, radio and press coverage of Britain has also seen a slight decline in volume, but recently the tone has been more positive. The very large German press corps in London (slightly larger than in Paris for reasons of international interest)[11] contributes to a thorough coverage of British events, with the economy a central focus. With some exceptions, the German media largely reflect British media criticisms, perpetuating to some extent the cumulative image of the 1970s of an economy in crisis and torn by strikes. There is strong interest in the British trades unions and efforts at curbing what is seen as their excessive power.

The image of Britain has improved in the 1980s, however, first because the Federal Republic is itself now experiencing some of the same symptoms of recession, and second because the British Prime Minister Margaret Thatcher is admired as an achiever, a *Macher* (even over the Falklands, although that raised severe misgivings about militarism and colonialism). Much of the German press (and the Kohl government) would like to imitate the Conservative government's efforts at privatisation. Nevertheless, with the incidence of strikes, for example in the car industry and coalmining where they are expected, old images recur very fast.

In the German press as a whole, there is little scope for political analysis of Britain, whose institutions remain unexplained except by a few major papers. There is curiosity about the Royal Family and about social and legislative matters, but European Community coverage in the German media is often critical of British *'non-communautaire'* positions, particularly where German interests are affected. Before Britain joined the Community, it was seen as a model of parliamentary democracy; since then, this image has been erased by Britain's intensified social divisions as well as by the FRG's own political consolidation. According to a French correspondent in London, for French readers, too, British institutions like the TUC, which differ markedly from those of France, need to be explained each time they are introduced. But explanations are not always given. Even in the case of *Le Monde*, an editorial could show a (fairly common) French dismissal of the British as different and non-Continental (for instance, Mrs Thatcher's 'incomprehensible' election victory despite 3 million unemployed). Like other French papers, *Le Monde* in its reporting and comments on British policy in the European Community has often been limited largely to stereotyped views rather than analysis.[12]

In the media as a whole there has been slightly greater interest in Mrs Thatcher and her policies since 1981, due in part to the fact that the right-wing press have tended to see in Britain a possible alternative economic example (although hardly a 'model'). This contrasts with continued criticism of British economic policies, most of it on the Left, which includes the drawing of unflattering comparisons with French success in holding down unemployment.

The two major French television channels, TFI and Antenne 2 both have news correspondents in London. TFI news bulletins show at most two short items (of 1½–2 minutes) a week from Britain, including serious political or economic items but with a leaning towards lighter pieces about Royalty, or 'scandals'. Antenne 2 attempts more serious and extensive coverage; an effort is made to convey British perceptions of events. The correspondent Bernard Rapp was attacked by some commentators in France for being 'a mouthpiece of the British government' for his Falklands coverage. Lighter items and 'British views of the French' are popular, as well as examples of British experience in some areas of legislation under discussion in France (for example, transport or social policy). The comment of experienced observers is that little time is given to placing the news in context (a criticism which is, of course, also levelled at British television). Like many of their German counterparts, the popular French press tend to 'personalise' news about Britain, and to echo the exaggerated interest of the British popular media in the personal role of Mrs Thatcher.

Turning to British mass media coverage (both press and television), the general level of news about other European countries is low, no doubt reflecting a belief that the British are primarily interested in domestic problems. The extreme national-centredness of the presentation is remarked on by officials at embassies in London, although they regard foreign coverage in the quality press as largely fair.

A clear distinction must be made between the 'tabloid' mass circulation press and the more serious dailies and weeklies. Among the latter, the daily *Financial Times* and weekly *Economist* with their international readerships, especially in the business community, have a special role, providing wider coverage and thoughtful analysis of European affairs.

Their editorial policy is partly aimed at foreign readers, including French and Germans, and attention is given to the internal affairs of those countries. A few other quality British journals, including *The Times*, also have European readerships, and cover French and German politics, but commercial pressures have in general led to a reduction in coverage of foreign topics other than the superpowers, trouble spots or stories of direct domestic relevance, an approach echoed in the broadcasting media.

It is worth noting that there are no resident British television correspondents anywhere on the European continent, so that what coverage there is comes either from foreign networks or from 'crisis reporting' by a journalist sent to cover an event − be it a summit conference, election, major strike or violent demonstration. He may lack the background knowledge to set his report in context unless he is one of the few correspondents specialising in French or German affairs for either the BBC or the independent channels. Even BBC radio now carries little political analysis of French or German affairs. BBC television news editors have long sought to base a correspondent in Paris, but so far without success.[13]

At intervals during the 1970s and 1980s concern has been expressed about the distorting effect of the continued showing in Britain of war films and documentaries, without a compensatory balance of information on modern Germany. Newer stereotypes can also emerge: a televised documentary series *The Miracle Workers* (September 1980) presented the 'disciplined and hard-working' Germans in a way which typified British admiration bordering on envy for their industrial success. These clichés may, however, be balanced by positive media coverage of the Anglo-German relationship at government level.

There is little coverage of France on British television, except for travel programmes, occasional films, and isolated documentaries (*The Year of the French* series, in 1983, gave a variety of sociological insights into French life). Many frivolous images are popular (beret, bread stick and Gauloises). The stereotyped responses of the popular press to French policy on European Community issues, especially on agriculture, are discussed further below.

A case study showing the 'personalised' approach of the French media to Britain, and the ethnocentricity and defensiveness of the British press, has been based on their respective coverage of the European Council meeting at Maastricht in 1981, where the main conflict was over fisheries policy.[14] The study examined six French and twelve British newspapers and, in brief, found that whereas 86 per cent of French headline coverage drew attention to European rather than national themes, 75 per cent of the British articles stressed national elements. The major stress in the French popular press was on Mrs Thatcher's intransigence and aggressiveness, and her betrayal of a 'gentleman's agreement' with Herr Schmidt (and the rest of the EC) in

May 1980 regarding an interim budget rebate for Britain. The two researchers found that the French press's unanimous characterisation of
Mrs Thatcher was a real obstacle to understanding of the issues which
were examined sparsely, if at all.

All the British press presented Britain's partners as being to blame
for the 'Maastricht fiasco', with a majority seeing France, and some
Germany, as the main culprit, and several, especially among the popular
and right-wing papers, discerning a Franco-German alliance against Mrs
Thatcher.

Criticism, which could equally be applied to the British press, was
that French journalists seem mesmerised when reporting on Britain and
Mrs Thatcher, making no effort to understand British positions, and
one simple idea predominates: that the British are difficult to get on
with. The attitudes which this study reveals still persist. A campaign in
The Sun, following the hi-jacking of British lamb lorries in January
1984, invited readers to submit anti-French jokes (*Le Monde* retaliated,
not very seriously, with its own competition).

Evidence from other sources suggests that the British public has
more interest in France and Germany, and perhaps in the Community,
too, than editors suppose. The striking number of 300,000 people (UK
viewing figures, 1981) stayed up until 23.30 to watch the adult education programmes *Heute Direkt* or *Télé Journal*, presenting news shown
by German- and French-language channels earlier that day: some indication of a level of interest that may grow with satellite broadcasting.[15]

Apart from the perpetuation of stereotyped views, sometimes with
long historical antecedents, the problems arising in media images between the three countries could be summarised by saying that the
media (particularly the British and French popular press) often assume
low public interest in the affairs of the other countries; that the other
countries are often presented in a personalised way, related to the
personality of, say, Mrs Thatcher or President Mitterrand; and that the
media in each country often tend to endorse the views put out in briefings by their own national government, rather than to challenge or
question them. On the other hand, they may have difficulty in gaining
access to official views at all. The readiness to speak to the press on the
part of French, and (more so) of German Ministers, and their spokesmen, contrasts with the habit of their British counterparts to say as
little as possible in public; foreign correspondents in Britain (and to a
lesser extent in France) find themselves with restricted access to official
information. The German system would seem to offer the best chance
of understanding by élite and popular foreign and domestic media of
official positions on specific events, while the Whitehall system is now
the most restrictive (see pp. 115–16 below).

These differences in official approach to the media are less marked
in Brussels, where British officials, like the others, must counter competing national versions of events. Foreign correspondents are not

excluded from the different national press conferences, although they may be presented by their own national delegation with harder national positions than are actually being taken by negotiating ministers. The resulting coverage, further sifted by editors in home capitals, is with some notable exceptions highly nationalistic, and allows little room for the interpretation of foreign viewpoints.

The media images of partner countries are directly affected by the way in which European Community issues are presented to the public. In the 1980s a trend towards the personalising of events was discernible, even in the serious press, with a harping on the budget theme and agricultural policy to the virtual exclusion of other topics. However, coverage by the British *Financial Times* and *Economist* with their wide European readership, was at least as comprehensive as parallel reporting by French and German newspapers, and often more balanced.

Public opinion polls and country images
The media are but *one* source of information and of stereotyped ideas which go towards the formation of the image which each individual holds of a foreign country. The complexity of these images, and the components which make it up, are illustrated, at least to some extent, by opinion polls. These polls are chiefly valuable in charting the development over time of broadly positive or negative views, and can also provide interesting insights into the public's opinion on some specific issues in bilateral relationships, despite certain contradictions.

General attitude trends
Questions about which country is the 'best friend' of one's own, or about various characteristics or attitudes, tend to be asked in ways which are not consistent between polls and cannot provide true indications of trends nor, often, of the broad range of public opinion at the point of enquiry. Confining our attention to the 1970s and 1980s, however, some general trends can be discerned.[16] Among the more reliable indicators are the EC-sponsored Eurobarometer polls of 1970, 1976 and 1980.

Trust grew between French and Germans between 1970 and 1980; using the index system evolved for this poll (Table 4.1), German trust in the French rose by 22 points during the period, and French trust in Germans rose by 33 points from the very low level of 1970.

Britain was not yet a member of the Community and was therefore not polled in 1970, although the existing members were asked for their opinions about Britain. German views of Britain fell from a high level of trust in 1970 to a low point in 1976 but recovered somewhat by 1980. British trust in the Germans was consolidated between 1976 and 1980.

The French expressed a low level of trust in the British in 1970 which slightly worsened in 1976, to fall back further by 1980. The

Table 4.1   *Trust/distrust between FRG, France and Britain, 1970–80, expressed as a plus/minus index**

Views about:	Respondents in:		
	Germany	France	Britain
Germans			
1970	-	−0.03	-
1976	-	0.25	0.33
1980	-	0.29	0.36
French			
1970	0.23	-	-
1976	0.15	-	0.16
1980	0.45	-	−0.37
British			
1970	0.53	0.16	-
1976	0.16	0.15	-
1980	0.40	0.13	-

Note:
* Questions asked whether a people is very trustworthy, fairly trustworthy, not particularly, or not at all trustworthy; the 'trust index' is derived from subtracting weighted negative from weighted positive percentage replies, resulting in scores ranging from −1.00 to +1.00. The UK was not polled in 1970 before membership of the EEC.

Source: *Eurobarometer*, 14 December 1980, pp. 46, 47.

Table 4.2   *Trust between Britain and France, 1984 (%)*

Question: Do you agree with the following statement:

'One cannot trust the French'   'One cannot trust the British'

British response		French response	
Agree	34	Agree	28
Disagree	45	Disagree	48
Don't know	20	Don't know	24

Source: *Franco-British Attitudes*. A survey for the BBC French Service and the Franco-British Council by Gallup in the UK and Faits et Opinions (France), November 1984. 2,000 interviews per country.

British, on the other hand, moved from about the same level of medium-low trust in the French in 1976 to one of strong distrust in 1980.

In 1983 and 1984 a number of different polls confirmed, first, the generally positive trend in Franco-German relations; second, the British regard for the Germans (as 'best friends' in Europe) and the more hesitant German feelings for Britain; and, thirdly, some diminution in Franco-British distrust by late 1984 following a gradual intensification of ill-feeling from the late 1970s (Table 4.2).

Some specific issues
Opinion polls on specific questions may shed further light on the development of these general attitudes.

The European Community   Interaction between countries as partners in the European Community has been a major source of public images and attitudes which have undoubtedly influenced feelings of trust and distrust.

French and German images of each other in the Community are, as expected, positive. In May 1983, in answer to the question: 'Which two countries within the Community show themselves to be most attached to European integration (*la construction européenne*)?' 56 per cent of French respondents mentioned West Germany, 53 per cent France, 10 per cent Belgium and 7 per cent Britain. A much larger percentage of Germans thought their own country the most devoted to building up the Community: 79 per cent, compared to 36 per cent who nominated France, 19 per cent the Netherlands, and 9 per cent each for Britain and Luxembourg.[17]

The Franco-German alliance is clearly vital to the Community's progress. Nevertheless, the French at least are under no illusion that the partnership 'is' Europe, or is sufficient of itself to guarantee its continuance. In February 1983, SOFRES found that only 26 per cent supported such a proposition, while more than double this figure, 56 per cent, thought that Europe would only be built with an *entente à trois*: West Germany, France, and Great Britain,[18] which should be seen perhaps as a realistic appraisal of Britain's political weight, rather than its 'nuisance value'.

However, by May 1984, a month before the European Parliament elections, patience with Britain as a partner was generally wearing very thin. Asked by Eurobarometer if there were any countries which respondents would be happy to see leaving the Community (multiple choice possible), 25 per cent of British named France, and no less than 41 per cent of French named Britain, as candidates for ejection. But while very few other countries' citizens shared Britain's opinion of France, every other country nominated Britain as least favourite partner, including 33 per cent of Germans, and averaging 25 per cent across the Community. These attitudes towards the UK may have primarily been based on views of its government and leadership as intransigent, especially on the budget issue.[19]

The public image in Britain of West Germany as a Community partner (generally reflecting the intergovernmental relationship) has been predominantly a positive one, in which Chancellors Brandt, Schmidt and Kohl, all popular in Britain, have been seen as conciliators between Britain and France.[20]

The causal connection between the reporting of events and the development of public opinion has been traced in a study of British attitudes towards the European Community in 1972 to 1979.[21] The authors noted that British attitudes towards Europe remained highly positive for several months after participation in the referendum on membership in June 1975. From 1976–77, however, there was nearly constant media criticism of the Common Agricultural Policy and continuing conflicts reported between the British fishing industry and the Community. From 1978 onwards came negative news about the Common Market impact on commerce and industry, and several Labour Party leaders stressed their opposition to the Community. Into 1979, both the General Election campaign and the campaign for the first direct elections to the European Parliament provided a forum for continued criticism. Even the new Conservative government, while supporting membership, stressed the costs to Britain which it was intending to reclaim. Thus the British public continued to acquire overwhelmingly negative views about the Community, and these were reflected in opinion polls, helping to give Britain in turn a negative image in the sight of its partners. Furthermore, those events presented in Britain in most negative terms were ones which particularly involved Britain and France as 'opponents', especially over the Common Agricultural Policy, fisheries, and budget rebate issues. The sequence of media-reported events (many positive aspects of Community relations attracted little attention) offers one explanation for the adverse trend in public attitudes towards Britain and within Britain towards France which the opinion polls illustrate from the late 1970s.

Historical images and bilateral relationships   While the above-mentioned study of British attitudes to the European Community pointed to the short-term effects of political events reported by the media, an earlier study had demonstrated the long-lasting influence of more traumatic events, such as wars, upon the images held of other nations.[22] Yet it also found that over time these stereotypes adapt to the quality of relationships, between governments and between people; liking and friendliness are symptoms and not causes of good political relations. How well have the enemy stereotypes of forty years ago been superseded, and how positive are popular views of the bilateral relationships, as reflected in the opinion polls?

Despite continuing exposure to media images of Nazi and wartime Germany, the association of such images with present-day Germans has constantly weakened. In Britain between 1968 and 1977 there was a 20 per cent decline (from 43 per cent to 23 per cent) in respondents who thought there was any chance of something like National Socialism recurring.[23] Even in France, in 1984, where memories had been recently revived through war crime trials, only 34 per cent could imagine such a possibility, 55 per cent being convinced that the likelihood was remote.[24]

As the images of German Nazism and militarism have been overcome, French and Germans now regard each other as close allies, with a mutual interest in peace. In 1984 52 per cent of French people favoured the idea of a common European defence force with West Germany sharing the French nuclear deterrent (28 per cent opposed).[25] Support in 1983 for a joint Franco-German defence system received almost equal support in both countries: 63 per cent in France, 61 per cent in Germany.[26]

The abandonment of older images has been paralleled by the development of positive views concerning each bilateral relationship, although the two sides of each 'pair' are not always evenly matched. The British not only believe the Federal Republic to be Britain's best friend in Europe, they also believe that the relationship has improved in recent years (in 1979 57 per cent thought so).[27] Yet this feeling was reciprocated by only 26 per cent of Germans, more of whom thought relations had stayed about the same (41 per cent). Whereas the British are positive in their liking of Germans, the latter are unsure of returning the compliment and compare Britain less favourably with other countries (Tables 4.3, 4.4). Even though there is almost equal confidence in each as an ally in any future conflict (Table 4.5), the Germans simply have a higher degree of confidence in the USA and France, the British being possibly still regarded as 'unpredictable'.

The Franco-German relationship, on the other hand, is remarkably mutual with as many as 70 per cent of Germans and 69 per cent of French, in May 1983, expressing themselves in favour of close political union between France and West Germany.[28] Both liking and the sense of friendship and trust are high on each side (Tables 4.4, 4.6), as is confidence that the other will help in an hour of need. In the French case the percentage relying on German help is higher (53 per cent) than the 41 per cent of Germans counting on France (Table 4.5); for Germans, American protection is far more important. The slightly higher reliance by France upon Britain than upon the Federal Republic as a potential ally early in 1984 is not easily explicable, given other findings (Table 4.6), unless it is related to an overestimation of the influence of the West German 'Peace Movement'.

British attitudes to France have also clearly been influenced by historical developments. Even in November 1956, immediately after the Suez crisis, Britain's 'best friend', apart from Commonwealth countries

Table 4.3   Britain's best friend on the Continent of Europe (Selection from countries nominated)

	1963 %	1969 %	1977 %	1983 %
West Germany	7	12	25	27
France	4	5	10	5
Holland	11	13	8	8
Denmark	12	10	4	1
Belgium	7	5	1	1
Italy	2	2	1	0

Source:
Gallup Poll, *Attitudes to European Countries*, August 1983 and other polls.

Table 4.4   Germany's best friend

Question: Which country in the world do you consider to be Germany's best friend? (Selection from countries named by respondents)

	1965 May %	1977 Sept %	1980 Sept %
USA	49	54	51
France	9	10	17
Austria	5	6	6
Switzerland	3	3	2
Great Britain	6	2	2

Source:
Institut für Demoskopie Allensbach: E. Noelle-Neumann (ed.), *The Germans*, p. 408.

Table 4.5   Allies in a crisis (January 1984)

Question put to respondents in each country: Can we count on each of the following countries in any future conflict?

Allies to count on:	As seen by each country (% positive replies)			
	by USA	by FRG	by GB	by France
USA	-	67	56	60
France	60	41	13	-
Britain	81	37	-	57
FRG	60	-	39	53

Source:
Gallup International for Radio France-Inter and *L'Express*, 27 January 1984. Other countries were included.

Table 4.6   France's two best friends (May 1983)

Question: Among the following countries, which two do you consider to be the best friends of France?

	Total*	Age group				Party preference			
		18–24	25–34	35–49	50+	PC	PS	UDF	RPR
West Germany	48	45	47	49	47	41	46	59	56
Belgium	38	31	40	38	39	24	42	40	35
USA	33	37	35	37	29	35	28	41	47
Italy	16	17	18	18	14	20	21	10	10
Great Britain	16	23	15	14	16	14	18	13	17
USSR	2	1	2	3	3	20	2	-	-
No opinion	16	17	14	15	18	16	17	8	11

* Percentages total more than 100, since respondents could give two answers.

Source: SOFRES, *L'image comparée* ..., pp.1, 3.

Table 4.7   British views of the French and Germans

The French	1968	1977	1983	The Germans	1968	1977	1983
Like them	64	74	64	Like them	66	74	75
Dislike them	29	21	33	Dislike them	28	21	21
Don't know	8	5	3	Don't know	7	5	4
	101%*	100%	100%		100%	100%	100%

* Column in originally published report totalled 101%.
Source: Gallup International polls.

Table 4.8   French views of four countries (November 1978)

	FRG		Britain		USA		Italy	
Très sympathique	7	53	7	60	8	54	5	50
Plutôt sympathique	46		53		46		45	
Plutôt antipathique	15	22	9	12	15	19	18	22
Très antipathique	7		3		4		4	
Ni symp., ni antipath.	17		19		16		18	
Ne sait pas	8		9		11		10	
	100%		100%		100%		100%	

Source: SOFRES, *L'opinion française et l'Allemagne*, February 1979, p. 5.

and the USA, was France.[29] Although no longer regarded as Britain's chief partner in Europe by the early 1960s (Table 4.3), France continued to be seen as the most influential country in the Community (by 26 per cent in 1967, with Germany second at 8 per cent). Following French rejection of Britain's second Community candidacy that year, however, attitudes towards the French became more critical. By 1969 Germany was regarded as Britain's 'best friend' in Europe and as having a more powerful voice in the world than either France or Britain. This assumption combined with other factors, such as the negative perception of Britain's European Community membership, to lower British interest in France at most levels of the population, as reflected in the decrease in French news coverage. At the same time memories of the humiliation suffered at the hands of President de Gaulle retained a powerful influence over stereotypes of French perfidy.

The seemingly anomalous recovery in mutual regard around 1977 (Tables 4.3, 4.7, 4.8) may have been due to attempts by President Giscard d'Estaing and his government to revive the Anglo-French relationship. Again, by 1983, President Mitterrand and Mrs Thatcher had been seen to make renewed efforts at entente. More positive popular attitudes emerging during 1984 (Table 4.2) may be due to these efforts, to the popularity of President Mitterrand and to the resolution of the Community budget issue. It would seem to be true that the more stable long-term disposition of both peoples is to like each other and to value being liked by the other.

Conclusions

Attention has been focused on the historic, political and economic aspects of the images of other countries because these are most relevant to the political judgements made by decision-makers, politicians and the public. They give only a partial glimpse of the whole range of country images, which vary with political viewpoint, educational and other experiences. On the lighter side, the image would include way of life, perceived personal traits, sporting prowess, and the merits of actors and entertainers, landscape and cities, food and drink.

The *durability of historical stereotypes* has been shown, both in media presentation of events and the record of public opinion trends. Although it appears that in both France and Britain even long-lived negative images of Germany have faded with time, they may have been superseded by newer stereotypes of 'discipline' and economic success, sometimes with positive, sometimes with negative associations.

Another observation was that the *self-image of a people* has a profound influence upon the kind of image held of others; in the Franco-German partnership, for instance, exploration of France's own war history has influenced views of German history; changing French economic policy criteria have also altered the German 'image'. Similarly, the poor British economic image has been modified partly because of

German and French economic worries.

In general a better understanding of domestic problems and national interests can assist bilateral understanding. When the flow of information about foreign countries is limited, however, stereotypes may still persist. They may affect not only popular images but the understanding of decision-making élites. When foreign attitudes and reactions are understood in terms of received stereotypes, these in turn mould future expectations and behaviour; this seems to have occurred frequently in the Anglo-French context, where the public opinion trend of mistrust and the media reporting and interpretation of events appear to have both reflected and reinforced official viewpoints. This interconnection does not appear so close on the other two sides of the triangle (and one hopes, may already be past between Paris and London).

The media provide the major source of information on day-to-day political and economic events, and also of stereotypes, not only for popular audiences but also in some of the key quality press, like *Le Monde*; this newspaper has occasionally presented a problem in Franco-German and Franco-British relations, because of its close relationship with the French government and élites. By contrast, the international readership of top British business and political journals requires and obtains a more balanced range of information and opinion for élites in all three capitals.

The volume and quality of mass media information exchanged between France and Germany have improved over the last ten years to a level where it probably reflects fairly the intensity of the interchange between ministers and officials, and in business, down to local levels. To this extent the awareness in the media of Franco-German cooperation, although it has often lagged behind the intergovernmental relationship, contributes to positive images.

The positive image of the Federal Republic shared by most Britons is largely centred on economic success. In addition, all German Chancellors since Erhard have enjoyed a highly popular personal image in the media. The apparent closeness of the two governments also feeds popular approval of 'Britain's best friend in Europe'. However, stereotyped wartime images of Germany still recur, even though British journalists seem less ready than French to exploit them. The prevailing German image of Britain as an outdated, inefficient and strike-torn economy, and a bad European partner, has been somewhat modified.

Even the more serious reporting of a dwindling French press and broadcasting corps in the United Kingdom is sometimes overridden by the stereotyped view of editors, dominated in the early 1980s by the unpopular figure of Mrs Thatcher and an image of the British as bad Europeans, which the British media and public opinion often reinforce. While this view by no means necessarily reflects élite French opinion, there has been a discernible decline over perhaps a decade in the level of serious media interest in Britain, probably coinciding with disillusionment with its claimed European commitment. The loss of interest is mirrored in most British media.

A further question explored was the relationship between media reporting of foreign events and public opinion trends. The study of British attitudes to the European Community found a strong correlation between published events and opinion polls. This association with the EC also explained the poor development of Anglo-French mutual attitudes in the same period. On the other hand, a conclusion to be drawn from the experience of French and German media coverage is that the popular relationship is now so close that published opinion has little effect upon public opinion. In the cases cited, neither the events reported nor the prejudiced reactions to them (with support in some élite circles) were perceived by the public as typical of the general development of the relationship. Public images have both a long-term and a short-term aspect: public opinion may react in the short term to media-reported events, but if these do not accord with the long-term trend (either negative or positive), opinion will revert more or less quickly to an established equilibrium.

In the history of all three bilateral relationships, intergovernmental relations have led, rather than followed, public opinion. Nevertheless, British public opinion, say, about their French or German partners and above all about the Community, is not a negligible factor in the dealings of political leaders in Paris and Bonn with counterparts in London, any more than in the Franco-German context, particularly when elections could bring changes in the party in power or when strong local or sectional interests can affect policy decisions.

Popular opinion apart, the persistence of erroneous historical 'lessons', or the recurrence of stereotyped reactions to events among political élites and opinion formers, must create concern in all three relationships for the quality of information available not only through the media but in education, through travel and through cultural contacts. The varying approaches of the three governments to improving mutual understanding are outlined in the next chapter.

Notes
1. Alfred Grosser, 'Vive la Différence', *Zeitmagazin*, 28 January 1983, pp. 4–5.
2. This section is by Roger Morgan, based on a paper presented to a seminar at the Deutsch–Französisches Institut, Ludwigsburg, in November 1983.
3. For analysis of the problem of officials' expectations based on historical precedent, see R. Jervis, *Perception and Misperception in International Politics*, (Princeton, New Jersey, Princeton University Press, 1976).
4. See H. Ménudier, *Das Deutschlandbild der Franzosen in den 70er Jahren*, (Bonn, Europa Union Verlag, 1981); K.-P. Schmid, 'Le Monde und die Bundesrepublik Deutschland', *Aus Politik und Zeitgeschichte*, Beilage zur Wochenzeitung *Das Parlament*, B 12/79, 24 March 1979.
5. See SOFRES, *L'Opinion française et l'Allemagne entre 1973 et 1979*, pp. 9, 27; Hans Hörling, 'La réalité politique allemande vue par la presse française', *Documents* special issue, December 1979, p. 116.

6. R. Stephan, 'Über die Macht der Bilder', *Dokumente* special issue, February 1984.

7. In the 1970s, these images were summed up by such features as 'Faut-il craindre la puissance allemande?', *Le Point*, 31 May 1976.

8. Interview in Paris, June 1983.

9. Ménudier, op.cit., pp. 42–3.

10. H. Ménudier, 'Die Information, Quelle für Konflikte oder für Kooperation?', *Dokumente*, December 1978, p. 127.

11. London attracts correspondents as a major financial centre, as well as a centre for the English-speaking world; Paris has a similar role as the centre of the French-speaking world. It is estimated that in 1983–84 there were 70 German and 20 French correspondents in London; 60 German and 20 British in Paris; about 10 each of French and British correspondents in Bonn, with a number in other German cities.

12. The responsibility may lie less with correspondents than with home-based editors.

13. There are Paris and Bonn correspondents for BBC radio.

14. Annie Cohen-Solal and Christian Bachmann, 'L'Angleterre face à la France: insulaire ou communautaire?' (unpublished report, September 1982, for the Commission of the European Communities).

15. Ian Boyes, 'Modern Language Broadcasts', in *Broadcasting and School Education in Scotland* (Edinburgh, Scottish Education Department, HMSO, 1984).

16. For the earlier development of attitudes in the three countries towards each other, see R.J. Shepherd, *Public Opinion and European Integration* (Farnborough and Lexington, Mass., Saxon House/Lexington Books, 1975); J.E. Farquharson and S.C. Holt, *Europe from Below* (London, Allen and Unwin, 1975), Chapter 10.

17. SOFRES, *L'image comparée de la France et de l'Allemagne de l'Ouest*, Montrouge, May 1983, p. 4 ff.

18. SOFRES, *L'image de l'Allemagne fédérale*, Montrouge, February 1983, p. 7. See also Chapter 8 below.

19. *Eurobarometer*, Commission of the European Communities, no. 21, special issue, May 1984, Table 19, p. 39, and no. 22, December 1984.

20. See survey by Research Services Ltd and Institut für Demoskopie, Allensbach, *Stern* magazine, 15 February 1979, pp. 52–5, and survey by Market and Opinion Research International (MORI) for *The Sunday Times*, 17 June 1984. In the latter poll Britons placed Kohl top, Mitterrand fourth, as most popular statesman, FRG third but France twelfth, as most liked country. Cf. *Le Nouvel Observateur*, 8 June 1984, where a similar poll in France placed Kohl high, Thatcher very low.

21. R.J. Dalton and R. Duval, *The Political Environment and Foreign Policy Opinions: British Attitudes toward European Integration 1972–79* (Tallahassee, Florida State University, and Morganstown W.V., West Virginia University, 1984). See J.G. Blumler (ed.), *Communicating to Voters. 'Television in the First European Parliamentary Elections'* (London, Sage, 1983) for comparative European analysis.

22. W. Buchanan and H. Cantril, *How Nations See Each Other* (Urbana, Unesco, University of Illinois Press, 1953).

23. Gallup International Polls, Social Surveys (Gallup Poll) Ltd., London, 1968, 1977.

24. Poll by SOFRES for Radio France-Inter and *Le Nouvel Observateur*, 10 February 1984, p. 39.
25. Ibid.
26. SOFRES, 'L'image comparée', op.cit., p. 13.
27. *Stern* magazine, 15 February 1979, p. 53.
28. SOFRES, 'L'image comparée', op.cit., p. 12.
29. G.H. Gallup, *The Gallup International Public Opinion Polls: Great Britain, 1937–1975* (Westport, Ct., Greenwood Press, 1976) vol. I, p. 393. This volume is also the source of the other figures cited.

5 Cultural and Information Policy in Bilateral Relations
Caroline Bray

The objective of cultural foreign policy (and information policy) is to win the 'hearts and minds' of foreign populations, generally in order to promote trade for one's products or a favourable disposition towards one's policies. The aim of bilateral cultural cooperation can go further: to create mutual understanding between societies and ultimately to enable them to face jointly common aims and problems. The receptiveness of a people towards cultural relations efforts from abroad depends partly on the level of their interest in cultural and educational matters generally, and partly upon their predisposition towards the country concerned. Cooperative or national effort at building up interest and improving the images is a long, constantly renewed process, closely linked to the developing political relationship. What actions do the three governments considered here undertake in order to promote their respective images in the eyes of their partners?

This chapter begins by outlining briefly the national characteristics which may condition responses to contacts and to cultural relations with other countries, and some of the social influences which underlie these responses. The main section of the chapter then sketches the broad approaches of the three countries' governments to cultural foreign policy and information policy, and goes on to examine impacts and responses within the three bilateral relationships at popular and élite levels. Finally, some conclusions are drawn concerning the appropriateness of these approaches and their possible impact upon bilateral relations at the level of governments.

Popular contacts and cultural attitudes

Several social influences since the Second World War, shared to varying degrees in all three countries, have helped to determine cultural attitudes and the growth of contacts. A most important movement in post-war Europe was the widespread impulse towards reconciliation and friendship, spread by individuals, churches and political parties. Early contacts between French and Germans were arranged by organisations founded by individuals of faith and vision, many of them writers. The Comité d'Echanges avec l'Allemagne Nouvelle, the Deutsch—Französisches Institut in Ludwigsburg, the Cologne-based Gesellschaft für übernationale Zusammenarbeit (with its French counterpart BILD, Bureau International de Liaison et de Documentation) began to create the network of contacts, mutual cooperation and trust which laid the basis for the political *rapprochement* of the 1950s and 1960s. In addition, a number of societies sprang up with membership in the two countries. Among the most important is the Arbeitskreis der deutschfranzösischen Gesellschaften, which links Franco-German associations.[1] BILD and its counterpart publish the journals *Documents* and *Dokumente*, which along with several other French journals devoted to German affairs and German publications on France, have maintained a small but informed readership. These have no counterparts in the Franco-British and German-British relationships, except for more specialised or official publications and association journals.[2]

Reconciliation was also the motive for creating in Germany a Deutsch-Englische Gesellschaft in 1949 and in Britain the Anglo-German Association. The former was especially active in efforts to bring the two peoples together through local groups and visitors from Britain as well as running the Königswinter conferences (see below, pp. 132–3). Anglo-French relations had less need of reconciliation as such, but to cement their alliance a Franco-British Society was created in 1944, followed by the revival of the Association France–Grande-Bretagne in France. Both the above sets of organisations promoted friendship, cultural appreciation and knowledge of each other's society, but their membership has declined over the years.

Linked to the friendship movement was the twinning of towns and communities throughout Europe. The 1963 Treaty of Cooperation gave impetus to Franco-German twinnings, which rose from 126 in 1962 to more than 1,000 links in 1983. British local partnerships are fewer with either country: about 530 with France and 355 with Germany in 1983, the fastest increase having occurred with European Community membership. Not all partnerships remain lively after changes in local politics and interests, but between France and Germany they have been the basis along with the associations for a great network of school and youth links, and popular and professional contacts. Notable geographical differences are the North German preference for links with the Paris region (or with Britain); South German interest in the South of France; Bavarian links with Scotland; and links between French and English Channel ports (most areas have links with *both* the other countries).[3]

Another social development affecting intercountry relations is the growth of mass tourism. The lifting in July 1984 of passport controls at the Franco-German border for citizens of these countries was of both symbolic and practical importance. So, also, would be the building of a cross-Channel link for Franco-British relations. Yet cheap air tours have also raised the sights for all three nations far beyond each other's frontiers. Ease of travel has greatly increased the mobility of young people, with a huge volume of official and private school visits between the three countries. The majority of young people travel without being organised, although many young French and Germans visiting Britain come to learn English at a college or to stay in a family. In the 1960s, the Beatles, Rolling Stones and Carnaby Street gave Britain the lead in a European youth culture, which has remained international. Sadly, football hooliganism has since tarnished Britain's image.

Perhaps the key post-war development to affect communication between these countries is the advance of English as an international language. Despite official commitments, in neither France nor Germany is the language of the other spoken really fluently by more than about 2 per cent of the population (in France mostly in bilingual Alsace and Lorraine, although perhaps 30 per cent of Germans claim to speak French fairly well). Popular preferences on the part of parents and children for English as the principal second language have been too strong for education authorities to ignore them. Increasingly, language studies compete with technical subjects. In the United Kingdom, the incentive to learn any language is reduced, particularly among boys, who are heavily outnumbered by girls in language classes. The majority learn French first, with German second for some; and few reach any degree of proficiency or learn a language in adult life.[4]

The effect of the language situation upon academic cooperation and the exchange of ideas between the three countries will be discussed below. Traditionally, each has a leading place in the intellectual life of the other two through its literature, political thought, philosophy, religion and science.

A fourth social development affecting cultural attitudes has been the growth of the mass media culture. Television and, to a lesser extent, radio and the press are the chief sources of cultural or artistic diet for most of the population, as they are for information about other countries. A high proportion of popular entertainment derives from America. The encroachment of English and of the Anglo-Saxon media culture has particularly affected French attitudes towards foreign cultural influences. National pride still forces many in official and literary circles on the defensive against such threats to the national identity; war is waged against 'franglais'. Nevertheless, there is increasing French interest in the arts from abroad, which are an important means of intercountry communication, given the place of the arts in the lives of educated French people. Germans, too, have a strong interest in the arts with cities and towns throughout the *Länder* supporting their own theatres and opera companies, orchestras, choirs and galleries (as do many French local authorities). Britain also has some lively regional centres for the arts, but these are more dependent upon central government finance, which has never given high priority to the arts and tends to be concentrated upon national activities in London.[5]

These are among the factors which influence reactions in the three populations to contact with the other two countries, their culture and society. They also have a bearing upon the way in which each country approaches its promotion of bilateral relations through cultural and information policy.

National cultural and information diplomacy

The next sections outline first the way in which the three governments have promoted their own countries through cultural and information policy, and second, how this has worked out in broad terms in co-operation with partners.

Both 'cultural' and 'information' policy aim to create positive attitudes abroad and they are discussed in juxtaposition here, although they are organisationally distinct and the latter is more directly 'political' in purpose. Each country's work with foreign press and broadcasting media at home and abroad is of different scope. All three also maintain institutions which disseminate material in their own and other languages to different media and audiences: in Bonn *Inter Nationes* and the *Bundespresseamt*, in London the Central Office of Information (British Information Services) and in Paris *la Documentation Française* and the Service d'Information et de Diffusion. London and Bonn, but not Paris, have departments organising visits for foreign journalists and other opinion leaders.

Broad comparisons can be made between the three countries' organisation of their cultural work: French secondment of education officials to embassies and institutes, German reliance upon career diplomats in embassy cultural work but with independent institutes as well, British separation from its Foreign Ministry of most cultural work in one organisation combining specialists from many fields. There are differences in function and numbers of institutes and personnel, often arising for historical reasons or geographical necessity. The British Council has four centres in the FRG, and five in France; there are seven Goethe Institutes in France, three in Britain; there are 17 French Institutes in the FRG, two in Britain. The picture is balanced by the inclusion of private organisations.[6]

Mutual expenditure between France and Germany is hard to estimate since many different departments and private organisations are involved besides Foreign Ministries. It includes approximately £8 million spent jointly on youth exchanges. Cooperation with Britain is not really comparable: in 1982—83 France spent about £3 million on Britain, Britain £1.5 million on France (British Council only); Britain spent £2.2 million on Germany (British Council); Germany £3.57 million on Britain (1982).[7] Part of these differences arise from local conditions, as in the case of numbers of institutes. They are not necessarily decisive for the relative effectiveness of policies, the main barriers to the success of which may lie in the other country's societal attitudes and domestic institutions.

One such domestic factor, dominating the cultural relations of these three countries, is the issue of language. The domination of English boosts Britain's cultural promotion and Britain's desirability as a partner for educational cooperation, the low interest in each other's language in France and Germany makes cooperation doubly difficult. Trade and cooperation generally between all three would be enhanced by better linguistic skills.

West German cultural diplomacy

Cultural relations have been an essential part of the Federal Republic's foreign policy from its earliest days when, because of post-war national unpopularity, 'culture took precedence over foreign policy and opened the road for it'.[8] In an unfriendly world, where even the German language was unpopular, music became the basis for early cultural contacts. As the new West German state grew in economic and political stature, cultural relations remained 'a pillar of foreign policy', along with information work abroad.[9]

The broad aims of this policy have been clear: to win respect and friendship for the new Germany among allies and trading partners, to replace negative memories and stereotypes, and to promote the German language and culture. Where European Community partners are concerned, and especially in the case of France, the further aim has been to create understanding sufficient for the needs of close cooperation.

Accordingly, the main emphasis has shifted since the 1950s from a concentration on élites to a broader approach, and from the arts to the presentation of the modern Federal Republic, its democratic institutions, way of life and cultural vitality. At the same time, the avoidance of an overtly nationalistic stance has encouraged cooperation with foreign cultural and educational institutions in response to their needs, a response often generously supported financially. Only in the 1980s have cultural budgets been constrained, partly by the recession.

A variety of institutions exist to further this work. The Goethe Institutes (Foreign Ministry-financed but independently run), created initially to support German language teaching abroad, have also been cultural centres, providing libraries, conference and exhibition venues and collaborating with local institutions from universities to art galleries. University exchanges are arranged by the German Academic Exchange Service and for teachers and schoolchildren by the Pädagogischer Austauschdienst, or PAD. The decentralisation of German education and cultural administration was one reason for the creation of a Franco-German Youth Office to facilitate all such contacts, financed by Ministries for Youth in both countries.

There are German historical institutes in both France and Britain, the former founded in the 1960s as a Federal Institution (Bundesanstalt), the latter originating in 1974 from a group of historians in both countries, and supported by the Bonn Research Ministry.[10] Both assist research cooperation by historians of the two countries involved.

In addition there are many institutions, public and private, for specifically bilateral work, the greatest number by far being for Franco-German cooperation.

French cultural diplomacy

For over a century, the strong sense of a national culture has given French foreign cultural policy a missionary zeal, and in the post-colonial decades it became an important focus for the national self-image, although becoming increasingly on the defensive against the advance of English and the 'Anglo-Saxon' media culture. Alongside the presentation of classic arts and language were current affairs and modern French government and policy. However, France's place in the forefront of international academic and scientific exchanges suffered, to some extent, from the focus upon the French-speaking world, which in some spheres isolated it from the main advances in international exchanges (conferences, publishing, and so on). At the end of the 1970s, however, there was a shift towards equality of exchange in cultural relations and increasing access to the cultural and technical achievements of other countries.

This new approach stemmed in part from domestic needs, and paralleled the longer-established pursuit of industrial cooperation with technologically advanced foreign partners. A Report in 1979 by Conseiller d'Etat Jacques Rigaud sparked vigorous debate in France and led to the adoption in 1983 of new Guidelines for French Cultural Foreign Policy.[11] The first objective of the new policy was to combat the continuing parallel decline of French language learning abroad and of interest in French affairs by a more lively presentation of contemporary France, especially through the audio-visual media of mass communication (television and cinema). Secondly, so far as Western Europe was concerned, the policy was intended to enrich French academic and scientific research especially in the social sciences, through bilateral cooperation programmes, while simultaneously promoting French achievements abroad. The quality of France's artistic presence in Western Europe was also to be maintained. This cooperation was to be developed with countries long neglected in favour of West Germany (which remains the principal partner). The large budget increases instituted by the Mitterrand government for cultural development at home and abroad have not, however, been maintained at their early level apart from special programmes.

The new programme has already had some success. It is coordinated by the department in the External Affairs Ministry responsible for relations in the cultural and scientific sphere, which coordinates bilateral contacts made by a wide range of other ministries and government bodies including the Ministry of National Education. The Ministry of Culture also has an International Section dealing with arts and theatre visits.

The role of the French institutes abroad, partly staffed by seconded teachers and lecturers, is primarily to provide French courses, lectures, theatre and cinema. There are differences in French organisations and institutional approach to cultural work in Britain and in West Germany, for instance in education, and a larger number of organisations for bilateral cooperation with the FRG.

British cultural diplomacy
Three main factors, not shared in France or Germany, affect the British approach to cultural foreign policy. First, there is a division between political and operational responsibilities: the bulk of Britain's cultural work is carried out by the British Council, a Foreign Office-financed but operationally autonomous body. The longer-term vision of its professional staff has sometimes been at variance with the political and economic priorities of the government. A linked factor is the peripheral place of the arts and intellectual life in British affairs; the notion of cultural diplomacy and the positive impact of British artistic and technical achievements abroad have not always been understood by politicians or the public. Third, ideas of Britain's international role (and with it, the national self-image) have undergone several drastic upheavals since 1945, reflected in shifts in policy related to Europe and including cultural policy. Charting these shifts are a series of inquiries and reports.[12]

Cuts from about 1948 in cultural activity in Western Europe (with the exception of West Germany) were endorsed in the 1953 Drogheda Report recommendations that greater effort was needed in the increasingly independence-minded Third World. Consequently, British cultural action in France was minimal for twenty years. Official recognition of the effect this possibly had upon Britain's subsequent efforts to enter the European Community and of the greater importance given to cultural relations elsewhere in Europe, was reflected in the Duncan Report of 1969 which recommended increased attention to Western Europe and a change in emphasis from the English language towards the arts and scientific achievements. A cabinet interdepartmental study on Anglo-French cultural relations in 1970–71 made recommendations which were eventually incorporated in a joint programme agreed between the two governments. In addition, on the recommendation of Mr Geoffrey Rippon, Britain's ministerial negotiator for entry to the Community, £6 million was made available in 1972 over four years for a 'European Extension Programme' designed to increase British awareness of Europe as well as to improve Britain's image abroad, and with an emphasis on expansion of youth exchanges and civic links, alongside arts and book promotion, and technical cooperation.

In 1978 the government re-affirmed its faith in the value of cultural diplomacy, rejecting the 'Think Tank' recommendation to abolish the British Council.[13] The need for a renewal of the earlier dual policy towards Europe became apparent and in the 1980s a much smaller European Awareness Programme was introduced, again with a stress on cooperation with the major bilateral partners, France and Germany. Mrs Thatcher's government showed appreciation of the value of British Council activities by moderating budget cuts.[14] However, with regard to its relations with its major sponsoring department, the Foreign and Commonwealth Office, an internal inquiry, chaired by Lord Seebohm, found in 1981 that 'the FCO do not appear to have . . . any clear cut policy on the contribution to be expected from cultural diplomacy to the government's overseas representation'.[15]

In addition to the British Council, several government departments and semi-official bodies are concerned with international exchanges and contacts or act as national coordinating points. The Department of Education and Science has high-level contacts with the French Ministry of National Education for cooperation and exchanges, and has further developed contacts in the FRG. Responsibilities for youth exchanges formerly under the British Council and the Central Bureau for Educational Visits and Exchanges were combined in April 1985 in a Youth Exchange Centre, with the Central Bureau retaining its advisory role for school exchanges.

Cultural cooperation

Germany and Britain

In the governmental perspective, Anglo-German cultural relations mirror the development of the political relationship and each government's view of the receptiveness of the foreign population to the desired image. The developments in popular terms are in opposite directions: German admiration for Britain has waned as British admiration for Germany has grown. British cultural and information work in Germany has shifted in focus and volume from the early days of occupation and reconstruction when a 'market' was created for British information, through periods of greater reliance on German financial support; now that this is restricted, there is a more clearly targeted current approach aimed at influencing the élite and correcting popular images. The German approach has always had more central concern with popular images and stereotypes, particularly among the young of all classes; Britain has been second only to France as a target for cultural and information work in Europe.

There is no doubt that the factor which has most assisted Britain's efforts at cultural and information work in Germany has been the legacy of goodwill stemming from cooperation in reconstruction. The main consequence of the work of 'Die Brücke' (the Bridge), the information and education centres founded under the Allied Control Commission, was the German openness to the British example in democratic institutions, including those of parliament, education, the press and broadcasting; and the importance to Germans of the English language. Many German local bodies demonstrated their feeling for Britain by taking over Die Brücke institutes as these were reduced from 34 to 10 in 1951 and later to six in 1959 when responsibility for cultural work was transferred from the Embassy to the British Council. British cultural policy in Germany was not significantly affected by the 1953 Drogheda Report, since an exception was made for Germany. A Cultural Convention was signed in 1958 pledging educational and cultural cooperation, and the Goethe Institute in London opened that year.[16]

Because of the Federal Republic's decentralised educational and cultural administration, work in Germany has always been expensive for the British Council which was obliged to close the offices in Stuttgart in 1960 and in Frankfurt in 1974, retaining only those in Hamburg, Munich, Berlin, and the Cologne headquarters. Yet a small injection of money for an arts tour or an exchange between technical institutions has often evoked generous and longer-lasting German support. Even in the 1980s with the cutting of local cultural budgets, the British Council needs on average to pay under ten per cent of the cost of the 40 or 50 British exhibitions, opera, music, theatre and ballet performances which it organises or supports in Germany each year.[17]

Educated Germans and experts in their fields find British literature and theatre, education, science and technology (all of which are promoted by the British Council) accessible to them through their knowledge of the English language. Book sales remain high, from fiction to scientific texts. Interest in British education led to following British models for the introduction of microcomputers in schools and for reform in university education. Collaboration, supported by both governments, in scientific and technical research and teaching allows experts in both countries to exchange ideas or to study solutions to common problems. There is some admiration for British 'post-industrial' values.

German students' greater confidence in English and the flexibility of their degree courses has encouraged many more to join in British non-language courses than is the case the other way round. The balance of advantage in broadening of educational experience is thus on the German side, the advantage of being more known – and possibly better understood – on the British side. This pattern is borne out in other spheres.

The only direct English language teaching by the British Council in Germany is in specialised courses in Munich for bankers, lawyers, doctors, teachers and others; at the same time these give influential people increased knowledge of British culture and achievements. Also in Bavaria, and likely to be copied elsewhere, are regular British Council courses and biennial three-day seminars about contemporary Britain for *Land* civil servants.[18]

Concentration upon the élite has long been a necessity imposed by

British government financial stringency in cultural work, reflecting the level of British popular commitment to contacts abroad, which has never matched German popular or official interest in either youth exchanges or town twinning, for example. Anglo-German youth exchanges began in the late 1940s mainly for schoolchildren and students and largely funded by Bonn. Only in 1965 was British government money made available at a fraction of the German contribution, and even in the 1980s it represents a little over 25 per cent of the latter contribution for youth groups.[19] There is nevertheless an awareness, at least among the professionals of British information work, that the young are an important target for influencing opinion. In Germany the British Council has assisted in creating video programmes on modern Britain for schools, and supplies background material for English teaching designed to counteract the unbalanced media image of endless strikes, football hooliganism and un-European attitudes.

The main problem in improving the media image of Britain is the decentralisation of the West German press and broadcasting organisations in the *Länder*. The most effective approach is found to be sponsored visits to Britain for editors and journalists.[20] In addition, the German correspondents in Britain can be offered facilities. However, the lack of openness of the British government information system means that, apart from a few highly experienced correspondents, the German popular and middlebrow press depends excessively for its information upon what is published by Fleet Street.[21] What 'foreign' information policy can achieve here is strictly limited; on the other hand, a more open information policy in British government and institutions generally could, while improving the quality of domestic political debate, also benefit understanding abroad, particularly in the Federal Republic where there is a widespread interest in European and British affairs.

The infant Federal Republic enjoyed no such advantage of popular admiration in Britain in the 1950s, but with rising economic prosperity was soon able to devote considerable funds to its cultural work. Apart from the promotion of German language teaching in schools and universities, German music was the primary vehicle for creating interest in Germany among the educated élite.[22] The establishment of only three Goethe Institutes (the first in London in 1958, followed by Institutes in Manchester and Glasgow, with small offices in York and Birmingham) reflects the relatively limited British 'market' either for cultural activities or the German language, which persists to the present day.

The change in German cultural policy in the early 1970s coincided with recognition by Bonn, at least, of the need to bring both societies closer as Britain entered the European Community. The emphasis shifted to a policy of cooperation with British institutions in mounting joint conferences, exhibitions, and other events, to a more popular approach, seeking wider audiences, and to the projection of modern

German society and technological achievements, rather than classical culture. The success of these approaches is inseparable from the growing public awareness in Britain of the Federal Republic as a major political force and leading partner in Europe; cultural policy could build upon this just as Britain had earlier been able to build upon German goodwill.

British interest grew in German art (with the 'discovery' of Expressionism) and in German cinema, modern music and literature (in translation). The 1970s saw the creation of a UK Association for the Study of German Politics (its activities often supported by official German funds), a German Historical Institute and library in London, and the Anglo-German Foundation for the Study of Industrial Society. British interest in learning from modern German example has tended to centre first on industrial relations and co-determination and secondly on vocational training and apprenticeship schemes (other aspects of German education failing to excite so much interest). Despite a gradual decline in German language study in schools, which causes disquiet, there is a lively and growing demand for adult courses largely for business, and some hope that the development of integrated courses at degree level could widen the appeal of the language to boys.

Nevertheless there is some German concern that the mutual interest between élites and governments does not extend far enough into wider intersociety understanding, despite the vague expressions of admiration and friendship in British public opinion. Youth exchanges and school exchanges have declined in volume in the 1980s, not only because of the drop in British language learning, but also because Bonn has less money available and also has higher political priorities in influencing new generations in the United States and France.[23] Thus, levels of exchange with Britain are unlikely to rise in the foreseeable future. Another area in which German official efforts have been frustrated is in attempts to widen the appeal of the Anglo-German Association and affiliated groups in Britain.

German officials are also concerned at the lack of political news and information about the Federal Republic in the popular press and on television. There are indications that younger British people in particular would like to know more about everyday German life, and the barriers to their doing so appear to lie within the British popular media and the school education system.[24]

British lack of knowledge of German is a limiting factor in Anglo-German communication but not a decisive one. Much exchange of ideas does take place in English, primarily between the better educated. The German concern is that the lower level of British visits, and the British inability to read and listen in German, make for less understanding of their country's problems than is necessary to withstand possible international strains in the future, or to meet the demands of European cooperation in the present.

Although popular mutual understanding may be unattainable, mutual reliance and a sense of partnership are feasible targets for Anglo-German bilateral cultural and information policy. Partly for this reason the two heads of government agreed in May 1984 to develop these aspects of the relationship, and later that year each appointed a special official to review all the opportunities not only for improving each other's country image, but for giving greater public prominence to the concept of the German-British partnership *per se* and within the European Community. In Bonn, the appointment also symbolises the equal importance of relations with Britain as compared to relations with France and the USA, for which Coordinators already existed, albeit with more extensive roles.[25]

Britain and France
These two countries' cultural relationship since the war is also closely connected with their political relationship. Despite the long period of Entente and the signature of a Cultural Convention in 1948, for the best part of twenty years thereafter Britain virtually neglected to 'cultivate' the French people and France devoted attention to an art- and literature-loving élite, the latter declining together with the popularity of the French language. School, private and tourist contacts in this period were, of course, numerous. But where they did not exist, or where no particular effort was made to acquire understanding of each other's society or way of thinking by those educated during the period, the effects might be long-lasting. The revival of cultural cooperation in the 1970s has been less successful for France in terms of popular response; the effects on the relationship of an intensification of élite contacts are not yet clear.

The advantages which the British have over the French in cultural diplomacy, and which they failed to exploit for so long, are the importance of the English language and the receptivity of the French to the arts. However, the issue of English language domination also adds considerable problems, and calls for sensitivity of approach.

The British Council began work in France immediately after the war, when interest in Britain was intense. The large staff and regional network of centres were cut back to one small office in Paris in the 1950s following the Drogheda recommendations. The immediate effect in France was in English teaching, but the lost opportunities for appreciation of Britain's scientific achievements and artistic heritage among educated French citizens were possibly as damaging. After the 1970–71 Working Party on Anglo-French Cultural Relations was set up it was found that French scepticism as to the true attachment of Britain to Europe had been reinforced by the cultural withdrawal of the 1950s and 1960s.[26] Also, many in French literary circles, and President Pompidou himself, were concerned about the effect upon the Community of the accession of the United Kingdom (together with three other countries whose second language was English). Reassuring them on both points was a major task, led by the Prime Minister, Edward Heath, and the British Ambassador Sir Christopher Soames. Following Mr Heath's successful meeting in 1971 with President Pompidou, talks in London with Foreign Minister Maurice Schumann resulted in a Joint Anglo-French Declaration which, among other things, announced measures to foster in both countries greater knowledge of each other's language and culture. The British Council received a prestigious new building in Paris, shared with the British Institute,[27] and an extra £100,000 annually for work in France — its first increase in Europe for 23 years. It was to be used to increase youth exchanges and civic links, both of which had been pressed for by France. A senior scholarship scheme for British postgraduates in France was started. The emphasis on the English language was kept down.

As well as the 'Heath—Pompidou' money, as it became known, part of the 'Rippon money' benefited British efforts in France (see p. 84). From Paris, the British Council expanded its work again in the French provinces and, while avoiding overt language promotion, an English Language Advisory Service was set up in 1974 to work with teachers, universities and education authorities throughout France. The industrial and commercial aims set by the French government under President Giscard d'Estaing encouraged the acquisition of English and of information published in English. The British Council's six libraries (later five) were developed and, by the late 1970s, were providing an information and reference service linked by computer to the British Library network: a demonstration of British technology. By 1983 over 33,000 enquiries per year about British education were handled; the exchange of specialists in all levels of education was promoted, and support given to the development of links between educational establishments.[28] These programmes ran in parallel to the large volume of school and teacher exchanges facilitated by the Central Bureau, and reflected the place played by both languages in each other's education system. Closer collaboration between education ministries from 1979 continued with the Mitterrand government. (In 1982, M. Savary was the first French Education Minister to make an official visit to London.) However, cooperation became harder following reorganisations in Paris and budget cuts on both sides. Nevertheless, some new bilateral programmes were established, such as exchanges of technical college trainees.[29]

The British Council has helped to develop collaboration between specialist colleges and universities in fields such as medicine and engineering, with a scheme to exchange students from the *Grandes Ecoles* with engineering departments in Britain. British interest in learning from the French has equalled reciprocal French interest in many spheres, with successful collaboration over some years between their respective national academic and science research bodies. The importance of the arts in presenting Britain to France is demonstrated in the demands by galleries to show British work. Especially successful have been the major single-artist showings in Paris of Gainsborough, Reynolds and Turner, but neither the French provinces nor British modern art have been neglected. The two Ministers for the Arts, Lord Gowrie and Jack Lang, had a good personal relationship. British musicians and British theatre are also popular. Since 1979 special book promotions have increased sales for British authors and publishers in English and in translation.

French receptivity to British cultural and information promotion may well vary with class and political viewpoint. In the 1970s, the growth of middle-class and élite interest in English — largely for commercial and technical purposes — centred on the United States' technological lead and domination of popular television and cinema, rather than on Britain, whose old-fashioned media image had hardly recovered from the comparison by the 1980s (although Britain's official information services now show consistent success in the French technical press). In response to the need to create better understanding of Britain among politicians and officials, journalists, editors and broadcasters, the Foreign Office increased the volume of sponsored visits from France from 72 in 1982–83 to 119 in 1984–85. The declining number of French journalists in Britain makes such visits the chief means of influencing the important French regional press.

Besides the arts, French cultural efforts in Britain in the 1950s and 1960s were concentrated on language work: exchanges of teachers, assistants and pupils, courses at the French Institute and assistance to teachers with, in addition, the non-government Alliance Française and its membership throughout Britain. The traditional British admiration for French culture and the French way of life, and the educational and social value placed upon the French language made for wide receptivity among the better educated. The arts, especially French cinema, found a steady if small market, as did French books.

By the 1980s, however, the fall in numbers learning French in the later years of secondary education or at university caused anxiety, as did decreased education budgets. Cuts in the numbers of *lecteur* posts in university French departments, and of *assistants* in schools were also a setback for the promotion of French language and culture (and incidentally for the reciprocal employment of British language personnel in France). The practical responses adopted in cooperation with British authorities are: to improve teaching methods; to encourage the development of more imaginative combined degree courses; and in other ways to improve the image of France and the French language. One of the French Institute's longstanding successes has been provision of specialist French courses for scientists, politicians, the medical and other professions.

The boost to cooperation following the 1970–71 Anglo-French agreements has had mixed results for French policy. Although youth exchanges and town twinnings increased, and the huge volume of school exchanges continued, the British response has never matched French popular demand. In 1983 200 schools awaited links through the Central Bureau, and a long queue of towns sought partners. On the other hand, in the 1980s neither French organisation nor finance has been sufficient fully to maintain agreed youth exchange programmes, partly because of the huge drain on resources of Franco-German exchanges. The hoped-for improvement of personal contact at wider social levels has been frustrated by British inhibitions about accepting foreign visitors in their homes. However, the French policy of promoting contacts between young professional trainees in colleges met with positive British response and the first exchanges took place in 1984 between students and teachers of hotel and catering management and computer studies. Language knowledge may not have sufficed for extensive interchange, but the motivation of shared interest would have been present.

Since 1983 the French government has sought cooperation between research centres identified for their quality in technical areas where British advance could save France costly duplication. The same aim lay behind the proposal of a Franco-British Association for industrial research.[30] However, as in more 'cultural' cooperation, it is perceived that benefits should be reciprocal and may go beyond the immediately practical to the creation of longer-term understanding. In the social science field these gains would be even more evident, since the exchange of ideas taking place, particularly with British experts in politics and social studies, economics, history, philosophy and psychology, could have wider repercussions through each country's educational and intellectual world. Following cooperation over some years, the Centre National de la Recherche Scientifique and the Economic and Social Research Council began a special programme for joint social science research, Britain being France's first partner country in 1983–84. Bilateral conferences have also been mounted in British universities. On the other hand, efforts to achieve equivalence of degree qualifications to facilitate student interchange have been less successful with Britain than with West Germany. Sadly, the high cost of imported newspapers limits this source of information for interested British students.

British interest in French art seems to be confined to the great artists of the past, as shown by the success of the Renoir exhibition in London in the spring of 1985, and there was an enthusiastic response to the Paris Opera Ballet's visit in 1984. But interest in French music or modern art is sparse. The French government made available extra finance for France's presence at the 1985 Edinburgh Festival. The French are disappointed at declining interest in their literature and theatre, along with their language. Although British television has brought wider audiences for the French cinema, occasional French opera productions, and documentaries about France, the quality of presentation of French affairs in British television and radio programmes (especially education programmes) and in the serious press contrasts with the stereotyped and commercialised approach of the popular British press, which remains impervious to cultural diplomacy. Another result of the 'Heath–Pompidou' agreements was the creation in 1972 of a Franco-British Council (see p. 134), which, besides mounting major conferences on 'Königswinter' lines since 1980, has developed contacts among experts through seminars in many topics, including agriculture, history, the press, industrial change, health and social security. Communication has become easier as more French experts speak English well. If France and the French language have become a specialist interest for the British, it is important for both countries to extend such interest to as broad a spectrum of expertise as possible, whether it be for purposes of collaboration in joint projects or for the broader understanding of each other's society necessary to support policy cooperation.

France and Germany
What chiefly distinguishes Franco-German relations in the cultural and information field is the fact that they are central to the purpose of bilateral cooperation as defined in the 1963 Treaty and before. There is a stronger political commitment than in other relationships to work for improved understanding between the two peoples, especially through the young, rather than primarily to promote intergovernment and élite cooperation. Secondly, this cooperation was intended to fit the two countries for close integration within the European Community.[31]

The development of official cooperation from the signing of the 1954 Cultural Accord by Robert'Schuman and Konrad Adenauer has in many respects followed the general lines for cultural cooperation with other partners (for instance, in the shift from artistic heritage to presenting modern society and institutions). However, the 1963 Treaty proved important not only for the political commitment it gave to relations between the two societies, but for the obligation it imposed on the governments to continue to seek improved relations in education (the only policy area under the Treaty in which cooperation is compulsory), although this has proved especially difficult to achieve. In many other areas successful progress has been made, but the two governments became sufficiently concerned at the situation in language teaching, academic cooperation and the media image to issue a Summit Meeting Declaration in February 1981 calling for action in these spheres.

The extra resources and institutional arrangements evolved to meet the mutual commitment have given a special character to Franco-German cooperation. The two Coordinators appointed in 1968 are especially concerned with the broader issues of popular opinion and understanding too easily lost from view by governments. However, a very active role is taken by the public and private foundations and institutes devoted to furthering the bilateral relationship, prominent among which in Germany are the Robert Bosch Foundation, which supports many schemes to help international understanding, and the Franco-German Institute at Ludwigsburg which conducts research, runs seminars, publishes books, develops language-teaching methods and promotes dialogue between experts from the two countries. In 1982 following joint decisions by Schmidt and Giscard d'Estaing, later confirmed by Mitterrand, a French counterpart institute was created in Paris with French public funds — the Centre d'Information et de Recherche sur l'Allemagne Contemporaine (CIRAC), whose role is similar but much more limited.

Also created in July 1963 as another byproduct of the Treaty, the Franco-German Youth Office is unique in its completely bilateral management, staffing and funds and in the mutuality of its work. It is not the only body promoting exchanges (for instance, the PAD arranges many school visits) but it covers a very wide range of young people and institutions: schools, universities, youth groups, sports and activity holidays, young professionals, and the all-important group leaders who facilitate communication. Intended to be open to all, it does not insist on prior language skills, but has developed language and other preparatory courses to make the encounter between the young more effective. It encourages discussion of current issues, and also insists on joint planning of the exchange between the two institutions involved.[32]

The huge joint endowment of DM 40 million per year in the early days was sufficient for annual exchanges of 300,000. Finance stagnated in the 1970s but a new joint commitment in 1982 of DM 35 million (£8—9 million) annually now allows fewer to stay but for longer periods (130,500 in 1983). As similar experiences elsewhere had shown, shorter visits may do no more than confirm existing stereotypes; prejudices acquired by each fresh generation are not eradicated without considerable effort. It has proved difficult to gauge precise results, yet officials of both governments affirm the value of their huge commitment of resources. The 4 million young people exchanged since 1963 must represent a stock of more open-minded citizens.

The two chief barriers to successful cooperation in education arise from the decentralisation of German education, and from the language problem. The solution arrived at in 1968 to ease intergovernmental contacts was to elevate one of the *Land* Minister-Presidents as national representative (*Bevollmächtigte*) of all the rest.[33] There are problems remaining, however, in trying to coordinate all eleven viewpoints and in getting the autonomous *Land* governments to accept the agreements arrived at between Bonn and Paris. Nowhere is this more evident than on the language issue, where despite solemn bilateral agreements to promote each other's language, French is not offered as the first language choice in some areas. Throughout the FRG, the vast majority of children study English first and for a longer period, about half taking French as second language. In French secondary schools, not only is

English learnt first, but increasingly Spanish is chosen as an easier second language than German.[34] Alarmed at this situation, the two governments called in 1981 for an action programme in both countries: as a result more *Länder* offered French as first option. But unless current proposals, to make obligatory the learning of two languages for an equal period of time, are adopted (in both countries) it is hard to see the present trend towards English dominance being reversed.

Other aspects of education cooperation have had success: there has been progress in revising school books to reflect modern realities, there is a large volume of school links and exchanges of teachers, *assistants* and *lecteurs* (although their numbers are lower than in English language exchanges, they stay for longer periods). Primary teaching of each other's language takes place in many border areas, and there are successful experiments in bilingual schooling. Nevertheless, poor language skills have wide repercussions. English predominates in most universities in both countries; only the French *Grandes Ecoles* make two languages compulsory. (There German is followed by 25 per cent and has acquired something of the traditional *cachet* of Classics in Britain, as a language for brighter students.) Most student exchanges are in languages despite the fact that, after long negotiation, equivalences of degree qualification have been agreed in the natural and some social sciences (but still not in medicine, politics or economics): for students of these subjects English may be more familiar than their partner's tongue. There are exchanges between the civil service colleges, but since the élite *Grandes Ecoles* have no German counterparts, links at this level are problematical. Problems also lie in differences in degree and research administration. For both countries, research cooperation in technical or social science fields has often been closer with American or British universities,[35] although the French CNRS scheme of joint projects is open to German researchers from 1984—85 on the lines established by France and Britain (see p. 92).

Thus lack of a common language has impeded the exchange of ideas between the two societies, both at élite and at other levels. It is borne out in the lack of interest in each other's literature (although a higher proportion of German books are translated into French, with government help, and there seems to be a higher level of French interest in German philosophy and other intellectual fields than vice versa). One avenue open to both governments is to attempt to foster interest through courses and lectures at the French or Goethe Institutes in the other country. Important contributions to academic cooperation and historical understanding have also been made by the German Historical Institute in Paris and its French counterpart at Göttingen.

German art, theatre and cinema also seem to inspire greater interest in France in the 1980s following the 'Paris—Berlin' exhibition of 1978, and with the continued vigour of German film-making. Over the decades artistic exchanges have been numerous in both directions, although affected in the 1980s by financial stringencies. Yet neither in the field of television nor the cinema have attempts by either government (pressed in particular by the French) resulted in close cooperation between producers. Exchanges and co-productions are outweighed by American competition for the increasingly commercialised channels. Cooperation on television broadcasting by satellite has been problematical, and only in radio has cooperation proved fruitful and easier to arrange, often between regional stations to mark a national or local event.

The appearance of negative stereotypes in the media in the late 1970s and early 1980s (see p. 59) aroused concern in both governments. On an initiative by the French Coordinator for Franco-German Relations a scheme of exchange placements for trainee journalists was introduced. The improved presentation of each country by the mid-1980s may stem from this and from the work of the Robert Bosch Foundation and the *Land* governments which since 1975 have organised seminars and visits to the FRG for French national and provincial journalists, resulting in balanced and informative published articles.[36]

The terms of the Franco-German commitment in the cultural sphere, which reflected widely held aspirations, emphasised the aim of popular reconciliation: this has now largely been achieved, as expressed in broad terms by public opinion. Yet the less clearly defined aim of strengthening European integration by bilateral cooperation is being frustrated in many ways by the barriers to dialogue and understanding on common problems. The effects of European integration had already changed the economic relationship between the two countries to one of close interdependence by the early 1970s.[37] Here the need ultimately is for popular understanding, but more immediately for dialogue between the élites and opinion-leaders of the two countries. Nevertheless there is insufficient communication between important academic and political élites, employers' organisations and trade unions.[38]

Action proposed by the two study institutes in Ludwigsburg and Paris would increase the dialogue between officials and experts in regular seminars and élite conferences. To counter the centrifugal forces in both societies, firmer action will be needed in the language teaching sphere, perhaps tied to European Community legislation. Ultimately, however, it is upon public opinion that official and private persuasion must work; a clearer expression by employers of the need for each other's languages, and not just for English, could provide motivation.

Conclusions
It is rarely possible to judge the effectiveness of official action in the foreign cultural field in terms of outcomes. Results tend to be in the longer term and to stem from a variety of linked causes. Thus a growth in public demand to link towns or to learn a language may be in response to the political symbolism perceived in cooperation between

government leaders, as much as to specific exhortation by government or private bodies. Success is largely dependent upon the receptiveness of target audiences, institutions and governments, a guiding principle being that 'the best cultural relations work is done when your host as a friend helps you to do it'.[39]

Criteria which can be applied within each of the three bilateral relationships focus on the responsiveness of national cultural policies to the mutual aims of the partnership and their appropriateness to the objective political and economic relationship between them.

The relatively successful *German-British* relationship in terms of cooperation has been so despite the imbalance of effort and resources put into it on the British side, and despite the difficulty with limited resources of reaching a German public dispersed among many major cities. Britain's poor political and economic image is perhaps balanced by admiration for its arts and for the 'post-industrial values' which it has had longer to develop.

The German image in Britain is good, if superficial and ill-informed in German eyes, and not free of the recurrent historical stereotypes. A large number of links exist in the business field particularly which are not charted here. The visible nature of the bilateral relationship has been promoted by various state visits and by a good image, in British eyes at least, of its quality and importance. What has not been evident is a deeper commitment on the British government's part to building a firm basis of understanding between the two peoples, and to publicising this commitment (summit declarations apart) in such a way as to make ordinary people in both countries more aware of its importance. The effect upon intergovernment relations is to impress the German side with the lower level of commitment on the part of the British to promoting both the national and the bilateral image. However, the joint review of policy in this area, prompted by a sense that the bilateral relationship is insufficiently visible to ordinary citizens, may lead to plans to improve the joint image. The implications of this for development of the relationship are hopeful, given that attention is being devoted to the longer-lasting people-to-people relationship, as well as to political dimensions.

The *Franco-British* relationship is in many ways the most contradictory and the most changeable of the three, at the level both of governments and people. Some of the reasons for this were outlined earlier. They combine a loss of admiration and interest on both sides and a long-held sense of political and cultural rivalry. Yet the enduring mutual interest on both sides of the Channel, the deep affection, for many, and the sense that a relationship has long existed and ought to be restored all contribute positively to the periodic recovery of esteem expressed in the opinion polls.

Government efforts devoted to the national image and to increasing mutual understanding have not been large or consistent on either side, except for the few years following the decision in 1971 by Heath and Pompidou that action in this sphere was necessary. The results of the extra finance then made available are hard to judge, but the very fact of the relationship *between the people* being given such a boost may have contributed — along with state visits — to the positive mutual public attitudes of 1977—78 (see p. 72). Since then, despite political vicissitudes and poor media images, Britain has enjoyed a growing success in the arts and literary fields, but continued incomprehension at the popular level. France's image in Britain is not so positive, because fewer people speak or read French and also, it must be said, because of some past misdirection of resources in the promotion of France's image. The marked popularity of Mitterrand in Britain may somewhat redress this imbalance.

The two governments have sometimes appeared to assign less importance to policies to foster deeper popular understanding than to cooperation in industrial and technical fields, but, judging by its more recent policy plans, the French government for its part seems to have a clear grasp of the need to improve its national image by means of cultural diplomacy. In both countries there may be an overemphasis on élites, partly for reasons of financial stringency.

Unlike when Britain joined the European Community, neither in the German-British nor in the Franco-British relationship is the concept of intersociety understanding in the interests of European cooperation or integration now emphasised. A stress on the Community dimension would seem more appropriate than the pursuit of primarily national cultural aims by France and Britain. A clearer role within overall foreign policy and a longer-term view of Britain's cultural and information aims would also be appropriate to the closer bilateral (or triangular) relationship recently aimed at.

The success of the German approach to cultural policy has in large measure stemmed from the projection of the FRG as a cooperative partner and ally, at the level of the political leadership and throughout its foreign policy, as much as in cultural and information policy.

Franco-German cultural cooperation should perhaps be judged by more stringent criteria, based upon the length of time during which the two countries have cooperated bilaterally and in the European Community, and their closer economic integration. Large resources of government finance, time and organisational effort have been devoted to cultural cooperation. As well as government agencies, private bodies committed to the relationship have exerted influence, initiated new ventures, drawn people together, educated and informed. Yet not even such resources as these could create a market for each other's cultural offerings or language against the pull of other forces. Mutual interest still varies according to geographical location. Despite all the exchanges of young people, town twinnings, links between associations and friendly encounters of all kinds, the occasional historical stereotype or uncharitable judgement still surfaces in the media. The work to remove prejudices among fresh generations is still vital.

Much of the cultural activity engaged in can only hope to provide an incitement to wider, popular action. And it is here that the success of the Franco-German record lies. Primarily the relationship between the two countries has become a real one because of the enormous number of links which have grown up between private individuals and organisations. They exist for three main reasons. First, because of the strong impetus towards reconciliation, now achieved. Second, because of the thorough-going political commitment to bilateral cooperation as part of European cooperation. And third, because the development of cultural and intersociety policies was central to that commitment. The combination of these factors — a visible relationship with a shared purpose, and a role given to personal contacts and understanding — provided the impetus for the gradual evolution of a myriad links at all levels of society and economic activity which is the real basis of the relationship. It is a relationship between peoples, and not only, or even primarily, a relationship between governments, even though the images of cooperation between leaders may have also been potent in creating a sense of mutual commitment.

Nevertheless, personal links and contacts do not necessarily contribute to the appreciation of each other's problems by political élites, union members or employers. There is very mixed ability to communicate between these important groups in the two countries, whose better understanding would assist and support intergovernmental cooperation on mutual problems. While the decline in language learning has affected the dialogue between experts at all levels, the economic recession has made domestic problems more acute and encouraged national protectionism. The need now is for increased dialogue between leaders at all levels, to create a network of opinion-formers who understand the interdependence of French and German society and economy, and can influence mutual cooperation on each other's problems.[40]

Notes

1. For the early history of these contacts and organisations, see W.E. Farquharson and S.C. Holt, *Europe from Below* (London, Allen & Unwin, 1975), Chapter 8.
2. For example, *The Journal of the Franco-British Society*.
3. See publications by the Joint Twinning Committee of the Local Authority Associations of Great Britain and le Conseil des Communes d'Europe, Paris. On Franco-German partnerships, see Farquharson and Holt, op.cit., and T. Grunert, *Langzeitwirkungen von Städte-Partnerschaften* (Kehl am Rhein/ Strasbourg, Engel Verlag, 1981).
4. Language problems in the Franco-German relationship are fully examined in publications by the Deutsch-Französisches Institut, Ludwigsburg, and the Robert Bosch Stiftung, Stuttgart. For Britain, see *Foreign Languages: A Survey of Schools*, Autumn 1982 (London, Department of Education and Science, 1983) and publications of the Centre for Information on Language Teaching and Research (CILT), London.

5. See J. Myerscough, *Funding the Arts in Europe*, Studies in European Politics no.8 (London, Policy Studies Institute, 1984).

6. The Alliance Française has about 65 local membership groups and 6,000 members in Britain, but for historical reasons none in the FRG. See also Farquharson and Holt, op.cit., Chapter 4.

7. Figures are from the British Council and from French and German Foreign Ministry sources (unpublished).

8. Heinz Kühn (Ministerpräsident of Nordrhein—Westfalen), 'Die deutsch-französischen Kulturbeziehungen in den letzten 25 Jahren' in *La réalité quotidienne des échanges franco-allemandes*, vol. II (Strasbourg, Istra, 1970), p. 15.

9. Farquharson and Holt, op.cit., p. 3.

10. One other German historical institute has existed in Rome since the 1890s.

11. *Le projet culturel extérieure de la France*, 1983.

12. For a history of Britain's cultural foreign policy see F. Donaldson, *The British Council. The First Fifty Years* (London, Cape, 1984).

13. See *Review of Overseas Representation*, Report by the Central Policy Review Staff (London, HMSO, 1977); and *The United Kingdom's Overseas Representation*, Cmnd 7308 (London, HMSO, 1978).

14. Donaldson, op.cit., Chapter 21. See also British Council *Annual Report*, 1984.

15. Review of the British Council by Lord Seebohm, Lord Chorley and Richard Auty, March 1981, para. 3.2; see also Donaldson, op.cit., Chapter 22.

16. See A. Volle, *Deutsch-Britische Beziehungen. Geschichte und Gegenwart*, Politik kurz und actuel 43 (Berlin, Landeszentrale für Politische Bildungsarbeit, 1985), pp. 187 ff.; Donaldson, op.cit., pp. 210—11.

17. See special feature on Germany in The British Council *News*, issue 6, November 1984, pp. 4—5.

18. Ibid.

19. For the early history of German-British youth exchanges and town twinnings, see Volle, op.cit., pp. 231 ff.

20. Visits are organised by the Central Office of Information on behalf of the Foreign and Commonwealth Office. Numbers invited from the FRG inclusive of politicians, officials, etc., were: 29 in 1982—83, 117 in 1983—84 and 33 in 1984—85. See also p. 91 (French visitors).

21. Interview sources among West German press in London.

22. Volle, op.cit., p. 204.

23. Interview sources. Israel, another priority country, also absorbs a high proportion of youth exchange expenditure because of high travel costs.

24. *The Attitudes of Young People towards West Germany*, Research Study conducted for the Embassy of the Federal Republic of Germany (London, MORI, 1981).

25. For the role of the Franco-German Coordinators, see Chapter 8.

26. Donaldson, op.cit., p. 259.

27. The British Institute in Paris is not run by the British Council; it is an independent university institute offering language courses, with 2,600 French and British students in 1983.

28. Richard Auty, 'The Council in the European Community', British Council *Annual Report*, 1978—79, pp. 19—20; 'The British Council in France', Note for the House of Commons Select Committee on Arts, Education and Science, March 1983.

29. Interview sources. See also Central Bureau for Educational Visits and Exchanges, *Annual Report*, 1983–84.
30. Press reports, 25 October 1984, on President Mitterrand's London visit and speech to Parliament.
31. See Treaty of Cooperation (Appendix), and R. Picht (ed.), *Deutschland–Frankreich–Europa. Bilanz einer schwieriger Partnerschaft* (Munich, Piper, 1978), pp. 189–90.
32. R. Picht (ed.), *Das Bundnis im Bundnis. Deutsch-französische Beziehungen im internationalen Spannungsfeld* (Berlin, Severin and Siedler, 1982), pp. 202–7. See also K. Wenger, 'Motivations et activités de l'Office Franco-Allemand pour la Jeunesse', *Allemagnes d'Aujourd'hui*, no. 84, April–June 1983, pp. 141–51, and publications by the Office franco-allemand pour la Jeunesse.
33. Farquharson and Holt, op.cit., pp. 49–50. See also interview with *Land* Plenipotentiary Bernard Vogel in *Dokumente*, 4/38, December 1982, pp. 309–18, and article by Ove Schlichting, pp. 319–24.
34. See especially Picht, *Das Bundnis im Bundnis*, op.cit., pp. 211–19; *Fremdsprachunterricht und Internationale Beziehungen* (Stuttgart–Ludwigsburg, Robert Bosch Stiftung/Deutsch-Französisches Institut, 1982); Paul Dehem, 'Les accords de 1963 et l'enseignement de l'allemand', *Allemagnes d'Aujourd'hui*, no. 84, April–June 1983, pp. 163–8.
35. Picht (ed.), *Das Bundnis im Bundnis*, op.cit., pp. 216–18; R. Stephan, 'Die akademische Beziehungen – Für eine transnationale Konzeption internationaler Zusammenarbeit' in Picht, *Deutschland–Frankreich–Europa*, op.cit., pp. 268–306.
36. Robert Bosch Stiftung, 'Séminaires d'Information pour des journalistes français sur la République Fédérale d'Allemagne', *Analyse et Documentation*, Stuttgart, Annual publications.
37. See Chapter 2 above; and D. Menyesch and H. Uterwedde, 'Partner oder Konkurrenten?' in Picht, *Das Bundnis im Bundnis*, op.cit., pp. 105–39.
38. Cf. R. Lasserre in Picht, *Das Bundnis im Bundnis*, op.cit., pp. 228–32, and Alfred Grosser, 'Was heisst Verständigung?' in ibid., pp. 233–9.
39. Unpublished paper by J. McDonaugh quoted in Donaldson, op.cit., p. 210.
40. See R. Picht, 'Die Versöhnung ist kein Grund zur Selbstzufriedenheit' in K. Manfrass (ed.), *Paris–Bonn* (Sigmaringen, Van Thorbecke Verlag, 1984), p. 76.

6 The Role of the Three Civil Services
David Gladstone

Introduction

Nobody who has had regular dealings with civil servants in the Federal Republic of Germany, France or Britain, or who has observed them operating in an international setting (particularly in Brussels), can fail to have been struck by the differences in their behaviour and in their approach to common problems. Similarly, anyone with direct experience of intergovernmental discussions and negotiations will be well aware of the crucial role that individual officials can play in either promoting or frustrating agreement. The pursuit of trilateral consultation and collaboration has been, and will continue to be, influenced as much by the attitudes and commitment to the task in hand of the officials concerned, whether as negotiators or executors, as by their professional competence. Their attitude and commitment will have been conditioned by education and upbringing — and all the ambitions, prejudices and assumptions so inculcated; their competence will have been formed by training and by experience gained on the job. Either form of conditioning may predispose them to favour or reject consultation and collaboration in principle. Once negotiations are under way or a project has been agreed, progress may be substantially advanced or retarded according to the degree of compatibility between the officials concerned.

Besides conceptual differences, the ease of longer-term contacts and cooperation may be influenced by organisational differences between civil services, as also by the differing operational methods and interactions with politicians, interest groups and the public in general. The aims of this chapter are to identify those characteristics of each national 'administrative culture' which may influence the way the separate services interact, and to suggest ways in which that interaction might be eased.

The term 'civil servant', which has no precise equivalent in French or German, is employed here narrowly to cover in the main *Beamte* in Germany, members of the *Corps* in Category A of the *Fonction Publique* in France, and public servants in the former Administrative and Executive Grades (or their equivalents) in Britain.

Theory and practice in the three services

The importance of tradition

One essential function of any civil service is to provide continuity. As a body, it will tend therefore to be conservative and must concern itself with questions of precedent and tradition, even while serving governments bent on reform. Civil servants will tend to perpetuate the values of their forebears, either through bureaucratic inertia, because they have become subconsciously steeped in those values, or because they are convinced of their continuing validity. National and constitutional histories have had a significant impact and have in turn been influenced by civil servants, even if their role is usually obscured by the much more visible activities of politicians. Furthermore, the very different constitutional experiences of the three societies have led to three very distinctive kinds of civil service today.

Germany

The German civil service model is the oldest of the three, having developed more or less continuously from the highly centralised and efficient administration created by the Elector Friedrich Wilhelm out of the ruins of the Thirty Years War. His successor, and first King of Prussia, Friedrich Wilhelm I, established Chairs in Administrative Science in the Prussian universities and required his civil servants to gain degrees in law. The Prussian civil servant came to embody the legendary Prussian virtues: thoroughness, integrity, impartiality, thrift and devotion to duty through service to the state rather than the monarch. Indeed, the status of the *Beamte* is still defined as one who holds office in the state.

Like Hobbes, Hegel, the most influential Prussian thinker, saw the state as the agency which reconciled public and private interests and imposed order on society but, unlike Hobbes, he preached its inherent goodness; it was the fount and indeed arbiter of all morality. The Prussian citizen's basic rights and freedoms were granted by the state, and guaranteed by the law which bound monarch and subject alike. The *Beamte's* first duty was to make and uphold that law. Thus, as we have seen, from an early date a law degree became a prerequisite for entry into the civil service. The *Beamte* was poorly paid, but enjoyed high social standing and a number of privileges (including job security for life), guaranteed by legal statute.

German public life still bears signs of Hegel's influence despite efforts to discredit or reinterpret his doctrines. His distinction between 'society' (*Gesellschaft*) and 'state' (*Staat*) is enshrined in the Constitution of the FRG, which contains numerous references to various aspects of 'statehood' (*Staatlichkeit*) and is rooted in the nineteenth-century concept of the *Rechtsstaat* — the state based on law. The two major post-war threats to the stability of the new German political system,

Communism and terrorism of the Baader–Meinhof variety, have each been stigmatised by the defenders of the establishment as enemies of the *Rechtsstaat*.

On the face of it, the federal system established after 1945 marked a clean break with the tradition of Prussian centralism by reverting to an older, regional tradition. But part of the Prussian inheritance has been handed down nevertheless. The intellectual underpinning of the Constitution is distinctively Prussian; and the legislation of 1953 establishing the new civil service virtually re-enacted Bismarck's equivalent law dating from the 1870s, itself derived from eighteenth-century Prussian traditions.

As a result, decentralisation and the devolution of real powers to regional governments, each with its own separate bureaucracy (and in southern and south-western Germany, some traces of French influence on the administrative style) go hand-in-hand with uniformity in the rules governing the activities and terms of service of officials at both *Land* and *Bund* levels. There is no central recruitment nor central management in Bonn; but for legal and practical purposes, one civil service operates countrywide.

The German civil service ante-dated by over two centuries the advent of political parties, which have thus grown up in the shadow of a bureaucracy wielding considerable authority and prestige. In popular mythology it was the politicians who fiddled while Germany burned in the 1920s. The civil service — even though it too failed to put the fires out — is seen as one of the few solid bridges between the nineteenth century and the post-war era. The politicians have asserted their primacy in the past 30 years, but have seen no advantage in distancing themselves from the bureaucracy in the process; on the contrary, about half the current members of the Bundestag started their careers as civil servants.

Officials with an eye to a political future see advantage in declaring their political allegiances openly, hoping for preferment when 'their' party is in power and able to switch to Parliament when it loses. This politicisation is taken for granted and it is rare for a senior official not to be openly associated with one of the three major parties.

France

The French civil service was established by the seventeenth century, but, unlike its German counterpart, it has not had a continuous development. Traces of the *ancien régime* survive in the emphasis on specialised training and the strong centralist tradition. But the French civil service today is essentially a Napoleonic creation underpinned by Jacobin theory, which vested sovereignty in the 'will of the people', and translated the 'general will' into action via the state. The centralist tradition established in the seventeenth century was, if anything, strengthened by the Revolution whose leaders argued that all political issues were, in the last resort, national issues, and thus too important to be left to the provinces. Napoleon's reform of the bureaucracy made the state a practical and indeed rather Hobbesian machine — 'that coldest of monsters', as de Gaulle was to call it. And it was, and is, run by the *Fonction Publique*.

This new executive power became a highly disciplined, centralised, efficient and expert service, modelled in many respects on the army, with an élite *corps* of officer status and a specialist *corps* corresponding to the army's engineers, and so on. Central government control was assured via the agency of the Prefect, belonging to the Prefectorial corps and posted rather like a Governor-General by Paris to each of the newly-formed *Départements*. Recruitment to the *Grands Corps* was based on educational qualification. The Ecole Polytechnique was added to the Grandes Ecoles of the *ancien régime* in order to train the new breed of specialist administrator, although, until the Ecole Nationale d'Administration was founded in 1945, the only school specialising in general public administration was the private Ecole Libre des Sciences Politiques (re-named Institut d'Etudes Politiques after the Second World War). Consequently, the civil service in France came to enjoy considerable prestige and its leading officials saw themselves — and were generally seen — as a social and political élite.

From the 1970s onwards, the *Fonction Publique* increasingly began to function with a momentum of its own sometimes in partnership with, sometimes independently of, National Assemblies which even in their hey-day have never succeeded in asserting their control over the bureaucracy. The state, in the guise of the civil service or executive power, has continued to make many of its own assumptions about the best interests of the people. From the time of Colbert onwards, *'dirigisme'*, particularly marked in economic affairs, rested on the state arrogating to itself the task of promoting economic activity at all levels of society, and not on partisan ideology.

Constitutionally, the Executive has even managed to distinguish its role from that of 'government': one commentator has described it as floating 'in an ambiguous limbo below' the latter. The distinction underlines the degree of independence even from ministerial oversight enjoyed by the civil service and helps to explain why no French government in living memory has attempted to reduce the size, influence or privileges of the *Fonction Publique*. As in the FRG, many French deputies have been *fonctionnaires* (usually from one of the *Grands Corps*, although the 1981 elections brought an influx of teachers) and they retain the right to revert to their former status. Indeed, two Presidents, most Prime Ministers and many ministers under the Fifth Republic started life as *fonctionnaires*, and President Giscard d'Estaing reverted to that status on losing office.

Constitutional theory thus conspired with administrative practice to place French civil servants at the hub of the political process. Not surprisingly, they have been much sought after by concerns outside government, by political parties and big business in particular, helped by their right to move freely out of the civil service — a procedure charmingly known as *pantouflage*. (Such moves into the private sector are usually intended to be definitive, but *détachements* to the public sector are vulnerable to changes in the political wind and the right to move back into the *Fonction Publique* has often proved almost equally valuable.) A member of a *Grand Corps* enjoys a high social standing and is allowed to play an active part in politics — at least at the local level — while still employed by the *Fonction Publique*. Like his German counterpart, his position is defined and guaranteed by statute — the Civil Service Law of 1946, which codifies long existing practice — and he is subject to administrative law which differs from that applying to private workers.

Britain

The British system of government is different in several fundamental respects: first, in its reliance on unwritten conventions rather than on a written constitution; second, in its rejection of any constitutional role for 'the state' as such; third, in its vesting of sovereignty not in 'the people' but in their elected Parliament; fourth, in its retention of the monarch as Parliament's partner in sovereignty; fifth, in its granting of supreme judicial authority to Parliament (in the shape of the House of Lords); sixth, in its failure to give civil servants any clearly defined legal status.

Inevitably these features engendered a distinctive kind of civil service, able to operate without fixed legal points of reference as the handmaid of a Parliament — or rather of ministers-in-Parliament — whose own preoccupations were political rather than legal. For nearly 200 years following the Restoration in 1660, while its German and French counterparts were developing into powerful, centralised bureaucracies serving the state, the British civil service was treated as the personal property no longer of the monarch but of the politicians and an important source of patronage. Even the limited Macaulay—Trevelyan reforms of the 1850s, which aimed at making the service more efficient, met with determined opposition from those politicians who placed a higher premium on personal loyalties than on efficiency. Selection methods were improved and patronage was almost eliminated. But no attempt was made to define the status of civil servants in law and to this day they remain technically members of the Crown's household, akin to domestic servants, who may not sue their employer. The very existence of the civil service derives from the prerogative powers of the Crown and is governed by common law: its activities have never been regulated by Act of Parliament.

This very personal concept of service is central to the British *modus operandi*. British officials serve ministers — to whom Parliament (that is, the Crown) has delegated the task of managing the civil service — and not, as elsewhere, the state or society. Ministers in turn look after, and answer for, their servants, thus relieving the latter of final responsibility for their actions and assuring that they remain anonymously in the background. It is in Parliament that the real political, legislative and judicial action takes place and, once battle is joined there, civil servants have no further part to play. The official's job is to prepare his minister for that battle, arming him as best he can with advice, but thereafter watching from the sidelines. This emphasis on political combat has determined the civil servant's approach to his work and indeed the whole organisation of Whitehall, and has meant that senior officials have to assign a higher priority to the political than to the legal or technical issues at stake. British ministers have traditionally enjoyed very broad discretionary powers in law — it is almost impossible to challenge a minister's decision in the courts — and the only serious threat to their position will be posed by Parliament, or by their own Prime Minister. The most successful civil servants are the ones whose political advice — always deployed *in camera* — best protects their masters from censure from either of these political quarters.

A further constitutional convention which bears directly on the way British officials perceive or perform their jobs is that of collective ministerial responsibility. The practice which evolved during the eighteenth century of government by cabinet, in which the Prime Minister is in theory only *primus inter pares* with no separate department of his or her own, has traditionally placed a high premium on coordination of policies between ministries. As far as possible, issues affecting more than one department are resolved either through interdepartmental bargaining or through the medium of the Cabinet Office. Those issues that cannot be resolved at official level are discussed at Committees of Cabinet Ministers, serviced by the Cabinet Office. Viewed in this way, Whitehall is one vast piece of coordinating machinery which, if it did its job properly, would leave nothing for the cabinet proper to discuss. In practice, ministries have increasingly compartmentalised themselves in order to cope with the growing complexities of modern government and coordination has become a secondary function. But requirements of cabinet still make themselves felt in every corner of Whitehall and by the time they have reached the higher levels of the civil service, officials have perforce developed an instinct for consultation and coordination if not an awareness of the likely impact of their proposals on the interests of other departments.

Translating theory into practice

The traditions compared
It is hard to escape the conclusion that today's French and German civil servants are likely to share many more common assumptions than either will with their British colleagues. In particular, the French and

German official will take for granted the following, which do not apply in the British case:

(a) a written constitution and a corpus of administrative law defining the status and role of the civil servant;
(b) relatively wide areas of authority and responsibility for civil servants in their own right, including a significant role in the political and legislative process;
(c) the central part played by the law in the political process and a civil service trained and qualified accordingly;
(d) a broad equality of status, or a shading of the boundaries between officials and elected representatives.

Other things being equal, these factors would lead one to expect French and German officials' instincts to bear a close resemblance. A common land frontier and the strong influence of the Code Napoléon on the German legal tradition point in the same direction. But pointing another way is the fact that, for all their long tradition of antagonism, the political histories of France and Britain have not been dissimilar and set them apart from Germany to a large extent: both have been nation states for much longer and they share a centuries-old tradition of government from the centre.

Qualifications and training
The way officials of the three countries mesh with each other in practice depends mainly on the sort of people they are; how they are organised; and what role they are expected to play.

What sort of people are the civil servants concerned? As a body they will tend to conservatism, but in both France and Germany the greater degree of in-built politicisation has resulted in the recruitment, at least in the administrative grades, of a number of individuals with pronounced political views of all shades. This willingness on the part of individual officials to contemplate more radical political solutions to problems combines or contrasts with a more technocratic and juridical bias in the selection and training of candidates in Germany and France by comparison with Britain. Although a law degree is no longer a prerequisite for becoming a *Beamte*, the latter, once selected, has to undergo a lawyer's training for 2–3 years before starting work in his ministry. In France, since 1947 most candidates for the more prestigious *Corps* have to pass through the Ecole Nationale d'Administration (ENA), which gives them intensive legal and administrative training, as well as a practical *stage* or apprenticeship. In both countries administration is regarded as a subject of academic study in its own right, in which the law plays a crucial part, and the state expects its administrators to be specialists in their field.

This is not so in Britain, where administration has traditionally been regarded as an art rather than a science and good administrators as being born rather than made. Until relatively recently no service-wide training was provided for Administrators or Executive Grade Officers either on entry or later on in their careers. Their previous academic experience still need have no relevance; in 1981, 66 per cent of entrants to the Administrative Grades came in with Arts degrees. Nowhere on the continent would that figure have exceeded 10 per cent and in France and Germany the overwhelming majority of successful candidates hold degrees in Law or Economics. Greater emphasis is now being given to in-service training at the British Civil Service College, but this arguably serves mainly to broaden educations which at school and university had been much narrower than in France and Germany, or to teach specialist skills to those doing jobs for which experts might well have been recruited by the other two countries in the first place.

This latter point reflects another basic difference in recruitment and training policy between Britain and the other two countries. The traditional British assumption has been that a good practitioner can turn his hand to any aspect of administration. This presumption in favour of the generalist accords with the perceived role of the senior British civil servant as adviser to his minister not only on the substance of the matter under discussion, for which purpose specialist (and almost by definition subordinate) advisers may be called in to help, but, equally importantly, on how to pilot it through cabinet and Parliament. For that purpose a wide view of the world is required. By contrast, on the continent specialists occupy a much higher proportion of senior posts. Even though ENA graduates may be regarded as generalists, a number of Grandes Ecoles of much greater antiquity than the ENA train these élite technocratic administrators who in later life dominate whole sectors of the economy (the railways are, for example, regarded as a *chasse gardée* by the Grande Ecole concerned). In Germany, where there are no Grandes Ecoles, specialists are recruited direct from Universities and Technical High Schools. In France it is intellectual brilliance and technical skill that count; in Germany it is experience, thoroughness and professional expertise. In practice, the judicious addition of experts to a British negotiating team usually takes care of the technical side; but it is harder to guard against misunderstandings arising out of a 'culture gap'.

Structures
The British system does have one inherent advantage over the other two in a collaborative context, in that *conceptually* it predisposes officials from different ministries to think collectively, and *structurally* it provides instant machinery for preparing a coordinated British line in any negotiations. Neither Bonn nor Paris has an equivalent of the Cabinet Office nor the attitudes of mind that go with it. In Bonn coordination is effected partly by the Chancellor's Office and partly by lead ministries, in Paris by the Prime Minister's Office at the Hotel Matignon or by the Elysée; but in neither case is there a collective

reflex to agree a common line which can guarantee to bring recalcitrant ministries into line.

The French system is both hierarchical (President — Prime Minister — Ministers) and segmented as in Britain; but also *ad hoc* coordination is either imposed (by Presidential decree) or effected informally via private meetings of representatives of ministers' *cabinets* (see below) with the Prime Minister's Office, or via special non-ministerial agencies. The most relevant for this study is the Secrétariat-Général du Comité Interministériel pour les Questions de Coopération Economique Européenne (SGCI) which, by and large, has succeeded over the years in maintaining a consistent overall French approach to major Community issues. It suffers (as French officials are the first to admit) from two drawbacks however: the tightness of its control which reduces negotiating flexibility in Brussels, and the fact that the most carefully concocted and coordinated strategems can be overturned without warning by an edict from the Elysée.

German officials are apt to complain that their coordinating machinery is by contrast rather too weak. This is partly due to the Federal Constitution, which deliberately eschewed tight central control and removed whole areas such as education and culture from the purview of central government, and partly to the ability of the separate ministries to deploy superior expertise at the various coordinating committees chaired sometimes by the Chancellor's Office and sometimes by individual ministries. Despite these difficulties, which show up clearly in negotiations *à dix*, with German officials sometimes taking contradictory lines in different groups, there is little evidence that German interests in, say, the agricultural field have suffered as a consequence.

It is indeed arguable that coordination may be subject to the law of diminishing returns. The British Cabinet Office machinery is without question highly efficient and probably coordinates a greater number of instructions for British negotiators on a wider variety of topics in quicker time than any of its Continental counterparts. But the team is small, the ground it has to cover is limitless, and its remit and powers are not always very clearly defined. Consequently, the respectable mantle of 'coordination' may be thrown over a sectional departmental brief which has gone unchallenged either because that department is particularly persistent, or because no-one in the Cabinet Office sufficiently understands the issue, or because another interested department has by oversight not become involved. By a similar token, the underlying doctrine of collective ministerial responsibility both justifies and powerfully reinforces departments' instinctive tendency to build a consensus around a single compromise formula rather than to identify and elaborate distinct options.

The ease of communication between ministries, both nationally and internationally, is ultimately determined, however, more by their internal structures and dynamics than by the nature of the external machinery devised to monitor or control the process of consultation. On the face of it, all three national government structures are similar: in each country there is a broadly similar set of ministries with comparable hierarchies of officials. But these superficial similarities conceal major qualitative differences of organisation, behaviour and style. The principal lines of demarcation in Continental ministries are vertical, dividing them into clearly, and as far as possible logically, distinct departments — *Abteilungen* (German) or *Directions* (French). Each is headed by a Director (a Deputy Secretary) who is completely responsible for the work of his department and will typically exercise tight control over its activities. The sections within it are normally small and encouraged to work upward rather than sideways: coordination, in practice as in theory, tends to take place at a higher level within the division or, more particularly in the French case, at the level of the minister's *cabinet* (see below).

In Britain, the vertical lines are much less distinct and sections or departments headed by Assistant Secretaries play a much more important role. Being grouped by subject rather than by broad category, they are more fluid, and are created and disbanded, or moved from one division — or even one ministry — to another, depending on the evolution of the subject-matter. It is hard for a British Deputy Secretary to exercise such close supervision over these mobile cells as his French or German counterparts; consequently low-level lateral communication is much freer in Whitehall and most coordination is effected at the level of Assistant Secretary or below.

The relative fluidity of the British system is accentuated by the rapidity with which British civil servants at all levels move around from job to job with the aim of 'broadening their experience' (that is, becoming better generalists). In France the products of the ENA also expect to tackle a wide variety of jobs in the course of their civil service careers, but those belonging to the lesser *Corps* tend to operate within a much narrower waveband. In Germany, officials in all streams move relatively slowly up a well-ordered ladder within their chosen ministry. A secondment to the Chancellor's Office provides a break for the most able; otherwise they, like the others, will typically spend many years in each job and their entire career within their chosen ministry and often predominantly in one area of activity. This reflects the premium placed on knowledge and expertise; the emphasis is on deepening rather than broadening experience.

A peculiarly French phenomenon is the important part played by the minister's *cabinet*. In contrast to the situation in Britain, or indeed Germany, where the Minister's Private Office is typically staffed by only two or three fairly junior civil servants who owe the minister of the day no political allegiance, a French minister will gather round him as many loyal followers as he is allowed, some of them civil servants, some not. His *Cabinet* is the real powerhouse of the ministry, interfering constantly in all aspects of its work and issuing instructions even to the very senior directors of divisions. No policy which does not enjoy the support of the *cabinet* is likely to survive for long. This system can pose problems for both British and German collaborators, since neither of these will normally be able to field negotiators who enjoy such a close political relationship with their ministers as the Frenchman — assuming, as is often the case, that the latter is a member of a *cabinet*. *They* may be more expert in the subject under discussion; *he* will often wield more political authority.

The political process

So far we have looked at the civil services from the inside. It is now time to locate them in their political settings and compare the ways they relate to politicians, parliament, pressure groups and the public. It is their intimate interaction with the political process that distinguishes them from other professional classes, quite as much as the actual content of their work. The professional judgement of senior officials is under constant pressure from subjective assessments of what is politically feasible. At the same time, their actions are generally shielded from public scrutiny more effectively than those of other professions.

Relations with politicians

The French system encourages close interaction between officials and politicians as between equals. They have come to regard their jobs as almost interchangeable. Ministers' *cabinets* are engaged in political work as a matter of course; French Presidents and Prime Ministers have made a regular practice of turning *hauts fonctionnaires* into ministers without prior election to the National Assembly; on the other hand, officials have not traditionally declared their party affiliation openly, although there has been movement in this direction since 1981.

In Germany the separation is slightly clearer in that ministers are almost invariably professional politicians of long standing and there is no equivalent of the French *cabinet;* a clearer distinction is drawn between the party political and governmental aspects of a minister's work and his civil servants can concentrate on the latter. But the relationship is close; appointment to senior posts is subject to political considerations, and officials may, for example, contribute to the formulation of party policies.

In Britain, by contrast, the dividing line between politicians and officials remains unequivocal. By tradition, election to Parliament confers a different kind of status and it is understood on both sides that officials defer to their political 'masters'. The ending of the system of patronage in the 1850s and the substitution of a new code of impartial service had the effect of removing party political pressures on the civil service. Apart from a small number of political advisers in Private Offices, clearly identified as such, and an occasional Ambassador, appointments have traditionally been treated as an internal affair of the civil service and, more particularly, of each individual department. Despite their proximity to the political stage, British officials do not normally aspire to become actors, and they keep their party political sympathies (if any) to themselves.

Parliament

These various distinctions become most clear when the roles of the various national Parliaments are considered.

In France, the Constitution of the Fifth Republic sought deliberately to strengthen the hand of the Executive *vis-à-vis* the National Assembly. The latter has not yet succeeded in imposing its will on ministers, and their civil servants do not therefore have to assign a high priority to Parliamentary Questions or political debates. Parliament functions mainly as the legislature, enacting framework legislation to be fleshed out and implemented by the Executive in accordance with the doctrine of the separation of powers. Thus the civil servants, who drafted the original legislation and played an active role (often via the minister's *cabinet*) in seeing it through the Parliamentary committees (Bills being rarely debated on the floor of the Assembly), are responsible for putting it into effect. In addition, there is an ancient tradition of government by Executive Decree (*Décret*) in which the Assembly plays no part.

The Bundestag plays a more important political role than the French National Assembly: Ministers and Chancellors (who after all are made and unmade by the Bundestag) treat it with respect and the government's programme is exposed for debate annually as in Britain. But plenary sessions are relatively infrequent set-piece affairs, and most parliamentary business is transacted in committee. Here civil servants play an active, if not equal, role explaining, defending and piloting through the legislation they have drafted: there is no obvious barrier between elected and non-elected in this setting. Once through its three readings in the Bundestag (which are normally a formality) the resulting Bill goes back to the ministry responsible, for the same civil servants to fill in the detail. Its actual implementation awaits the 'Administrative Decree' which is signed by a senior official.

By contrast, at Westminster, despite apparent similarities in procedure, statute law is regarded essentially as a political matter, the outcome of a tug-of-war between government and opposition. Bills may be drafted by civil servants, but once they reach the floor of the House the politicians take over and officials resume their constitutional role as advisers to their ministers. The latter aim to enact laws which are complete and self-contained down to the last dot and comma, since thereafter nothing stands between them and the judges who may be called on to interpret them in a court of law.

The word 'interpret' is significant in this context. As noted earlier (p. 107), it is almost impossible to challenge a minister's decision in the courts and the same is true *a fortiori* of decisions or Acts of Parliament. A judge's task in cases of doubt is seen as being rather to understand what Parliament intended than to substitute his own view of what it *should* have intended. In Germany, by contrast, the Constitutional Court has often overruled Executive and Parliament. Similarly, in France, legislation enacted by the National Assembly is subject to scrutiny by the Conseil d'Etat which may strike it down if it finds it unconstitutional. In both these countries there is a strong in-built incentive for those preparing legislation (that is, the civil servants) to pay attention to the purely juridical aspects.

In general, since Parliament itself plays a much more central role in the British Constitution than its French or German equivalents, civil servants in Whitehall are bound to devote what often appears across the Channel as a disproportionate amount of their time attending to its needs, just as British ministers' lives are dominated to a unique degree by the division bells at Westminster. Parliamentary Questions and Early Day Motions take first call on civil servants' time whatever else may be going on, at home or abroad.

The public
Broadly speaking the public (apart from the press) impinges on the administration in two shapes or sizes: individuals and corporate bodies. It is important to make the distinction because the two groups fare differently in each country. A British citizen can exploit the constitutional pre-eminence of Parliament by invoking the help of his MP, who may not always gain satisfaction for his constituent, but can at least guarantee a considered and usually speedy response from the government department concerned. French and German citizens are at a comparative disadvantage: in the former case because of the weakness of the National Assembly and its members *vis-à-vis* the Executive; in the latter because of the weaker link between the German MP and his constituency inherent in the German electoral system, under which half the MPs are elected on a regional list.

In the case of organisations, the boot is on the other foot. Bonn is a lobbyist's capital, if not quite on the same level as Washington. (The capitals of the *Länder* are important too.) There is virtually untrammelled access to officials as well as to politicians and it does not take long for a skilled representative to get to know everyone who matters in his own field of interest.

In Paris, French (but not foreign) corporations' access to the levers of power is facilitated by the 'culture' of government described earlier: the leaders of the main corporations, whether public or private, will have been to the same Grandes Ecoles as the 'Enarques' and specialist administrators who run the government either as ministers or senior officials. The long tradition of central government involvement in national economic affairs ensures that these ministers and officials remain closely attuned to the needs of industry even if they do not always see eye to eye with its leaders' wishes.

In London matters are much more complicated. In the first place, trade and industry associations are much less highly organised and therefore less powerful than their Continental counterparts. And secondly, gaining access to the policy-makers in Whitehall requires rare gifts of skill and tenacity. Partly because of their Parliamentary obligations, ministers with industrial/economic attributes are usually too busy to see any but the most important of their 'clients', and then not for long. Moreover, since, according to constitutional convention, they and not their officials are the policy-makers, the officials have , in theory at least, nothing to say to outsiders. Practice varies, but in some ministries it can indeed be very difficult to gain access to officials (although paradoxically it may be easier for real outsiders than for opposition MPs who are obliged to deal with the minister's Private Office). The proliferation of quasi-autonomous non-governmental organisations ('Quangos') in recent years has erected a further barrier, in that constitutionally these bodies respond only to the minister who set them up and not to his officials: often therefore the latter may not know what is going on in some important areas within their department's general remit and for that reason alone will not be *interlocuteurs valables* for lobbyists. The latter quickly learn to deal direct with the Quango itself, thus bypassing the executive as well as the legislature.

The press
To a greater extent than in France or Germany, the British press has traditionally seen itself — and been tolerated by Parliament — as a 'fourth estate', defending the rights and liberties of the common man against the other three. It has always enjoyed a confrontational relationship with the Executive, and in particular the bureaucrats in Whitehall on whom it has pinned the label 'faceless' and whom it can attack with impunity since they are not allowed to answer back. British constitutional conventions require ministers alone to defend their policies, and the execution of them, in public — that is, before the press as well as in Parliament — and the latter objects if officials assume too high a public profile. Civil servants are further inhibited in their public utterances by a very wide-ranging Official Secrets Act, itself the product of the long years of confrontation between a succession of governments and the self-appointed press watchdogs.

Inevitably, Whitehall's on-the-record press conferences tend to be ritualised and uninformative affairs. The press is more extensively briefed than is often supposed, but the briefings are necessarily unattributable and the public appearance (and indeed often the reality) of confrontation is maintained.

French and German officials — particularly the latter — enjoy a different kind of relationship with their press. In Bonn, the large Press

Centre occupies a commanding position between the Chancellory and the Bundestag; German officials are deliberately less secretive and argue that the role of government is less omnipresent than in France or Britain. In contrast to London, there is an official government spokesman who briefs the press fully and on the record after cabinet meetings and whenever the government judges necessary in between. Senior officials, who are often publicly identified with certain policies, may contribute articles explaining or defending them to newspapers or learned journals.

French governments have always accorded a high priority to guiding (the opposition parties of the day would say 'manipulating') the media. They control the national TV networks and most of the radio stations and usually employ a senior politician as government spokesman to deal with the press. Besides briefing journalists fully on discussions in cabinet, the spokesman adopts a generally high profile, entering or stimulating public debate via the columns of national newspapers. Within ministries, officials have, by contrast, normally adopted a more distant attitude to the press, leaving it to the staff of the ministers' personal *cabinets* to do the bulk of the briefing. Unlike their British counterparts, these officials have been subject to a Freedom of Information Act since 1978, but their relations with journalists seem still to be somewhat selective.

The discrepancy in national practices becomes most marked in European Community gatherings. Depending on the progress of discussions, French and particularly German negotiators give their own journalists full and up-to-the-minute briefings almost as if they were backstage members of their national delegations. British spokesmen also give copious briefings, but are less selective in their audience, being prepared to talk to all comers, and are more inclined to stick to the line agreed at the meeting.

Conclusions

'In Britain, everything is allowed if it is not forbidden; in Germany everything is forbidden if it is not allowed; in France everything is allowed even if it is forbidden.' The grain of truth in this old chestnut lies not so much in the precise nature of the purported national characteristics as in the perception that the three countries are administered in strikingly different ways on the basis of different assumptions, not least about the nature of government itself.

These differences, as indicated at the outset, may be grouped under three main headings:

— *conceptual*: embracing the inherited and inducted attitudes of the administrators;
— *organisational*: that is, the internal structures of the separate administrations, recruitment, training and so on;
— *operational*: that is, the ways in which the civil services interact with the 'real' world outside, both governors (the politicians) and governed.

This chapter has tried to show both *how* the three civil services differ under each of these headings and *why*. The question remains: how much do these differences matter in practice? Are they a barrier to intergovernmental cooperation? Do they perhaps favour cooperation between two of the three to the detriment of the third? Leaving aside the question of whether intergovernmental collaboration is always necessary or a good thing, it is not difficult to find a number of examples of bilateral collaboration which show clearly that, whatever difficulties the national administrations may experience in understanding or adapting to each other's ways, they can be overcome given the political will on both sides. What is less clear is how many potential joint projects have *failed* to materialise, or which of these failures can be ascribed to lack of political will rather than of administrative rapport.

Nor can it always be safely assumed *a priori* that a given pair of countries will collaborate more easily than another pair because their administrative traditions and systems seem to 'fit' better. Franco-British cooperation should arguably be easier to achieve than Franco-German because France and Britain both have highly centralised government systems and closed socio-political structures by comparison with the FRG. Sometimes French officials do indeed find the German system confusing. But in practice French and British civil servants have found it at least as easy to deal with the relatively 'open' and decentralised German system as with each other's. To take only two examples, Anglo-German cooperation on the MRCA (multi-role combat aircraft) project has functioned as smoothly over as long a period as has Anglo-French cooperation over a succession of helicopter projects, although the minutes of relevant committee meetings would no doubt disclose fascinatingly different discussions held within and between the national bureaucracies *en route*.

In short, it may be misleading simply to equate differences with difficulties, and more rewarding to think in terms of complementarity. Fruitful international cooperation is a form of arbitrage, secured by trading each partner's strong points. Viewed in this way, British, German and French officials may often cooperate successfully with each other because, rather than in spite, of their contrasting backgrounds and styles. Each group appreciates that it has much to learn from the others and profits in unexpected ways from the exchanges.

- *conceptually*, the tendency of Continental systems toward formality, legalism and a certain *'esprit de contradiction'* can be fruitfully matched against the Anglo-Saxon tendency toward flexibility, pragmatism and compromise;
- *organisationally*, the more logical but also sometimes more rigid and compartmentalised Continental structures which encourage a narrow definition of each department's 'competence' (in the juridical sense) complement the sometimes excessively fluid and random nature of British structures with their greater propensity to coordinate;

— *operationally*, each national group finds something to envy if not emulate in the others: Germans envy the British ability to keep a wide range of government business clear of public scrutiny; Britons envy German and French officials' closer involvement in the political process; the French envy the success of German administrators in protecting national interests while simultaneously extolling the free market; Germans and Britons envy French ability to rally industrial and other private forces behind the government line. And so on.

But alas, complementarity is not always enough. Mutual incomprehension can, on occasion, breed a mutual mistrust which is stronger than the desire to learn what the other partner has to teach. And this danger appears to grow almost in proportion to the square of the number of partners involved. The sort of informal atmosphere in which two teams of negotiators usually meet once they know each other is much harder to create when a third team is introduced. Moreover, the two teams with the most obviously similar interests or attributes (the two things are of course not necessarily synonymous) will always be tempted to gang up against the third. This phenomenon is a familiar one in the wider context of the European Community as a whole, but is also likely to make itself felt whenever the three countries seek to cooperate *à trois*. In these circumstances, a natural distinction between the real *interests* of the two Continental partners and those of island Britain can only be exacerbated by deep-seated contrasts in thought-processes, working methods and constitutional arrangements. In these too, as we have seen, the British tend to be the odd men out. It is ironic, and unhelpful, that it is precisely they who have the greatest proclivity to compromise.

There is a widely held belief that if the French and German governments tend to gang up against others it is largely on account of the Franco-German Treaty of 1963. This belief is not always soundly based (Franco-German understanding is more often based on shared interests), but certainly the joint commitment of the two governments, enshrined in the Treaty, to consult each other at all levels on all major issues of mutual interest continues powerfully to influence the way in which European cooperation develops both inside and outside the Community proper. The Treaty came about, and continues to operate, essentially for political reasons, but for the purposes of this study it is important to bear in mind that its successful conclusion depended, as does its continuing effectiveness, quite largely on the fact that both the French and German administrations were and are geared to coping with formal, detailed Treaty commitments. It is almost impossible to imagine a similar treaty being concluded by either France or Germany with Britain, whose politicians and administrators are instinctively averse to such formalism and who tend to regard the law — and especially international law — as an adjunct to political action rather than as its absolute arbiter. Be that as it may, the existence of the Treaty will continue (whatever individual German or French politicians and administrators may think of it) to favour Franco-German cooperation at the expense of British cooperation with either of them.

That being so, only the continued and consistent exercise of political will on the part of the British government can counteract this permanent tendency to find itself on the outside. Given the relatively modest constitutional role of civil servants, and their lack of clearly defined legal status, the onus for sustaining a trilateral cooperative effort thus rests in the British case with politicians – that is, ministers.

All this assumes that the principal characteristics of the three systems of government (and hence their principal differences) are immutable. In fact, all three are evolving (France in particular is steadily devolving power to the regions and is shortly to have a new Civil Service Statute) and there is no reason why they should not, by agreement, evolve in a common direction. Harmonisation of this process could itself be the subject of trilateral discussion, if not actual negotiation. But if, as this study suggests, it is Britain that is farthest out of line with its closest European partners, then a special effort is perhaps needed here. What could realistically be envisaged by way of reform? A written constitution is not a realistic option, nor is a wholesale revision of the relationship between the legislature and the executive. But that between Parliament and the civil service has been slowly changing (in a 'European' direction) with the expansion of the Select Committee system, and this process could be furthered by the enactment of a Civil Service Statute which would define, for the first time, the civil servant's position in law. This move, which would be but a logical extension of the reforms initiated 130 years ago (and perhaps of the Fulton reforms of the 1960s?) would not only bring British practice broadly into line with that on the Continent but would also help to remedy the disadvantage under which the British civil servant labours *vis-à-vis* his Continental counterparts, namely his lack of authority. And a British civil service with greater authority could surely relieve ministers of part of the onus for sustaining trilateral cooperation.

Notes

1. The author, who is a member of the British Diplomatic Service, writes here in a personal capacity.

7 Communication Between Political Elites
Roger Morgan

Introduction

Cooperative relationships between states depend not only on the administrative arrangements existing between governments, but also on the attitudes and the degree of reciprocal understanding between the politicians in charge of national policies. This chapter explores the patterns of communication between political leadership groups in London, Paris and Bonn in order to establish what attitudes are likely to influence the intergovernmental consultations and negotiations analysed elsewhere in this book.[1]

The chapter begins at the top: it considers Anglo-Franco-German relationships at the levels, in turn, of heads of government, ministers, parliamentarians, political parties, and politically important interest groups, such as employers' and trade union organisations. (The civil services and the media of the three countries have been considered in Chapters 6 and 4 respectively.) At the higher levels, the main question is how much knowledge and understanding of the other two countries is likely to have been acquired by major office-holders in the course of their earlier careers; as far as the parliaments, parties, and interest groups are concerned, the focus is on the degree of relevant communication each organisation undertakes, and the effect of this activity on the bilateral relationship as a whole.

Next there is a brief survey of channels through which the political élites of the three countries may encounter each other in broader multilateral contexts. The chapter ends by assessing the principal efforts which have been and are being made, in each of the three bilateral relationships, to improve the quantity and quality of dialogue between the political élites. One point which underlies a good deal of the argument is that the composition and influence of these élites vary widely from one country to another: this is part of the broader problem of developing really intimate links between three such diverse national cultures.

Political leaders, ministers and parliamentarians

The most important inter-élite relationships are, of course, those at the top level of government. Although good personal relations between rulers are no guarantee of good relations between the states they rule, they obviously play a decisive role. Adenauer's close affinity with de Gaulle was important, and so was Schmidt's with Giscard d'Estaing. Indeed, in Franco-German relations, recent years have seen a succession of top-level partnerships with an apparently high level of personal compatibility: Kohl's relationship with Mitterrand is not the first case of a CDU leader having a good personal relationship with a French socialist (Adenauer got on much better with Guy Mollet than with his Christian Democratic counterpart, Georges Bidault), and the only recent period of top-level personal difficulty between Bonn and Paris appears to have been that between Brandt and Pompidou in 1969–74. Anglo-German relations, while showing nothing like the quality of personal rapport which existed between Schmidt and Giscard d'Estaing, seem to have been marked by a fair degree of personal understanding at the summit, especially perhaps between Callaghan and Schmidt, and again between Thatcher and Kohl. Anglo-French top-level relations, in contrast, have been less fortunate: President Giscard d'Estaing is said to have felt disdain for the 'bourgeois' Wilson and Callaghan, and got on very badly with Mrs Thatcher, whose relationship with Mitterrand appears to be much better.

Apart from the strictly personal element in these top-level relationships, there is of course the question of how much real understanding each leader has for the political situation and objectives of his or her partners, and of their countries. Promotion to the top level of government is essentially the culmination of a career within a national political system, although it is rare to get so high without *some* involvement with other countries. As it happens, both Britain and the Federal Republic, after being governed by a succession of leaders with a fair degree of international experience (Heath, Wilson and Callaghan in the one case, Brandt and Schmidt in the other), now have heads of government whose contacts with foreign countries on their way to the top were exceptionally limited. France, in contrast, after the administrations of Pompidou and Giscard (the latter very experienced internationally), now has another President whose involvement in international affairs has been fairly intensive throughout the 30 years since his first ministerial responsibility for overseas relations.

The personal attitudes of heads of government are of course important not just because they can personally promote (or inhibit) agreement with their partners, but also because their general attitude will be felt at lower levels of the machinery. If it is known that the will for an agreement is strong at the top level, attitudes of ministers and officials will be adjusted accordingly, and some of them may even use the situation to promote causes going rather beyond what the leader had in mind.

At the level just below the summit, the attitudes and experiences of individual ministers are important factors too. It obviously makes a difference to the readiness of a national government to communicate internationally (at least to understand and discuss problems, if not to resolve them) if a number of its leading members have wide international experience. At the time of the Mauroy government of 1981–84, France was again in the lead on this score: leaving aside the Prime Minister (whose exposure to 'abroad' before taking office was as limited as Mrs Thatcher's), the Finance Minister, Foreign Minister and Minister of the Interior (Delors, Cheysson and Defferre) had collectively had considerably more experience of high-level international dealings than their British counterparts (Lawson, Howe and Brittan), or the Germans (Stoltenberg, Genscher and Zimmermann), with the striking exception of the ten-year Foreign Ministry tenure of Genscher. The replacement of Mauroy, Delors, Cheysson and Defferre in 1984 (by Fabius, Bérégovoy, Dumas and Joxe) has put France back in a situation similar to that of Britain and Germany.

It is of course true that significant international experience for a politician may come in unexpected forms. The Minister-President of a German *Land* is likely to be involved in substantial international dealings: this is true by definition of Governing Mayors of Berlin, but it would be true of any Minister-President with a leading role in the Bundesrat or with international ambitions for his *Land*. In addition, many British, French and German ministers of 'home' departments will now have intensive contacts with their counterparts through the EC Council of Ministers. It even appears that Council meetings in areas where EC business is at times minimal or routine – meetings, say, of Ministers of Transport, Energy or Education – provide the best occasions for informal or relaxed encounters which will enable participants to absorb the general preoccupations of their counterparts, and to know who they will be dealing with on future occasions.

Although it is clear that encounters between ministers of the British, French and German governments are more intensive than they have ever been (and that the exchanges of views between their respective officials have grown correspondingly), it is also the case that contacts between the parliamentarians of the three countries are much less significant than they might be, and arguably less significant than they were in earlier decades. (There is, of course, the separate question of how important national parliaments and their members actually are in themselves.) In particular, the practice whereby influential members of national parliaments were also members of their country's delegations to international assemblies – the Council of Europe's Parliamentary Assembly, the North Atlantic Assembly, the WEU Assembly, or the pre-1979 non-elected European Parliament – has gone into a distinct decline.

The British delegation to the Council of Europe Assembly, which was formerly led by a junior minister and contained a number of up-and-coming members of future cabinets, now tends to consist of MPs who, worthy as they are, are marginal in terms of Westminster politics. Again, since the introduction of direct elections to the European Parliament in 1979, today's MEPs are full-timers, whose role in national and party affairs is an isolated one. There are also no British counterparts to the French and German cases where high-level experience in the Community institutions has been a prelude to national ministerial office, as with Deniau and Delors in France or Bangemann in Germany. This means that, instead of considerable exposure to the politics of other European countries being a normal part of the experience of many significant members of national Parliaments (and future ministers), the only parliamentarians to have considerable dealings with their foreign counterparts are either the professional international assemblymen of the kind sketched above (who will develop close international contacts, both personal and organisational), or else those with a specific interest in contacts with one or more particular foreign country.

There have for some years been bilateral Anglo-French, Anglo-German or Franco-German Parliamentary Groups, which are more or less active, but the parliamentarians involved in their work tend to be a self-selected and not very representative sample, who are brought into this field of activity by a personal interest in the other country concerned. The membership of these bilateral parliamentary associations, and participation in their activities, also tends to fluctuate from year to year and from meeting to meeting, according to the topic under discussion. The Franco-German Parliamentary Working Group, although it provides a channel of communication for the discussion both of bilateral and European Community problems, is said by close observers to be incomparably less important than the official governmental channels in shaping the substance of relations between Paris and Bonn. The Franco-British Parliamentary Group, again, has allowed a select group of British and French legislators to maintain contact during the ups and downs of Anglo-French relations (the group includes a small number of faithful and long-serving members), but it has not made a decisive impact on policy transactions between London and Paris. The activities of the Anglo-German Parliamentary Association, in contrast, are more structured: in the late 1970s and early 1980s, with the administrative and financial support of the Anglo-German Foundation for the Study of Industrial Society, groups of parliamentarians from the two countries have engaged in joint studies of specific policy issues, some of which have led to written reports. However, even these efforts cannot be said to form more than a marginal strand in the overall pattern of relationships between London and Bonn.

The activities of those groups specifically devoted to bilateral relations is, of course, only a part — although an important one — of the spectrum of parliamentary contacts as a whole. Quite apart from the heavy intensity of ministerial visits between the three countries — which may amount to dozens or even hundreds per year, even without counting multilateral meetings in the EC and other contexts — there is a steady flow of visits by individual parliamentarians between London, Paris, and Bonn. The occasions for these visits are diverse: a British backbench MP may undertake a one-week lecture tour in Germany for the Deutsch-Englische Gesellschaft; an influential German or French parliamentarian may be invited for discussions in Britain through the Visitors' Programme of the Central Office of Information; or parliamentarians may travel for business purposes. However, the experiences gained on visits of all these kinds will play some part in the course of the politicians' parliamentary or other political work in their own country.

Perhaps the most significant dimension of international parliamentary contacts — at least in terms of influence on the making of policy — is the practice of visits by specialist committees of national parliaments. Such visits have been a feature of relations between the parliaments of France and Germany for some years, and in the case of the British Parliament they have been facilitated by the establishment of a new system of departmental Select Committees since 1979. As an example, a visit to Paris by the House of Commons Agriculture Committee is said by observers to have played a useful part in promoting mutual understanding of British and French views on the CAP. A visit to London by the Bundestag Foreign Affairs Committee in March 1985 again provided for a useful exchange of views with the corresponding House of Commons committee.

Political parties and interest groups
A further aspect of inter-élite contacts is that of links between political parties. The links between the parties of Britain, France and Germany contribute to the overall political relationships between the three countries in at least two important ways. First, the parties are among the channels through which the future political leaders may, or may not, communicate with their counterparts in the other countries. Second, the party organisations, through their committees or their officials responsible for relations with parties abroad, provide a structure for communication on policy issues. This may be relatively unimportant when two parties with the same general political orientation are in office (when, for instance, British Conservatives and German Christian Democrats find themselves in frequent contact in their capacity as ministers), but it can become very significant when parties tend to diverge on ideology or major policy issues when they are in opposition (as currently between the British Labour Party and the German Social Democrats on the EC), or when one party is in opposition and the other in office (as between the SPD and the Parti Socialiste on nuclear defence).

We need to keep in mind that fruitful communication between parties in different countries often has to overcome serious intrinsic obstacles. For example, the politicians who represent their parties in international discussions, while they may sometimes represent the party's official policy, are not always in line with its more powerful leaders, especially when it is in office: between 1974 and 1979 the Labour Party was often represented in the Socialist International by Ian Mikardo or Tony Benn of the NEC's International Subcommittee, while the foreign policy of the Labour cabinets of the time was in the hands of James Callaghan, Anthony Crosland and David Owen. Again, different national political systems vary considerably: a 'backbench' member of the French National Assembly carries considerably less political weight than his German or British counterpart, both in parliamentary and in party affairs, so that a dialogue may be one between unequal participants. A third difficulty, the importance of which will be clear in the following discussion, is that the party system itself varies greatly from one country to another, so that some parties cannot easily recognise a counterpart abroad (this is indeed symptomatic of deeper differences between the political cultures of the three countries, which may affect every aspect of their political communication).

Despite these handicaps, the parties in the three countries have developed certain patterns of communication and cooperation. The discussion should start with the parties of the non-Communist Left (France is of course alone among the three countries in having an important Communist Party). These parties share a tradition of international contacts established by the First and Second Workers' Internationals in the years when all parties of the Left seemed condemned to permanent opposition. Through the Socialist International, the British Labour Party, the French Socialist Party and the SPD have had a long history of contacts, and these have been intensified within the Federation of Socialist Parties of the European Community (although it was important that the Labour Party participated fully in the latter only after the referendum confirming Britain's EC membership in 1975).

Despite the divisive issue of the EC, and other differences (including the relationship of the two parties to the trade union movement), the socialist parties of Britain and Germany have had closer relations in recent years than either have enjoyed with the French. Most of the SPD's leaders speak English (partly because of their interest in America), and the SPD has been a leading influence in the Socialist International, which has its headquarters in London. (The financial strength of the SPD and of its related political foundation, the Friedrich-Ebert-Stiftung, has helped the party to establish this high international profile). The International Subcommittee of the Labour Party's National Executive Committee and its staff, and the SPD Executive's Department for International Relations have maintained close contact in recent years, and certain relationships between individual leaders of the two parties have also been good. In particular, Denis Healey, now the only leading member of the Labour Party to speak German (Patrick Gordon-Walker and Richard Crossman were the others in recent years), has maintained close relations with Germany since his days as the party's International Secretary (1945–52), notably with Helmut Schmidt, with whom he shared the uncomfortable experience of being Minister for Defence and for Finance in left-wing governments.

A new element entered the relationship between the Labour Party and the SPD with the creation in 1981 of the British Social Democratic Party (SDP), a party which modelled itself to some extent on the German social democratic movement. Many of those who left the Labour Party to found the SDP had exceptionally close links with Germany, in particular Shirley Williams and William Rodgers and, in turn, many leading members of the SPD went out of their way to show active sympathy for the SDP (partly out of exasperation at Labour's negative attitude to the European Community). However, the SPD's official partner in Britain is still very clearly the Labour Party: it is significant that during the European Parliament election campaign of June 1984 *The Times* carried a photograph of a visiting Helmut Schmidt together with Denis Healey, and it is even more significant that Willy Brandt was filmed for British television in the company of his host and fellow party-leader, Neil Kinnock.

Between the German and French socialist parties there has also been a flow of communication which has varied in intensity over the years, with a mounting sense in the early 1980s that a crisis of confidence required urgent attention. An earlier crisis in the mid-1970s, when the SPD (then in a coalition government with the German Liberals) was very concerned by the French socialists' incipient alliance with the Communists, was overcome when this alliance temporarily collapsed in the autumn of 1977. After 1981 it was the turn of the French socialists to express their alarm at the apparently neutralist direction of their German comrades' defence policy, as the SPD's opposition to Euro-missile stationing hardened towards the total rejection of November 1983. (By this time, ironically, France's socialists were leading a co-alition including the Communists, who were obliged to accept a strong-ly anti-Soviet defence policy as well as an increasingly 'orthodox' economic policy as the price of office.) The dramatic misunderstand-ings and even conflicts between the French and German socialists were a sign of faulty communications between the two parties at all levels, from the top downwards: President Mitterrand's pro-missile declaration to the Bundestag in January 1983 amounted to an intervention against the SPD in the current Bundestag election campaign, and was seen in part as revenge for Schmidt's tacit support for Giscard d'Estaing against Mitterrand in the presidential election of May 1981.

In this situation (French concern about the dangers of German neutralism reached a peak in 1983), the two parties agreed to establish high-level committees of influential politicians to tackle their differ-ences both on security and on economic issues. It is also noteworthy that the Friedrich-Ebert-Stiftung, whose research efforts and inter-national conference debates gave high priority to these issues, concentrated heavily on Franco-German discussions. The Foundation itself, it could be said, was in a very loose sense copied in Paris, where the government-financed 'Forum pour l'indépendance et la Paix' was established in 1983. The debates and publications of this body (which, although its principal intellectual *animateur* is the dissident Communist historian, Jean Elleinstein, is close to the thinking of the French government and the Socialist Party) have given a clear priority to questions involving Germany: the Forum's major conference on 'Europe and the German Question' held at the European Parliament in Strasbourg in January 1984 with the participation of parliamentarians from both countries[2] was followed in the ensuing months by discussions of related issues in Paris and in Vienna.

The British Labour Party has so far played no part in these French-led discussions, and this may be symptomatic of the poor communications between the two parties. The French Socialist Party has risen from a position of relative impotence in the early 1970s to the triumphant tenure of power after 1981, while the Labour Party's fortunes have correspondingly declined (especially since it lost office in 1979): this difference, combined with wide divergences between the two parties on EC affairs, on defence, and increasingly on economic policy, have tended to produce a relative lack of contact. The fact that no major efforts have been made by either side to bridge the gap – in sharp contrast to the situation in the Franco-German relationship – suggests that socialists in London and Paris do not give a very high priority to their relations with each other.

When we turn from the left towards the centre of the political spectrum, party relations are seen to have been complicated by the different conceptions of liberalism prevailing in the three countries, and the contrasting fortunes of the parties representing it. The British Liberal Party and the German FDP have maintained good and close relations, their solidarity being cemented not only by general ideological affinity and good relations between their leaders, but also by the German Liberals' misfortune in winning a precariously small proportion of electoral votes, and the British Liberals' misfortune in winning an even smaller proportion of parliamentary seats (and no ministerial posts whatever). This relationship, embedded in the strongly 'European' orientation of both parties, means that a high proportion of parliamentarians and other leading figures in each party are usefully aware of the preoccupations of the other. In recent years there have been differences on economic policy, since the FDP under Genscher and Lamsdorf, in its post-1982 coalition with the CDU, has adopted explicitly 'liberal' positions, while the British Liberals, in alliance with the SDP, have reinforced their already more interventionist approach: the relations between the two parties appear to be sufficiently close for these difficulties to be managed relatively easily.

Both British and German Liberals, however, have found it difficult to identify counterparts in France, particularly since the virtual demise of the Radical Party (or parties) of the Third and Fourth Republics. One group of possible allies, the descendants of the MRP led by Jean Lecanuet, although acceptable on political and 'European' grounds, is ineligible because of its religious affiliations (which align it with the German CDU), and the main force of the 'Giscardian' UDF presents problems both for German and for British Liberals because of its reactionary image on questions of law and order. The FDP and the UDF have indeed maintained contacts, both bilaterally and in the European Liberals' and Democrats' Group in the European Parliament (from 1979 to 1984), but these contacts, like the French contacts of the British Liberal Party (which prefers the Movement of Left-wing Radicals to the UDF) could hardly be described as cordial or systematic.

On the right and centre-right of the party spectrum, the main problem is that of finding common ground between the specific characteristics of British Conservatism, German Christian Democracy, and the mixed Gaullist/'Giscardian' heritage of the centre and right in France.

The British Conservatives and the CDU/CSU, the undisputed right-wing parties in their respective countries, have developed a fairly close partnership over the years, especially since both parties have simultaneously held power in the 1980s, in a period when the word 'conservative' has lost some of its pejorative connotations in Germany. Contacts between leaders, parliamentarians, and officials of the two parties have been extensive. The CDU's party Foundation, the Konrad-Adenauer-Stiftung, has played an active part in familiarising British Conservatives with German problems: for instance, the Foundation's London office, established in 1981, has promoted cooperation (including a joint study with the Bonn Group of European peace movements)[3] and has organised visits for the new Conservative MPs of 1979 and 1983 to the Federal Republic and to Berlin. It may safely be expected that Christian Democratic and Conservative ministers of the late 1980s and 1990s, and their political advisers, will be sensitive to each others' concerns.[4]

Between these British and German Conservatives on the one hand, and their putative French counterparts on the other, difficulties arise because of the specific character of this part of the French political spectrum, where neither the Gaullists nor the Giscardians, for one thing, are prepared to accept the label 'right-wing'. The British and German parties have developed a degree of contact both with the RPR and with the UDF, but these contacts seem to have been intermittent and often *ad hoc*: for instance, a tactical agreement on a specific issue in the European Parliament, or an *ad hoc* study group on defence policy which brought together Conservatives and Gaullists in 1981–82. The establishment by the Konrad-Adenauer-Stiftung of offices both in London and in Paris in the early 1980s (of which the Paris office has greater difficulty in establishing systematic party contacts than the London one) is a clear indication that the links between right-wing parties are regarded as unsatisfactory. With France in particular, they have hitherto depended on the personal contacts of individual grandees — Lord So-and-So, 'Le Président Un Tel et ses amis' — and have not yet found a form appropriate to the more professional political parties of the 1980s.

Turning from political parties to other élite organisations which play a part in communications between the three countries, it is necessary to mention the role of the organisations representing what the British call 'the two sides of industry', and which both the French and the Germans call 'the social partners'. Employers' organisations and trade unions are essentially concerned with promoting the interests of those they represent within the industrial, economic, and political life of their own countries. The European Community, rather than any strictly bilateral interests, is by far the most important factor to have brought both the employers' and the trade union organisations of Britain, France and Germany into close contact — although a degree of bilateral *ad hoc* consultation on specific issues has naturally developed as well. The growth of Community legislation in many areas, particularly in those of direct concern to industrial interests (the Fifth Directive on Company Law and the 'Vredeling Directive' are obvious examples), has led the representative national organisations not only to establish their own offices in Brussels (in the case of the employers' organisations, at least), but also to join together in Community-wide bodies: UNICE (Union of Industries of the European Community) for the employers' organisations and ETUC (European Trades Union Confederation) for the unions.

While UNICE and ETUC, from their respective viewpoints, each try to present a united front to their interlocutors in the Community institutions, their statements are naturally preceded by bilateral discussions between the major national organisations, including those of Britain, France, and Germany.

The CBI's Director for International Affairs, for instance, maintains close contact with his counterparts in the CNPF (Conseil National du Patronat-Français) in Paris and the BDI (Bundesverband der deutschen Industrie) in Cologne, and UNICE issues which require special consideration (at a higher level than that of the representatives in Brussels) are discussed in bilateral telephone conversations. It should in fact be noted that the degree of the Community's involvement in economic and other policies has not increased as was expected in the early 1970s, so that the representation of employers' organisations in Brussels has been maintained at a relatively modest level (this is not, of course, true in the agricultural sector, where COPA's (Comité des Organisations Professionnelles Agricoles) importance reflects the domination of farming policy by the CAP). Recent research on the political activities of the BDI, for instance, shows that, even when its aim is to influence Community policies, its efforts are nowadays directed at the Federal government in Bonn (on which the BDI counts to represent the interests of German industry), rather than at the Community institutions. One reason for the failure of UNICE's role to develop is that EEC policy initiatives have often been sectoral (for example, the Davignon plan for the steel industry), rather than global.

The employers' organisations in the three countries, while they may make common cause on specific bilateral issues (for instance, the intervention of the CBI and the CNPF in favour of the Channel Tunnel), appear overall to act as lobbyists for certain general lines of policy (on reduction of corporation tax, or the safeguarding of industrial secrets from 'excessive' disclosure to employees, *à la* Vredeling), rather than as lobbyists for the development of the bilateral relationships we are considering. The industrial sectors which are interested in bilateral or broader cooperative ventures will tend to pursue them spontaneously (see Chapter 11) and the overall employers' organisations are, in most cases, not involved.

On the trade union side, the Community is again an important factor in international contacts, although the relative organisational and financial weakness of the unions (especially in Britain and France) limits their presence in Brussels, in comparison with that of the employers. Rather than having permanent representation in Brussels, the British and French unions rely on frequent contacts at the meetings of ETUC (usually at the level of permanent officers responsible for international contacts, but sometimes involving elected leaders too), and in the framework of the Community's Economic and Social Committee.

There are, in addition, important differences in organisation between the trade union movements in the three countries (the German movement consisting of 17 industrial unions, the French movement of 3 ideologically-opposed central bodies with very diverse affiliated organisations, and the British movement of 126 individual unions loosely linked together in the Trades Union Congress), and this makes organised international cooperation difficult. In particular, the fact that the Communist-inspired union organisation of France, the CGT (Confédération Générale du Travail), is not affiliated to the ETUC, and has no official relations with the DGB (Deutsche Gewerkschaftsbund), creates a substantial gap in the structure of possible cooperation.

The unions of the three countries have been able to coordinate their public declarations and demonstrations on specific issues – for instance, in the well coordinated protest campaign against unemployment in June 1983 at the European Council meeting in Stuttgart, or in the more recent and more diffuse demand for a shorter working week. There have also been numerous cases of bilateral or more general trade union contacts in specific sectors: for instance, cross-frontier cooperation between French and German unions in adjacent regions, solidarity of port workers in cases of seamen's strikes, or gifts of food and so on from the CGT to the striking British National Union of

Mineworkers. It is hard, however, to find evidence that the trade union organisations, any more than the employers, have acted as a force impelling the governments in Britain, France and Germany towards closer policy cooperation.

Channels of communication: multilateral and bilateral

As well as the bilateral contexts which may bring members of national political élites together, and the Community or other official 'networks' through which they may meet, it should not be forgotten that they may encounter each other in certain organisations which specialise in promoting policy debates among leading figures from the whole of the North Atlantic or even OECD regions. The most prominent of these bodies are the Bilderberg Conferences (established by Prince Bernhard of the Netherlands in the 1960s), the Trilateral Commission (founded by David Rockefeller and other prominent Democrats in the early 1970s), and the Atlantic Institute for International Affairs (established in Paris in 1961).

In all of these organisations, political figures from Britain and Germany have been much more actively involved than their opposite numbers from France, partly because of the dominance of English as a *lingua franca* in any organisation with strong American involvement, and partly because of the reticence of most French politicians towards any organisation smacking of 'Atlanticism'. Even though the Atlantic Institute was deliberately located in Paris in order to facilitate communication with the French élites, its political orientation, and the fact that all its directors have been Americans, have limited its main local connections to a small and unrepresentative section of French political life.

France's limited representation in international circles of this kind is illustrated by the membership list of the Trilateral Commission for a typical year, 1975 (the Commission's membership has changed relatively little over the years). Among the 76 European members there figure five members of the German Bundestag (including one ex-minister and two future ones), five British parliamentarians (four of them past or future ministers), and only one comparable figure from France — admittedly a future Prime Minister, Raymond Barre, but the contrast is still striking. (Significantly, the membership also included three trade union leaders from Germany, one from France, and none from Britain.)[5]

In terms of the direct involvement of political élites, the impact of these multilateral 'Western' policy discussions in France has thus tended to be less than in Germany or Britain. (The same is true of the work of the International Institute for Strategic Studies, where the involvement of 'working politicians' from Britain and Germany has been ensured by its location in London and a strong German presence on the directing staff, while France's intellectual contribution, from

Raymond Aron and others, has not been matched at the level of political practice.) This means that politicians from Britain and Germany, when engaged in international discussions — whether bilateral, trilateral, or multilateral — will often tend to refer (explicitly or not) to a common stock of discourse and attitudes, which their French counterparts will often not share. There are, of course, exceptions to this general rule — for instance, the former French Foreign Minister Jean François-Poncet, who speaks fluent English and German, agreed in 1983 to become Chairman of the Brussels-based Centre for European Policy Studies — but these exceptions are rare.

The picture that emerges from this diverse array of connections and interactions shows some positive elements, and some negative ones. It is fairly clear that *ministers* of the three countries, in their official capacities, have considerable contact with their counterparts, both bilaterally and otherwise (although the role played by their *officials* in preparing and following up these meetings is obviously of critical importance). In contrast, *parliamentarians, party officials*, and *interest group representatives* have relatively less contact across frontiers. Although the networks of bilateral and trilateral understanding may be substantial enough to sustain harmonious day-to-day intergovernmental cooperation, they are evidently not always effective in cushioning the shocks that may arise from unexpected crises (sharp currency fluctuations, or diplomatic episodes such as Afghanistan in 1979 or Poland in 1981). Neither are they often strong enough to give significant support to governments in the exploration of decisive new steps in European cooperation or integration, let alone to impel governments to take such steps against their own inclination.

Within each bilateral relationship under discussion here, certain initiatives have been taken — in some cases starting several years ago — to supplement the existing flows of communication, and 'thicken-up' the substance of mutual knowledge and understanding so that the political élites of each country (whether in or out of government office) are sufficiently sensitive to each other's concerns not to be taken unawares by new developments or differing reactions.

Probably the most effective attempts at promoting understanding and bringing together influential people who would not necessarily meet their counterparts from the other country are those to be found in the relationship between Britain and Germany. At the summit of a whole network of visits, exchanges and contacts promoted by the Anglo-German Association, the Deutsch-Englische Gesellschaft and other bodies, are the annual Anglo-German Königswinter Conferences. At these gatherings, which started in 1950 in Königswinter near Bonn and since 1978 have been held in alternate years there and in England, a group of over 100 participants from the two countries meets for informal and genuinely frank discussions of current domestic and (mainly) international issues. They normally include at least a dozen active and fairly prominent politicians from each country (including a sprinkling of ministers, past, present and future), as well as senior officials, business leaders and some trade unionists (more German than British), academics, and contributors to the quality media.[6] The 'family' or 'club' atmosphere of Königswinter is at the same time a great strength and a potential source of weakness: the very success of Königswinter in attracting a group of politicians and others with friendly feelings towards each others' countries and the continuity of much of the membership does something to deter attendance by those with more sceptical views, although it should be noted that regular attenders from the Labour Party have included some very hostile towards Britain's EC membership, including Barbara Castle, Peter Shore, and the late Richard Crossman. The fact that much of the discussion at Königswinter takes place in English may deter non-English-speaking German parliamentarians and others from attending, and it may also inhibit the totally fluent and accurate expression of all the nuances of German political attitudes.

However, despite these marginal limitations on the value of the Königswinter forum, there is no doubt that it has played a uniquely important part in contributing to a shared understanding of European and international problems by a significant section of the German and British political élites. In recent years the Königswinter discussions have been supplemented by smaller and more specialist meetings of parliamentarians and others, sponsored by the Anglo-German Foundation for the Study of Industrial Society: this body, set up in the early 1970s on the initiative of the Federal President Gustav Heinemann, has developed a programme of Anglo-German research and discussion on current policy issues (in a few cases reinforcing the existing activities of the Anglo-German Parliamentary Group).

The Franco-German relationship exhibits something of a contrast to the fairly intense network linking the German and British political élites. There are of course many political leaders in France and the Federal Republic who have known each other well for a considerable time — in some cases they have worked together in Brussels, in others they have been involved either as ministers or as officials in the intensive bilateral consultations laid down by the Treaty of Cooperation — but interviews and observation suggest the relative absence of the kind of informal exchanges of view made possible by, say, Königswinter. There is, as noted earlier, a Franco-German Parliamentary Group which has continued to spread mutual understanding among a small but sometimes significant group of members of the Assemblée Nationale and the Bundestag, and there have also been occasional attempts to promote broader Franco-German élite encounters on the lines of Königswinter. However, because of a combination of linguistic problems, organisational difficulties, and social and structural differences between the political élites of the two countries, these efforts have not been of long duration. The latest attempt at reviving the Franco-German dialogue at this level

— a high-powered gathering held at Bad Godesburg in November 1984 — may be more successful than its predecessors.[7]

Probably the most effective non-governmental channel of continuous communication between France and Germany is the Franco-German Institute in Ludwigsburg, near Stuttgart. Mainly devoted to research and publications, the Institute also holds frequent symposia devoted to a comparison of French and German experience on such issues and topics as foreign, economic and industrial policy, social structure, and the policy-making process. The participants in these gatherings have included several members of the political and administrative élites of the two countries — indeed the subject of élites itself has been intensively discussed — and the Ludwigsburg Institute has a unique importance among the large number of bodies, at all levels, devoted to Franco-German contacts.

Anglo-French relations, at the level of political élites, are characterised by a sharp contrast between the good relations which prevail within the specialist and already committed bodies (such as the Anglo-French Parliamentary Group, the Anglo-French Association, or the Association France—Grande Bretagne) and, on the other hand, a marked degree of misunderstanding and even mistrust among the political élites as a whole. The reasons for this include the historic rivalry between the two countries (see Chapter 1), language difficulties (some French politicians speak English fluently but badly, while very few English politicians speak French at all), and the differences between the composition and social habits of the élites on each side of the Channel.

It was the realisation of a serious gap in mutual comprehension which led President Pompidou and Prime Minister Heath, in 1971, to establish the Franco-British Council, a body with influential representatives of many sectors of public and economic life, to promote the comparative discussion of common problems. After a number of relatively small expert meetings devoted to particular topics (industrial policy, regional planning, the publishing trade, and so on), the Council embarked in 1980 on a series of high-level and well-publicised conferences of the 'Königswinter' type, designed to promote closer understanding of how the two countries saw the state of the world and their respective places in it.

At the first and second of the conferences, held in Bordeaux in September 1980 and in Edinburgh in May 1982, a number of politicians, officials, academics, publicists and businessmen from the two countries were assembled. They included the ruling Prime Ministers (Thatcher and Barre in Bordeaux, Thatcher and Mauroy in Edinburgh), who delivered formal speeches in settings which also tended to be very formal. The conferences were characterised by a level of sumptuous hospitality which certainly contributed to bilateral goodwill, and the exchanges in debate were often sharp and direct (this was helped by the provision throughout of simultaneous interpretation, so that all participants spoke in their own language). The time available for intensive group discussion was limited (in Edinburgh the group dealing with world affairs had six hours to discuss an agenda which 'covered' East—West relations, the two superpowers, the Middle East, the Falklands, Europe's relations with developing countries, and the political, financial, and institutional prospects of the EEC). However, there is no doubt that these events (a third was held late in 1984 in Avignon) have improved Franco-British goodwill and understanding at the level of the political élites, and done something to fill the gaps in knowledge and trust which continue to be a marked feature of the Franco-British relationship.[8]

The conclusion emerges from this survey that, of the three sides of the London—Bonn—Paris 'triangle', the London—Bonn one appears to be marked by the greatest *ease* of inter-élite communication, while the Bonn—Paris one is characterised by a pattern of *intensive* relations created by proximity and history, and actively cultivated for mutually agreed purposes of policy. The London—Paris relationship, at the levels discussed here, is marked by failures both of communication and of mutual confidence.

Notes

1. The author's sources for this chapter are best described by A.J. Petrie's statement in Jolyon Howorth and Philip G. Cerny (eds), *Élites in France* (London, Frances Pinter, 1981), p. 195: 'the generalisations contained in this paragraph . . . are a distillation of years of accumulated snippets and impressions from a diversity of sources.' As well as this important book on the French élites, the reader should refer to Dietrich Herzog, 'The Study of Élites in West Germany' in M. Kaase and K. von Beyme (eds), *Elections and Parties* (Beverly Hills and London, Sage Publications, 1978) and W.L. Guttsman, *The British Political Élite* (London, MacGibbon & Kee, 1968).

2. See *L'Allemagne et l'Avenir de l'Europe. Actes du Colloque de Strasbourg 27—28 janvier 1984* (Paris, Editions Anthropos, 1984).

3. *Playing at Peace*, Konrad-Adenauer Foundation jointly with Bow Group (London, 1983).

4. The attempt by the Konrad-Adenauer-Stiftung to do part of its international work in the German language clearly tests the linguistic capacity of both the CDU's British and French counterparts. It was noteworthy that in a German-language conference on 'Europe and the German Question' in November 1983, when several CDU/CSU spokesmen were able to converse with German-speaking parliamentarians from Belgium and the Netherlands as well as Austria and Switzerland, the participants from Paris and London were not party representatives but independent researchers.

5. Membership list in the Trilateral Commission's report *The Crisis of Democracy* by Michel Crozier *et al.* (New York, New York University Press, 1975).

6. See *Deutsche-Französische Konferenz* (Bonn, Forschungsinstitut der Deutschen Gesellschaft für Auswärtige Politik, 1985).

7. See report in *Dokumente*, vol.41, no.1, March 1985.

8. Reports of conferences and symposia published by the Franco-British Council.

8 The Conduct of Bilateral Relationships by Governments
Helen Wallace

Bilateral contacts between each of the three pairs of governments covered in this study have intensified to an astonishing degree in recent years,[1] with each relationship having a dense pattern of consultations amongst ministers and officials over an increasing range of policy issues. This chapter surveys the three discrete bilateral relationships, as they have been promoted and managed by governments, and their consequences in terms of the interests pursued by each government. Nevertheless, to impose a framework of bilateralism on the subject matter is to risk adopting a straitjacket which may distort the evidence and the analysis. 'Reality is not bilateral', as Richard Neustadt aptly commented on the Anglo-American relationship.[2] Policy-makers do not necessarily view their relationships with interlocutors from other governments in this way, and indeed the less so the further away one moves from foreign ministries. Despite this, the relationships covered in this study have, however, been characterised by a high degree of self-consciousness in that continual attention has been paid to the notion of 'good relations' in each bilateral pair even though it is not always achieved or achievable.

Defining bilateralism
Each of the three relationships is multi-layered and multi-faceted. Contacts and linkages span a spectrum from heads of state and government to the working level of junior officials and technical experts. Bilateral relationships between governments can take at least three distinct forms. First, pairs of governments engage in dialogue simply because transactions take place which involve those governments directly or indirectly, actually or potentially. But such relations may do no more than respond to events and keep lines of contact open. Second, and more important, some pairs of governments are *condemned* to consult and to cooperate, because the volume and complexity of transactions between the two countries are such that their governments have to appraise the bilateral relationships explicitly. 'Volume and complexity' may relate to any or all of the following: geographical contiguity; movements of people, goods, capital or services; historical, cultural and ideological affinities or security ties; and membership of the same multilateral organisations. Such interconnections may, how-

ever, produce a patchwork of disaggregated contacts pursued with different rhythms and intensities. Third, there is the concept of a 'special relationship', when two governments put their bilateral dealings on to a privileged basis.

Our concern is to identify into which categories the three bilateral relationships between Britain, France and the FRG fall, and whether the categories have altered. In practice we are excluding the first category of randomised connections and also the notion that good relations can be divorced from interdependencies, interests and national calculations. Three particular factors bring the relationships of our three target countries into especially sharp focus. First, Britain, France and the FRG are rough analogues in terms of broad political and cultural attributes, economic character, resource endowment, size and so on. The bilateral relationships thus rest on assumptions of approximate equivalence and parity, in contrast, for example, to the US— Canada relationship.[3] Indeed, a symmetrical relationship may be more difficult to manage and maintain, since the boundary between partnership and rivalry is easily crossed. Its maintenance requires a mutually acceptable reciprocity in the consequences of interdependence. Second, the identification of a bilateral relationship as 'special' may give it an exclusive character which prevents an equally intense relationship with the other partner in our triangle. Third, bilateral relationships in the London—Paris—Bonn triangle are affected by the relationships of each government with other partners (notably the USA) and by the operations of relevant multilateral fora.

Structures and processes

A key question is whether the formal requirements of the 1963 Elysée Treaty, which committed the French and German governments to systematic dialogue, endowed their relationship with a special quality different in kind from the Franco-British and German-British relationships. The Treaty requires the French and German governments both to communicate regularly and to establish effective management of the relationship in each capital. Interestingly, although Franco-British and German-British relationships lack this quasi-juridical base, in recent years both have been put on to a more structured and systematic footing. This imposes a regular rhythm of meetings both engaging the top levels of political leadership and 'routinising', to different degrees, cooperation at more junior and more technical levels. Structures are accompanied by timetables, explicit commitments, review procedures and a concern to throw into relief the outputs of collaboration — that is, activities which are visible, quantifiable and on the public record.

Tantalisingly more difficult to pin down are questions about the 'atmosphere' or degrees of mutual trust, the extent of informal contacts and understandings, the establishment of policy networks between national administrations, and changing political and bureaucratic habits.

Precise agreements can be identified, but a more gradual transformation of national policies towards those of the partner is often barely discernible. There is often a disjunction between structure and process — in other words formal structures are sometimes empty of content and of supportive attitudes — just as constructive cooperation may take place virtually without formalisation. The problem is to identify systematically attitudes, perceptions and behaviour, since we cannot chart accurately the volume, let alone the quality, of contacts beyond the formal meetings. Direct telephone dialling, ease of transport, conversations in the margins of other (often multilateral) meetings defy calculation. Indeed, embassies in Bonn can no longer keep track of all ministerial visits to the FRG: they are simply too numerous and often too informal. Practitioners in all three capitals agree that the intensive involvement of heads of state and government in the bilateral relationships is crucial. The requirement to brief for summit meetings, with their varied agendas, both penetrates each national administration and demands a coordinating point to pull together a concerted view. But though edicts from presidents, prime ministers and chancellors have a powerful driving force, obstacles may persist elsewhere in the governmental apparatus.

The way in which each relationship is managed in capitals suggests that a qualitative difference emerges between a 'special relationship' and a necessary but less elevated process of cooperation. A vigorous special relationship requires active nurturing by both partners, the strategic assessment of objectives, a long-term timescale for results, and a capacity to define broadly the balance-sheet of the relationship. It probably also requires governments not to be imprisoned by domestic political attitudes. Special relationships are unlikely 'just to grow'. They need a sustained investment and careful evaluation of the costs and benefits of partnership in terms of particular achievements and broader international interests. A less comprehensive approach will yield a more fragile relationship.

The opportunities and limits of partnership

Governments are not monoliths nor able to control events. Domestic problems force points on to the agenda; developments on the international stage demand responses; old problems fade in relevance; and new ones rise up the priority rankings. Agenda setting is thus a critical factor. This is bound to be partly a process of reaction, yet a cultivated special relationship implies a readiness to set part of the agenda by one's own action. The durability of a relationship depends on its ability to adapt to significant changes in the complexion of individual governments, since ideological differences influence fruitful areas for cooperation. There is too the elusive factor of personality and personal rapport, especially in the upper reaches of government. Thus the bilateral relationships demonstrate an interweaving of transient factors with the longer-term pressures to collaborate.

Above all, the life blood of bilateralism seems to lie in the way in which each partner defines its interests and in the extent to which bilateral channels offer a productive vehicle for pursuing them. Bilateralism is not an end in itself. Occasionally the two partners may have identical interests, more frequently they have compatible interests: either to generate a common interest in cooperation or to establish a basis for reciprocity. Sometimes the common interest lies in finding processes of conflict resolution and damage limitation. Geographical proximity may be the motor in particular collaborative projects. Interests may be defined within sectors or in an across-the-board assessment of different policy areas. The balance between the particular and the aggregate is struck differently in each of the three cases: a special relationship presumes a global appraisal of the aggregates. Equally important is the record of achievement; that is to say, to what extent interests are satisfied and how the outputs are to be measured. To the expert concerned with the fine print what looks like a doubtful benefit may appear useful to a senior politician or central coordinator in terms of harmony or valuable in opening a window of opportunity. Sometimes symbolic agreements serve a purpose. Ill-thought-out ventures with an uneven distribution of benefits may raise false expectations, produce unworkable arrangements or generate counterproductive competition.

The Franco-German relationship
This is the most formalised, most intense and most deeply embedded of the three relationships. The mystique of a special relationship between Paris and Bonn, combining the Elysée Treaty and the intimacy of the Schmidt—Giscard period, readily translates into the imputation of a Bonn—Paris axis, especially for the envious or resentful observer. History, geography and the interdependence of politics, economics and security led both governments to conclude that a very close relationship was desirable, as their efforts at cooperation in the 1950s testified. The step change lay in the commitments of both partners to manage their dialogue on a structured and privileged basis. Appraised retrospectively over some 20 years' experience, the Elysée Treaty marked a key stage in that process of dialogue — even a critical threshold.[4] The symbols, structures and disciplines of the Treaty have provided a useful motor to generate cooperation, a shared sense of purpose and developing habits in both governments to keep the relationship productive. In the early 1960s, especially after the departure of Konrad Adenauer, it was by no means all plain sailing. Significantly, contemporary policy-makers in both Paris and Bonn stress the importance of working at the relationship especially in difficult times and on awkward dossiers.

The Treaty could have lapsed into shallow symbolism, if it had not provided a focus for satisfying the interests of the two partners and if external pressures and constraints had not served from time to time to remind policy-makers in both countries that the devil you knew was to be preferred. Yet here there is something of a disjunction of attitudes between Paris and Bonn. Through the 1960s and early 1970s the French government had no other Western government competing with the Germans for primary attention. Attempts to improve the Franco-British relationship did not take root and there was always a distance from the US government. In the late 1970s the French government began to diversify its pattern of bilateral relationships but did not pursue this actively in the 1980s. In Bonn the choices have been more complex. At the level of high politics and ideological orientation the transatlantic relationship has remained crucial; politico-military links with Britain are very important; and the *Ostpolitik* has become a prime focus. The relationship with Paris is part of a larger pattern, although a necessary sheet-anchor.

The Elyseée Treaty framework conveniently encapsulated the commitments of both governments. Some 20 years on and 44 summits later, commitments have become habits for the most senior leaders, junior officials and technical experts in the two administrations. At the biannual bilateral summits, in effect, the French and German cabinets meet in joint session, with as many as 15 departmental ministers from each government joining in discussion. Over a six-month period most ministers and ministries from each side will have been involved in exchange visits. The dialogue consists of formal meetings, detailed joint studies, and substantive cooperation.

Meetings of ministers are prepared by senior officials, as for example Directors General from Finance Ministries, and as one participant put it 'the next deadline is never more than four or five months away'. Discussions rest on the shared assumption that collaboration can be made to work. Recognisable policy networks exist and the reflex to consult informally (including direct telephoning by ministers, even with simultaneous interpretation) is deeply ingrained. The rhythm of meetings has continued irrespective of changes of government and has indeed been supplemented by *ad hoc* meetings at the highest political level to affirm the continuity of partnership.

Some would argue that a key contribution is made by 'Coordinators' designated by each government since July 1967 to take an overview of the relationship.[5] Yet the evidence sheds some doubt on this. Each Coordinator has a small staff, loosely attached to each Foreign Ministry: German Coordinators usually have a political background, while the French have been senior diplomats. In neither case does the Coordinator sit at the real 'centre of decision-making' on substantive policy subjects outside the fields of education, cultural policy, and public opinion formation. They and their staff do look at the bilateral relationship in the round, and sometimes introduce initiatives. They also play the occasional role of firemen on issues which might otherwise escalate into conflagration. But the direct and recurrent attention of the most senior politicians and their staff in the Elysée and Bundes-kanzleramt has proved more crucial.

Both the Ministère des Relations Extérieures and the Auswärtiges Amt have traditionally powerful and prestigious Political Directorates. The Political Directors, as prescribed by the Elysée Treaty, continue to meet each other monthly in addition to their meetings in the margins of other fora. The Quai d'Orsay maintains a geographical department with five staff specifically charged with monitoring relationships with Central Europe, in effect Germany (West and East), while in the Aus-wärtiges Amt responsibility for France is combined with other Western European countries. The two Foreign Ministries generally meet at least once a week and speak on the telephone almost daily. Curiously both in the Quai d'Orsay and in the Bonn embassy there is an identifiable cadre of 'germanistes'. A striking proportion are of Alsatian origin and thus fluent in German; and a second group consists of those, often younger, high flyers for whom academic success consisted in doing well in German — a difficult and prestigious subject. No parallel cultural phenomena are observable within the German administration. The French Embassy in Bonn is the most diverse and most functionally oriented of all French diplomatic posts. Of the 200 staff many are primarily concerned with specifically targeted bilateral collaboration: some 30 deal with armaments, around 6 handle cultural matters, another 6 industrial cooperation, and new sections are created when necessary, as on the high-speed train project. The German embassy in Paris is a more conventional diplomatic post.

Elsewhere in both governments bilateral relationships are subsumed under particular subject heads and in neither capital do the major ministries systematically structure their contacts within a bilateral framework. In a few cases, such as education or trade, the character and volume of bilateral activities have required designated units in the relevant ministries. In yet other cases — agriculture, coal and steel — bilaterally focused units have in effect withered as the multilateral, largely EC, dimension has displaced 'pure bilateral' work. Language does not constitute the barrier one might expect, and productive collaboration often occurs in spite of laborious meetings with slow consecutive interpretation. Yet the rather modest and recent civil service exchanges (both short and long) have been impeded, especially on the French side, by a shortage of officials with good German. At ENA only some 33 per cent of students opt for German as a first language, compared with about 66 per cent taking English.

Rather more important has been the substance of the bilateral agenda which has not entirely coincided with the clauses of the Elysée Treaty.[6] Until recently defence cooperation was pursued on a very limited scale and intensive bilateral consultation on EC issues did not blossom until the mid-1970s, although foreign policy has remained a fairly consistent focus for dialogue. The cultural aspects of the relationship do loom large: educational and cultural cooperation have been core subjects throughout, with special agencies, joint committees and a programme of mutually agreed work, partly because the Elysée Treaty gave them a key role and partly because multilateral fora have not provided an attractive alternative. Interestingly the mismatch between the centralised French system and the devolved federal system of the FRG has been a potential, but not an actual, obstacle to collaboration. French officials and ministers have learned to live with the role of the *Länder* governments and the decentralisation among federal ministries, to the point of interpreting delays on the German side not as shilly-shallying but a constitutional inevitability.

Trade, economic and industrial issues have proved to be subjects of primary attention. The high level of trade interaction has perhaps been the driving force for this. However irrelevant bilateralism may be in terms of conventional economic analysis, policy-makers have believed that it was important to keep a close eye on the consequences of being each other's first trading partner. Nevertheless, there is a difference in perception on the two sides. The combination of a statist approach with a structural trade deficit with the FRG has made French policy-makers feel a sense of watchful vulnerability, even of obsession. The more generally export-oriented German economy, combined with much less explicit intervention by government, has led German policy-makers to see the trade relationship more as a consequence of market forces and comparative advantage.

During the period of sustained growth policy-makers in France could accept that there was reciprocity in the exchange of French consumer goods for German manufactures, although in the 1950s both French industrialists and policy-makers feared this German industrial competition.[7] These fears have resurfaced since the recession. In 1982 a real head of steam built up in the French administration, led by Michel Jobert, then Minister for External Trade, against the deleterious effects of German industrial standards on French exports to the FRG.[8] Across French ministries could be heard a chorus of criticisms and specific examples of effective non-tariff barriers, which could have erupted into a significant bilateral confrontation. Yet ways of smoothing over the problem were quickly found through a combination of bilateral discussion and intensified EC cooperation. The introduction by the French in 1982 of a customs requirement for import documents in French seems to have been less rigorously applied to German imports than to those of some other countries, which strikingly illustrates the predisposition of policy-makers on both sides not to let conflict escalate, fostered by the existence of trusted channels for managing the necessary dialogue.

This compulsion to find agreement derives from the effects of bilateral trade on broader economic interdependence. Policy-makers in both countries are well aware of the extent to which their policy options for macroeconomic and monetary management are circumscribed by each other, whatever their differences of doctrine.

In the 1970s there was considerable French envy of German economic performance and 'das Modell Deutschland' fuelled the determination of President Giscard d'Estaing and Prime Minister Raymond Barre to emulate their German partner.[9] These efforts had much to do with the drive towards the establishment of the European Monetary System, but were complemented by the bilateral dialogue. It is worth noting that the French reflex when assessing their economic performance is to compare French figures with American and German but not with British.

However, since the change of government in France in 1981, this dialogue has become rather more stylised, not surprisingly given the contrasts in economic doctrine and policies. Yet the modifications of French economic policy in 1982 and 1983 reflect an adjustment much encouraged by German pressures, in this instance strengthening the arguments of the more moderate members of the French government. German policy-makers have been prepared to make concessions to the interests and priorities of their French partners, notably on monetary issues, although with limited tolerance in the 1980s. Habits of co-operation provide a valuable insurance policy against open conflict, but convergence in the 1970s required compatible policy priorities as well as channels of dialogue.

As a counterweight to macroeconomic discussions, industrial co-operation between the two governments has been extensive. At one level, and especially on the French side, there has been an effort deliberately to seek out productive sectors and projects for detailed collaboration. Every policy-maker in Paris concerned with the Franco-German relationship can and does recite from an aggregated list of joint projects spanning nuclear energy, aerospace, space, transport and so on. Much of it reflects a French preoccupation with pursuing industrial goals in key sectors in which French resources alone have been insufficient and where a German partnership could make cherished aims viable. Projects are chiefly those in which governments have little option but to be involved, thus facilitating cooperation with German governments which have preferred to be less explicitly engaged in other industrial sectors. It is interesting just how far French industrial policy-makers have gone along with the concept of the FRG as a partner of first resort, even though in specific cases other partners — the British for Concorde, and sometimes Japanese or American links — have been preferred.

There are elements of mythology about the record; several projects involve other partners, as in the case of the airbus; there have been spectacular failures, such as the never-achieved Franco-German battletank; and, on occasion, the French themselves have pulled the rug out, as in the case of Unidata. Clearly success or failure depends substantially on the inherent soundness of the particular projects and on the extent to which different national interests and industrial enterprises can be satisfactorily combined. Some cases are essentially functional, such as the exchanges of electricity supplies between France and the FRG because their peak hours differ significantly. Geography makes high-speed trains a logical sector for cooperation. Cooperation in the field of nuclear energy has served both French and German interests relatively conveniently, especially given the various inhibitions on an independent German capability and the high profile which the French have accorded to it. The Elysée Treaty framework has helped policy-makers in both countries at ministerial and official level to look for suitable projects with initiative and with a fairly deep-rooted predisposition to evaluate the technical evidence positively. Space (Ariane), cable television and microelectronics were explored at summit meetings with commitments to follow up by technical ministers and their officials. Projects are a visible and solid demonstration of the commitment to privileged partnership. However, the mood has changed in recent years, especially on the German side. The relatively lush period of economic growth and high investment facilitated many of the projects on the list, but few new projects are now being added. Thinking inside the German Economics Ministry is becoming much more circumspect, although the Research Ministry remains more supportive. There is less willingness to accept the French tendency to use partnership to build a base for a project which will be marketed abroad as a predominantly French project (such as the airbus) or to give French companies an in-built advantage. Although the Franco-German summit of May 1984 focused on potential new projects, heavily biased towards defence, the follow-through has proved disappointing.

In the background is the broader issue of how far French and German policy-makers understand and empathise with each other's industrial policy. There remains a surprising degree of misperception and ignorance on both sides. In the Elysée Treaty framework, summits have generated imperatives to senior officials from each government to carry out joint studies with recommendations for ministerial decision. At senior levels free and frank discussion is now promoted, but it has not thoroughly penetrated either administration. Here there are elements of an adversarial relationship at the bilateral level with implications for the EC arena.

The bilateral relationship also has a less glamorous side. A long common border inevitably generates much, often mundane, business between the two governments and between adjacent local and regional authorities, as in the Alsace/Baden-Württemburg and Saar/Lorraine areas. The traces of occupation have left a legacy of practical issues to be resolved, and both sides have made real efforts to address practical cross-border questions. Such issues rarely surface in the Elysée Treaty consultations at the most senior level, although the readiness of heads of state and government to intervene should not be underestimated. To

take a recent example, President Mitterrand and Chancellor Kohl agreed
in May 1984 to reduce police and customs checks on the Franco-
German border, despite the fears of responsible officials in both
countries that dishonest rather than honest citizens would be the main
beneficiaries of this particular symbol of Franco-German amity.[10]

The Franco-German relationship at the level of intergovernmental
contacts has thus become a carefully cultivated and deeply embedded
process of *engrenage*. Structures, networks and joint activities have
combined to maintain a mutually relevant agenda and an acceptable
reciprocity of benefits. Not only is the relationship 'special' in the
sense of being deliberately given priority, but there is an acquired
willingness on both sides to treat the bilateral dialogue as a positive-sum
game. Although some issues and policy areas have not produced significant output and others have generated friction, channels have generally
— at least so far — been found to resolve conflicts or put them on ice.
Ministers and officials accept an imperative to maintain the quality of
the relationship in most fields of policy. These habits and attitudes
took root in the 1970s and they have survived the major changes of
government and personalities (both ministers and officials) remarkably
well in recent years. The Elysée Treaty was a crucial political investment, the pay-offs of which have matured over a 20-year period. Also
central to the relationship has been the conviction that both countries
are core members of the broader venture in EC cooperation. But the
bilateral enterprise still depends critically on the accumulation of pay-
offs for relevant interests on each side.

Tantalisingly elusive is the question whether the Franco-German
relationship is evenly balanced. Often, the French government has
appeared to have a higher profile, a more self-conscious role of motor,
a more conceptual orientation and a more calculating approach to ex-
tracting benefits. Successive German governments have been consistent
in their attachment to the relationship, but have become more adept at
genuflecting to French concepts while arguing hard the details of each
dossier. If necessary they have acted independently, as for example
when they unilaterally floated the Deutsche Mark in 1969. They have
used the bilateral relationship 'to save the French from protectionism'.
Both governments have from different standpoints endeavoured to
ensure that unavoidable interdependence could be fashioned into a
positive-sum game.

The Anglo-German relationship

On the surface the relationship between London and Bonn has been
calm, straightforward and mutually useful.[11] It lacks drama; perhaps a
sign of success, for rarely do direct bilateral frictions impinge; discourse
is open and satisfactory. Contemporary policy-makers in both governments argue that they manage quite adequately without the formalism
of a treaty framework. Some German participants comment almost

with relief that they prefer the flexibility and open-endedness which marks their relationship with Britain. In any case, so the conventional wisdom goes, the British, unlike the French, instinctively prefer co-operation to follow functional needs rather than stylised commitments. Yet this conventional wisdom needs close scrutiny. The British and German governments are enmeshed in a web of multilateral treaties, notably on defence and economic subjects, which commit them to collaborate bilaterally as well as multilaterally, the British commitments to Berlin and the British Army on the Rhine being crucial elements. In practice the British and German governments hold formal summit meetings with a rhythm, a predictability and a subject-range now at least broadly comparable to those of the Elysée Treaty. Yet there is a sense in both capitals that the relationship does not quite deliver the goods which have been ordered, notably in the EC context. On the German side there has been continuing disappointment at the perceived reluctance of successive British governments over the years to climb on board the Community ship as a wholehearted partner. British policy-makers have been first puzzled at, and more recently resigned to, the German government sometimes not endorsing in Brussels what they thought was an agreed and mutually beneficial line. These question marks about the other partner's 'reliability' in the EC have permeated the bilateral relationship, even though in other arenas, notably defence and security, British and German interests are largely convergent. It is a partnership characterised by variable-sum outcomes.

The traces of British involvement in the establishment of the FRG have of course engaged both governments in a continuous bilateral relationship. Throughout the post-war period, contacts between London and Bonn on broad political issues — defence, security and the crucial Atlantic dimension — have been intense and have rested on a cluster of shared or complementary interests. But until the mid-1970s the linkages consisted of meetings in the context of other multilateral (especially NATO) fora and *ad hoc* consultations. The other main issue on the bilateral agenda was when, whether and how Britain might accede to the EC. The relationship lacked the broader scope of the Franco-German partnership and the symbolism of a privileged dialogue. To some extent this was remedied by the existence of informal contacts among policy-makers in meetings such as the annual Königswinter conferences. But such discussions, even though they maintain open and important channels of communication, by no means necessarily translate into direct governmental action. Direct policy interdependence, most visible in the presence of the British Army on the Rhine, created significant bilateral interchanges, but these were largely self-contained and have occasionally caused friction, as in discussions of offset arrangements. On the economic, trade and industrial fronts, inter-governmental discussions were not strikingly intensive.

Once Britain had acceded to the EC in 1973 the pattern changed. From 1975 onwards an annual bilateral summit, initially modestly conceived, was gradually extended into a rhythm of biannual meetings of heads of government and departmental ministers with business to transact. Shared Community membership rather than any distinct bilateral motivation was the motor. Thus pragmatic bilateralism began to be practised on largely functional criteria, but within a political conception on both sides that the quality and intensity of the relationship could usefully be reinforced. But unlike the Franco-German dialogue, German-British consultations were, and have remained, more reactive than initiatory in character. Many of those involved on both sides proclaim the merits of this approach, since it does not saddle them with unrealistic commitments and allows collaboration to follow, rather than to dictate, functional requirements.

In other respects, both formal and substantive, contemporary Anglo-German summits closely resemble the Franco-German dialogue. It is now commonplace for a large team of ministers from each government to be associated with the meetings of the British Prime Minister and the German Chancellor. The agendas now range over a similar variety of issues, but with less work on cultural and educational topics. The limited financial resources available, even on the German side, have prevented ambitious and long-term exchange programmes. Keen attention is given to the preparation of summit meetings by the British Cabinet Office and Foreign and Commonwealth Office and by the German Bundeskanzleramt and Auswärtiges Amt. The embassies in both capitals operate at both the technical and political levels as valuable channels of advice and dialogue. Yet there are differences from the Franco-German model. There is no direct parallel to the role of the Coordinators, and preparations for Anglo-German summits and other bilateral meetings depend on the established processes and procedures for handling intergovernmental relations. No special units exist in either Foreign Office, but instead geographical units concerned with several other West European countries handle the detailed work, acting in close liaison with the British Cabinet Office and the German Bundeskanzleramt. Each government clearly treats the other as a primary not a secondary partner, but not on an especially privileged basis. While occasional *ad hoc* meetings of heads of government take place in addition to the biannual summits, they are both less frequent than in the Franco-German case and no overtly symbolic meeting takes place when a new head of government is elected as a pledge of continuing bilateralism. A recent development, prompted by the Germans, has been the appointment late in 1984 of retired diplomats as 'coordinators' charged with making a review of the relationship and reporting on possible improvements.

Thus the infrastructure for a close partnership is in place but both sides lack a developed conception that the partnership is 'special'. Each government sees recurrent dialogue as necessary, although there are signs of German incomprehension at the British preference for separating politico-military issues from economic collaboration, notably in the EC context. On specific and substantive issues the record of the bilateral relationship is patchy. Although the FRG has become more important to Britain as a trading partner, there is little evidence of any German inclination to accord Britain special treatment on economic issues. For a long time the Germans saw the British economy as both damaged by secular decline and wrong-headed, but to some extent, the robust economic policies of the British Conservative government since 1979 have begun to counteract this, even to the extent of stimulating some German interest in emulating British policies of privatisation and deregulation. On the other hand, while there has been much British admiration for German economic performance, there has been no direct British parallel to the French interest in 'das Modell Deutschland'.

Anglo-German consultations take place between the ministries responsible for monetary and macroeconomic issues, which are 'frank' and 'useful' but are more an exchange of views than productive of agreements to align policies or to launch initiatives. There is no clear and built-in reciprocity to the trading relationship. Privileged German access to British oil resources was discussed in the 1970s and early 1980s, but was not accepted by British governments as a sector for special arrangements. Considerable quantities of North Sea oil and gas are actually sold to German customers but on a commercial basis, and without the symbolism and rhetoric on which comparable French sales would undoubtedly have rested. Some government-led industrial collaboration takes place between British and German companies, notably in the defence field, but none is purely bilateral or with quite the symbolic bilateral lead — even on Tornado — which is evident in the Franco-German cases.

A broader dialogue with some governmental involvement and funding takes place through the Anglo-German Foundation for the Study of Industrial Society. But by and large cooperation follows the emergence of substantive requirements rather than from either of the two governments deliberately identifying shopping lists of items for collaboration. This shared preference for letting government follow, rather than lead, economic criteria is quite logical in terms of the two governments' economic doctrines, especially in recent years. Thus, although no monuments to dashed expectations figure on the bilateral agenda, as in the Franco-German and Franco-British cases, nor can either government make capital from any demonstrable industrial achievements of bilateral enterprise. Nor is there the underlying thread of exchanged benefits and costs across a range of sectors which provides a firm weft to the Franco-German relationship. The exception lies in the defence field with its range of bilateral exchanges on detailed cooperation, rendered vital by the existence of the British Army on the Rhine and the Berlin commitment.

This variegated pattern of consultations and contacts has produced contradictory consequences. Outside the EC context, the bilateral dialogue is sustained but intermittent. Within the politico-military arena there are first a set of networks which instill into both sides a reflex to consult, second, a willingness to be open and, third, important interests to be satisfied. Here we can discern tangible elements of a policy community which involves the main policy actors recurrently through a mixture of formal and informal channels. For the rest, the bilateral relationship is only marginally more intensive than would otherwise be the case given geography and history and given the level of economic transactions and the network of contacts among political élites in the two countries. Policy-makers on both sides insist that dialogue is easy and open in a way that neither achieves so readily with their French counterparts. Yet dialogue does not of itself generate outputs. The added intensity of the relationship over the last 10 years or so is primarily a consequence of British membership of the EC, but this latter has been so beset by problems that it has not yet served to create a step change in the intensity or the outputs of cooperation. If we compare the current character of the Anglo-German relationship with the Franco-German relationship of the 1960s it has neither the high points of symbolism nor the low points of outright friction.[12] But by the same token the relatively smooth and good-natured relations which obtain do not of themselves connote a partnership capable of yielding the maximum in mutual benefits.

The Franco-British relationship

The ambivalent record of relations between Paris and London bears little resemblance to either of the other two bilateral dialogues.[13] The overwhelming image is of periods of competitive friction interspersed with vigorous efforts on both sides of the Channel to upgrade the relationship. The story is one of paradoxes: bouts of mutual incomprehension and bilateral squabbles have too often set the tone of the relationship for both policy-makers and broader opinion, while the almost cyclical bursts of re-invigorated cooperation have not yet proved sufficiently durable to withstand countervailing pressures. In broad terms the two governments start from strikingly similar endowments. Both have a legacy of inherited global commitments and aspirations, with each maintaining a privileged place in international diplomacy. Both governments, under successive parties, have hung on to a nuclear defence capability. Each retains a post-colonial network of commitments to, and interests in, the rest of the world as a focus both for national action and for its preferred multilateral policies. Both have been under pressure to adapt to the position of a middle-ranking power. Policy-makers can thus engage in dialogue on this range of subjects on a basis of approximate parity and with a comparable agenda of interests to be taken into account. But there comparability runs out, since each government has retained a separate set of interests and an acquired view about the appropriate way to blend national interests and international cooperation. Indeed, it has often seemed that there was less a bilateral dialogue than a competition to see whether French or British definitions and interests would prevail.

These differences of approach have permeated the attitudes of policy-makers on the other issues where interdependencies exist and frontier management is essential. Politicians' statements, media coverage and evidence from interviews with officials in both countries testify to the extent to which both French and British policy-makers interpret their discourse with each other against a backcloth of competing interests and initial suspicion, and often without penetrating the fine print of the other government's detailed concerns. Of course these caricature images do not hold in all cases; there are many examples of productive cooperation and mutual respect. But, in both the bilateral relationship and in the EC context, a key difficulty has been the accumulation of enough items on the credit side of the balance-sheet to keep the bilateral account in the black. There lingers a sense in both capitals that explicit Anglo-French bilateralism is an option to be weighed and re-evaluated but not to be taken as given.

Policy-makers have occasionally worried about the consequences of a strained bilateral relationship. Over the last 20 years or so events and attitudes have conspired, roughly once a decade, to induce a change of gear. In the late 1950s and early 1960s a flurry of activity and meetings between Harold Macmillan, the then British Prime Minister, and President de Gaulle opened up the first close dialogue since the British had distanced themselves from the EC experiment. One element was the considerable effort invested in establishing bilateral industrial collaboration. The Concorde project was the most dramatic example — a case of pure bilateralism — with its careful division of anticipated benefits between French and British participants. The broader dialogue was brought to an abrupt halt when, soon after the US/UK Polaris agreement, President de Gaulle vetoed British accession to the EC in January 1963 just as the Elysée Treaty between France and the FRG was being concluded. Concorde would not have survived the 1964 Labour Government if there had been a break clause in the contract. From these episodes and the surrounding commentary, several lessons can be distilled. First, the Franco-British bilateral venture rested on flimsy underpinnings, and could not prosper against the disinclination of senior political figures on both sides to sacrifice other, and apparently exclusive, bilateral openings. Second, misunderstandings of the other partner's motivations and aspirations abounded. Third, the Concorde deal illustrated on both sides an approach to bargaining in which the reciprocating of advantages took second place to fears of being out-negotiated. The subsequent, and now well documented, Soames Affair of 1969 demonstrated *inter alia* just how much ground needed to be made up by the two governments in terms of communication and definitions of interest before a creative and rewarding dialogue could be established.[14]

But de Gaulle's initiative of 1969, before being recast as the Soames Affair, signalled a sea-change in French thinking towards acceptance of Britain as an important partner. In the early 1970s a much more sustained effort was made to promote a new era of bilateralism. Stimulated by the remarkably close convergence of minds between Edward Heath, as British Prime Minister, and President Pompidou, both governments began to define the relationship in terms which were quantitatively and qualitatively altogether more ambitious and far-reaching. Cooperation was promised on wide-ranging and finely detailed policies. Here, in retrospect, was a real window of opportunity. At their summit meeting of 1971, Heath and Pompidou unblocked the key obstacles to British accession to the EC. At their subsequent meeting in 1972 they laid out an agenda for bilateral cooperation containing the seed corn from which might have burgeoned a privileged relationship comparable to the Franco-German partnership. Multiple bilateral ventures were set in train: reciprocal exchanges of civil servants; funding for cultural cooperation; an Anglo-French Industrial Committee; the elements of government-induced pump-priming to breed an atmosphere over the longer term in which intergovernmental cooperation could be cumulatively pursued.

A wide range of policy sectors was brought within the ambit of cooperation under close scrutiny at the most senior level of government. Rapport was established at the top. The process of jointly identifying the scope for resolving difficult issues in the EC negotiations began to edge the two governments towards an acceptance both of shared interests and of the need for trading off the costs and benefits of closer association. The prior images on the French side of the British as 'not fit for Community membership' and on the British side of the French as determinedly resistant to British accession began to be displaced by an acceptance not just of necessary co-existence but crucially of other common interests. Unlike the earlier period of flirtation between Harold Macmillan and General de Gaulle, this time the new mood of bilateral understanding began to percolate government thinking on both sides, in spite of the difficulties of shaking off old attitudes and assumptions.

This new-found amity was to prove shortlived. Before French and British policy-makers had the chance to establish habits of cooperation, events intervened — the oil crisis, Pompidou's deteriorating health and the vicissitudes of electoral politics in Britain. The arrival in office of Valéry Giscard d'Estaing, whose reference points — especially economic — were German not British, proved a complication. The new and precarious British Labour government, committed to renegotiation of the terms of EC entry, saw no special virtue in a privileged dialogue with Paris. The recently-established formal structure of Franco-British cooperation was too fragile to constitute a countervailing pressure against either the residual suspicions of France within the British policy élite or the fissiparous inclinations of Labour ministers. Although the British

Foreign Office continued to argue for maintaining the relationship with Paris, it spoke to some extent 'with forked tongue' and was suspected by some of 'kowtowing to French interests'. Equally, in Paris, the Foreign Ministry had never warmed to President Pompidou's reversal of orthodox Gaullist thinking.

This episode illustrates vividly the dependence of sustained partnership on a mixture of political stimulus and ingrained habits. Remove either or both and the partnership vanishes, at least in the absence of clear interdependence of interest. Franco-British trade was too sparse to provide a significant counterweight, each partner's policy interests in fields such as money and agriculture pointed in directions that were apparently mutually exclusive. Joint industrial projects had proved divisive in so many respects that they could be easily disparaged, with Concorde again under critical scrutiny and proposals for ventures such as the Channel Tunnel overwhelmed by financial and technical obstacles. Instead of burgeoning, the tender plant withered. During the succeeding period old images became an easy alibi for policy-makers, as well as public opinion, to use to explain away the difficulties of building bridges between the two governments, in spite of the increased links necessarily established through joint participation in EC and other fora. The partial participation of the French in NATO and the particularly close Anglo-American links in defence compounded this phenomenon. Islands of cooperation did emerge but did not spill over into those policy sectors where conceptual and substantive issues divided the two governments.

Over the last five years the British and French governments have made considerable efforts to create an improved bilateral climate, nudged by changes of government in each case and prompted by the need to achieve a more productive relationship for both bilateral and multilateral reasons.[15] In part, the British feared that the Franco-German relationship was running away from them, and that it was becoming an exclusive and collusive partnership. Bilateral summits, more frequent meetings of ministerial opposite numbers and more regular contacts amongst officials developed from the mid-1970s and were treated with increasing seriousness. Early evidence demonstrated the limitations of relying on formal requirements to consult as the catalysts of cumulative agreement. In functionally discrete areas where there was a juxtaposition of enthusiasm and business of clear mutual interest — such as the cultural and research fields or the cross-Channel electricity link — networks of French and British counterparts were beginning to deliver results bilaterally. But in policy areas where definitions of concepts and issues of substance impeded dialogue, reluctant officials on either side were still not under a firm compulsion to make the relationship deliver. Several practical issues interposed themselves as sources of bilateral friction: in the EC context, sheepmeat, turkeys and UHT milk; and at the frontiers, problems such as the rights of entry to France for British citizens born abroad. Significantly the Franco-British relationship had not acquired the reflexes to enable those genuine conflicts of interest to be resolved smoothly without muddying the waters of the broader bilateral dialogue. Both governments were also seriously constrained by the press and parliamentary opinion. While the embassies in both capitals sought to mitigate these problems and to underpin efforts to improve the relationship, neither achieved the consistent rapport with the host government which has characterised the Franco-German and the Anglo-German relationships.

During 1981–82 much discussion took place in each capital and bilaterally about ways in which qualitative and quantitative improvements could be achieved in the relationship. The question was even aired of whether a treaty commitment, analogous to the Elysée Treaty, might usefully and symbolically contribute. In the event a different formula emerged which sought to combine what was seen as the kernel of Franco-German experience with a more flexible and less stylised approach. In the autumn of 1982 Mrs Thatcher and President Mitterrand agreed to intensify the dialogue and to take steps to ensure that their commitments of principle were translated through their administrations into practical and tangible collaboration. To this end they designated a handful of senior officials to manage the dialogue and to report back to them regularly on progress. In effect, the two governments were designating senior diplomats to add to their existing responsibilities the task of taking an overview of the relationship, identifying areas of cooperation and spotting tension points which should not be allowed to expand. This modified version of the role of the Franco-German 'Coordinators' was to ensure that the relationship was looked at in the aggregate in a way not previously attempted.

In London this was supplemented by structured efforts to improve interdepartmental coordination and monitoring of the Franco-British relationship through the Cabinet Office. In Paris, officials at the Elysée and the Quai d'Orsay began to focus more systematically on the evolving dialogue, helped by the resolve of the socialist government to diversify its pattern of West European consultations to which ministers at the Quai d'Orsay attached considerable importance. In parallel a cognate set of arrangements was established for handling critical issues on the EC agenda. In both capitals the message went out to other ministers and officials that they must work harder at making the relationship productive, by demonstrating progress where possible and by producing reasoned opinions for failures to agree.

One sign of this upgrading of the relationship has been the greater attention paid to practical areas of cooperation. In the industrial and technological field, projects have been examined with renewed interest and a greater willingness to find agreement. Lists are now appended to Franco-British summit communiqués reminiscent of the Franco-German dialogue. Despite a long history of aborted discussions, the Channel Fixed Link has re-emerged as a potential area of collaboration after being tabled by President Mitterrand as a priority topic. By late 1984 there was a feeling of satisfaction in both capitals that the investments were beginning to pay high dividends. Officials and ministers were happily surprised at the range of issues on which they could agree with their opposite numbers and reasonably confident that they had established an early warning system for potential conflicts and the means to assuage them.

It is too soon to judge the effects of this significant upgrading of the relationship. Much depends on the willingness of policy-makers to stick to their bilateral commitments even when the going gets hard. All the evidence of the Franco-German relationship suggests the existence of time-lags between commitments and outputs. The EC context is critical and it may well be the case that the resolution of the budgetary issues at Fontainebleau in June 1984 will allow the opportunity for the bilateral investment to accumulate dividends. Old habits in each capital of appraising the relationship in zero-sum terms will not die easily. Perhaps crucial to a shift from zero-sum to positive- or variable-sum outcomes is the question of whether the bridgeheads of functional collaboration and political agreement which exist in some fields can set the predominant tone of the relationship.

Conclusions
Of the three relationships the Franco-German remains the most intimate, the most 'special', but it has become much less exclusive than in the Giscard—Schmidt era. Neither the French nor the German government takes the view that operating à deux will achieve enough of their objectives. In both Paris and Bonn there is now an instinctive recognition of the need to tie the British government in more closely. The British government itself has edged towards a more intensive dialogue with both the German and French governments — steadily with the German, rather more adventurously with the French. If current trends continue we shall see a significantly different triangle of 'special relationships' emerge, but only if all three governments are willing and able to make the capital investments necessary both to maintain the infrastructure and to identify successful joint ventures. Managing a three-partner consortium is much more testing than maintaining a two-party contract. The ingrained reflexes of both the French and German governments to rely on their established relationship will not easily give way to a more finely-balanced triangle. Much will depend on how sensitively and vigorously the British cultivate their dialogues with Bonn and Paris.

Notes
1. Much of the data on recent developments was gathered from unattributable interviews with officials in the three capitals.
2. Richard E. Neustadt, *Alliance Politics* (New York, Columbia University Press, 1970), p. 5.

3. Robert O. Keohane and Joseph S. Nye, *Power and Interdependence: World Politics in Transition* (Boston, Little, Brown, 1977).

4. See 'Les relations franco-allemandes depuis 1963', *Documents*, November 1978 and the series of studies published by the Franco-German Institute at Ludwigsburg.

5. Horst Holthoff, 'Der Koordinator für die Deutsche-Französische Zusammenarbeit' in *Konkretionen politische Theorie und Praxis* (Stuttgart, 1972), pp. 424–31.

6. See the text of the Treaty, reprinted in the Appendix.

7. F. Roy Willis, *France, Germany and the New Europe, 1945–1967*, revised ed. (London, Oxford University Press, 1968), Chapters 4 and 9.

8. See the French press *passim* in October and November 1982, during the period in which the French government introduced several measures to curb imports, not only from Japan (videos via the Poitiers customs post) but also arguably from EEC partners, including the FRG.

9. Bernard Keizer, *Le modèle économique allemand: mythes et réalités* (Paris, La Documentation Française, 1979).

10. This initiative, announced in the summit communiqué, subsequently drew in the Benelux governments.

11. Karl Kaiser and Roger Morgan (eds), *Britain and West Germany: Changing Societies and the Future of Foreign Policy* (London, Oxford University Press for the RIIA, 1971) and Angelika Volle, *Deutsche-Britische Beziehungen – eine Untersuchung des bilateralen Verhältnis auf der staatlichen und nichtstaatlichen Ebene seit dem Zweiten Weltkrieg*, doctoral thesis (Bonn, Rheinische Friedrich Wilhelms-Universität, 1976).

12. William Wallace, *Britain's Bilateral Links Within Western Europe* (London, Routledge & Kegan Paul for the RIIA, 1984).

13. W. Wallace, op.cit.; and Neville Waites (ed.), *Troubled Neighbours: Franco-British Relations in the Twentieth Century* (London, Weidenfeld and Nicolson, 1971).

14. See Alan Campbell, 'Anglo-French Relations a Decade ago: a New Assessment', Part 1, *International Affairs*, vol.58, no.2, Spring 1982, pp. 237–53, and Part 2, vol.58, no.3, Summer 1982, pp. 429–46, and see also Chapter 9 below.

15. See summit communiqués and speeches and the speeches at the time of President Mitterrand's much heralded state visit to Britain in October 1984.

9 Bilateral, Trilateral and Multilateral Negotiations in the European Community
Helen Wallace

To the Community purist the notion that bilateral, let alone trilateral, relationships are an intrinsic feature of the system smacks of heresy. The mere suggestion of a relevant trilateral or triangular relationship between France, the FRG and Britain immediately brings in its train the rebuttal that a *directoire* would imply the end of the Community as we have so far known it. Yet bilateral alliances have always been important. After all, from the outset, the EC was in some senses a Franco-German creation, designed to cement Franco-German reconciliation by 'multilateralising' their historical differences, and built on a Franco-German contract about particular policy benefits. In the larger Community of the mid-1980s an organised pattern of coalition-building is probably unavoidable. This chapter explores the development of the relationships among the three governments in discussions within the EC Treaties and the potential relevance of the London—Paris—Bonn triangle for the EC at its current stage of development.

It is not easy to identify quite how bilateral and trilateral relationships and coalitions fit into the overall picture of the EC. First, there are many examples of bilateral alliances (not just alliances involving our three target countries) on individual issues critically affecting EC outcomes — a typical feature of all multilateral negotiations. Second, all the participants engaging in 'cooperative' negotiations have an interest in ensuring that their individual bilateral relationships should not be a source of friction in the broader EC forum. Nevertheless, the negotiating process changes if a particular bilateral coalition becomes a durable and predictable feature, especially if the two partners involved are in a position to exercise a predominant influence. Whether such a development is functional or dysfunctional will depend on the extent to which the predominant coalition produces results which give adequate political satisfaction in terms of the other partners' substantive interests.

In the Community of Six the core Franco-German relationship was set into a mosaic of policy concerns which satisfied the interests of the other four member states, either because their specific objectives lay close enough to those of the French and Germans or because the currency of negotiation was in sufficient supply to accommodate side-payments to other participants. When the Franco-German relationship was strained, as during the period following the Community crisis of 1965—66, all EC governments had an interest in reducing the friction.[1] French veto power was a threat to progress and the de-coupling of the FRG from the EC would have amounted to a failure of the system to achieve a key EC objective. Yet some, including many Germans, feared that the Franco-German Treaty, if taken too far, might undermine the original conception of the Community.

The Franco-German relationship in that period, however, did not in practice consist of a predictable alliance on every issue. The EC agenda was predetermined by the content of the Treaties which main-tained a balance among the member states. There was an equilibrium in Franco-German relations that was more subtle than the crude exchange of French agricultural interests for German industrial interests al-though, as most myths, it does contain a kernel of truth with regard to the initial negotiations within the Spaak Committee. However, the detailed negotiations on the Common Agricultural Policy in the 1960s, in which a high cereal price was set to help German farmers, in some ways distorted the alleged reciprocity. Reciprocity could none the less be found in the origins of the European Coal and Steel Community and the subsequent development of intra-Community trade in coal. In the 1980s, the French retain a commitment to import relatively expensive coal from the Saarland, because it is a lingering heritage of the way in which the Saarland was reabsorbed into the FRG under the shelter of the ECSC umbrella. In the EEC of Six any strong disagreement on an issue between the French and German governments could effectively prevent any broader EEC consensus, and the stalled discussions of the Werner Plan bore eloquent testimony to this proposition.[2] By and large good relations between Bonn and Paris were a precondition for the effective functioning of the Community.

British accession to the Community
As the enlargement of the EC approached, the correlation of forces seemed to be altering. Even though some precise Treaty commitments eluded progress, the EC agenda was rapidly expanding into other sectors, a development which would require a new set of trade-offs amongst member governments no longer necessarily tied to a Franco-German core contract. The German economy was very robust and German political interests were diversifying, especially as greater confi-dence took Germany into the *Ostpolitik*. Enlargement would bring into the EC another substantial member, Britain, with its considerable political endowment and economic resources. One kind of Community had been closed off by de Gaulle in 1965 and another was prevented by vetoes of British accession. For the other four founder members, British accession was anticipated as a valuable counterweight to undue French influence. Germany welcomed the entry of a new partner with many similar interests, although in the 1960s German politicians had

not risked straining relations with the French too far by supporting the British. French thinking shifted from the high Gaullist reluctance to contemplate British accession, which might disturb a Community anchored on the Franco-German relationship, to an acceptance, at the end of the 1960s, of partnership with Britain as a counterbalance to a Germany which might drift out of the French orbit. In 1969 President de Gaulle had already indicated to Sir Christopher Soames that Britain must now become an integral and influential member of the Community family,[3] but the British government shied away from the hint of a *directoire*, and the German reaction, other than irritation at the manner of the story breaking, was not fully probed. When enlargement occurred in 1973, there was, however, much talk of the British as potential bridgebuilders and as a countervailing influence to the French.

In retrospect, there was probably a window of opportunity to forge a new triangular relationship. The Franco-British relationship had improved immeasurably under the active leadership of President Pompidou (taking de Gaulle's initiative forward) and Prime Minister Heath. The more relaxed German-British relationship and the continuing Franco-German dialogue could have been harnessed to this new-found Franco-British amity. However, at that stage none of the three governments explored the scope for a triangular relationship, each concentrating rather on the individual sides of the triangle. Events then began to impose their own momentum. The combination of recession and enlargement presented obstacles to the effective expansion of the EC policy agenda. Instead, the locking of the Community into defence of the *acquis communautaire* further consolidated the old Franco-German core contract. From 1974 the British government tabled demands too large to be dealt with by side-payments, seeking both changes to the *acquis* and different policies. During renegotiation the British government was engaged in confrontation with the rest of the Community *en bloc* rather than inserting itself into the complex coalition pattern of Community negotiations.

The improved Franco-British relationship was rapidly undermined by three developments. First, British criticisms of the terms of accession often implied an antipathy to those features of the EC thought to be French-inspired. This suggested that only a zero-sum game could be played in which improvements for Britain would necessarily connote a diminution of French benefits. Second, there were competitive elements in the attitudes of French and British policy-makers towards each other. Third, President Giscard d'Estaing had little affinity for Britain and saw no attraction in extending President Pompidou's efforts to improve the bilateral relationship. There was a dismal sense of stereotyping in both directions at the level both of broad élite attitudes and of interpretations of substance. This had the deleterious effect of obscuring not only legitimate differences of policy interest but also areas of potential agreement.

Such appraisals, however, disguise some of the developments beneath the surface. For example, a ginger group in the French Ministry of Agriculture looked to British accession to nudge the EC towards a CAP based on sounder economic logic and away from the excessively high prices on which German negotiators had insisted. While this did not represent a majority French view, it was a seedling which could have been nurtured. But the perception in London of the French as Britain's chief adversaries on the CAP made it hard, if not impossible, for British policy-makers to read the signals they received on what lay behind formal expressions of French agricultural policy.

The example is indicative of the extent to which conventional assumptions needed to shift and political commitment to be sustained before a useful bilateral dialogue could develop on key EC issues. Yet on some important EC policies, notably within the GATT (General Agreement on Tariffs and Trade) agenda and on institutional issues, British and French interests were quite close and indeed were pursued cooperatively. On trade policy, however, a sterile debate continued about the extent to which the British were committed to trade within the Community, even though the statistics of the 1970s demonstrated that British trade was shifting remarkably rapidly to levels of Community preference broadly comparable to those of France. Issues of often rather confused principle repeatedly got in the way, with French policy-makers tending to interpret British moves as subversive of key Community doctrines, and British policy-makers tending to conclude that French support for the key tenets of the Community faith was a simple alibi for what substantively suited French domestic interests. Consequently, as the agricultural sector shows, French negotiators found themselves pushed into making the best they could of their bilateral dialogue with their German counterparts, including complicity in high agricultural prices, even though their substantive interests were significantly at variance. The history of Franco-German quarrels about 'green rates' for agricultural prices vividly illustrates this paradox. Meanwhile, too much British negotiating effort was attached to dealing with the French adversary. The debate over the establishment of the European Regional Development Fund (ERDF) demonstrated a preoccupation with finding a way of stitching the French into the deal, which distracted the British and the Commission from fully exploring German thinking.[4]

The German-British relationship should, on all the prior indicators, have emerged as more fruitful. The governments of both countries were oriented more towards industrial than agricultural development; both sought to keep EC cooperation on economic and trade issues within the bounds of what was acceptable to the United States; and both had substantial trading links with the remaining members of the European Free Trade Association (EFTA). In the mid-1970s, despite some ideological affinity between the German SPD and the ascendant group in the British Labour cabinet, the relationship proved disappointing to both sides. The German government, and indeed broader German opinion, took very ill the whole episode of British renegotiation and the British government's lack of interest in institution-building, notably British reluctance to accept direct elections to the European Parliament. Immediately on accession, the British had set much store on their aspirations to build a coalition with the German government to reform the CAP and to put the Community's budgetary house in order. However, British analyses had seriously underestimated the power of the German agricultural lobby and, equally importantly, British policy-makers found it hard to adjust to dealing with a German government which seemed to consist of different ministerial segments pursuing their own policy lines. Although the British government was used to working with a US government with similar characteristics, it was perplexed by their manifestation in Bonn and their preservation in the institutional processes of the EC.

While these broad perceptions of each other's policy profile and attitudes did not sour the whole German-British relationship, they helped to account for misunderstandings and mutual impatience on particular issues. The ERDF was almost strangled at birth by intense confrontation between the British and German governments in 1973–74, which consisted of outright animosity at ministerial level (during which Sir Alex Douglas-Home and Hans Apel were reported to have exchanged barbed remarks about Munich and the Second World War) and misunderstanding by each government of the internal differences of view in the other capital. No German-British coalition emerged on the question of reforming the EC budget, despite the domestic German criticism of the FRG as the paymaster of the Community and the British government's insistence in 1974 on budgetary reform as crucial to renegotiation. During the discussions following the EC's Paris summit of 1972 little evidence emerged of any consensus on new policy developments between the two governments. On the contrary, the energy dossier, which surfaced with some urgency after the Arab oil embargo of 1973, found British and German attitudes at variance.[5] The German government, acutely dependent on external energy sources, argued hard for a collective EC response and clearly looked to British oil resources as a secure source of supply from which the EC as a whole could benefit. But the British government, at least in terms of EC (as distinct from International Energy Agency) commitments, preferred to maintain the maximum possible national control, even though, as subsequently proved the case, considerable quantities of British oil were likely to be sold commercially on the German market.

During the 1970s German policy-makers began to develop a more robust political approach to their own position within the EC, albeit with continuing hesitations over how vigorously they could push particular lines of argument. This translated into an unwillingness to be taken for granted, especially financially, and into a greater inclination to promote particular initiatives, such as the EMS. Meanwhile, British policy was characterised by a sense of vulnerability and uncertainty about policy options, political leverage and the interconnections of EC and national policies. British policy-makers of the period were aware of their limited bargaining power in the EC and were not sure how or when to play the cards they held. The transitional nature of thinking in both capitals about their relative positions and scope for influence did not make it easy for either government to focus on the relevance and utility of the other partner to its Community ambitions.

The Franco-German entente

In contrast, the Franco-German link re-emerged, notably from 1974 onwards, as a much firmer focus of mutual understanding. The story has been carefully elaborated in Haig Simonian's study.[6] The EC was picking up the backwash of the troubled international economy, and hopes of moving ahead quickly to European union had been dashed. Making the best of unpromising circumstances and ensuring that existing commitments were not unravelled became crucial objectives, neither of which was obviously fostered by British demands during the 1974–75 renegotiation. Both French and German policy-makers were convinced of the importance of interweaving their bilateral dialogue with Community negotiations. Neither Helmut Schmidt nor Valéry Giscard d'Estaing had a sentimental attachment to the EC *per se*, but both were determined to maximise their returns from the EC arena and its bilateral underpinnings.

It is arguable whether either government explicitly sought to establish a Franco-German axis to the EC, since the relationship was probably never as collusive or exclusive as some observers asserted. But there was signal evidence of close bilateral cooperation and consultation before, during and after EC negotiations. At the top of the pyramid the relationship was intimate, intense and often disdainful of other, less serious partners. The proverbial fly on the wall at sessions of the European Council could, by some accounts, have observed Schmidt and Giscard d'Estaing sitting next to each other (through some distortion of the 'normal' seating arrangements) and locked in private conversation while others were speaking. The easily caricatured debate over how the name of Greece should be spelt covered a point of real significance (not only for the Greeks), since the agreement on Ελλας not Hellas meant separation of the French and German delegations by virtue of the alphabetical seating arrangements.

Further down the governmental pyramid the reflexes for consultation, fostered by the long-term investment of the Elysée Treaty, began to pay off across the EC policy agenda and across ministries. Participants admit that, by the end of the 1970s, it had become more or less automatic in national coordinating meetings on EC business to ask explicitly what was the known position of the other partner and to look for ways of accommodating it. Far less detailed attention was paid to the positions of other partners in general, although they were of course weighed in the balance on particular issues. Where French and German policies were irremediably at variance the next step was usually to warn the other partner that this was the case, at least to ensure that the bilateral divergence did not become a source of friction. Often this would be reflected in a deliberate decision not to comment too adversely on the other partner's position in EC meetings. Whether by luck or by good management — and the reality was probably a combination of the two — there were, in the mid-1970s, no serious bilateral grievances between the French and Germans on Community issues.

None of this should be interpreted as implying total harmony of views between the two governments. There were, and remain, serious differences of view on major as well as minor issues. In EC discussions of both the internal market and external trade, for example, the Germans remained unrepentant free traders, while the French maintained their instincts to protect sensitive industrial sectors. On agricultural and agri-monetary issues substantive and monetary interests diverged. In the ERDF case German negotiators were determined to prevent the French, yet again, from being net beneficiaries. Their responses to the energy crisis of 1973—74 pointed in quite different directions. But, although the list is much longer, it is striking how little these divergences eroded the core of the relationship. Significantly this pattern of bilateral empathy began to structure the expectations of other partners and of the Commission. No-one benefited from Franco-German discord except those who wanted no agreement on a given issue. If a Franco-German deal could be stitched together even on issues difficult for one or both, the other participants in the negotiations would generally fall into line. Often this would encourage French and German negotiators to prepare bilaterally the side-deals which would permit a broader compromise to emerge. Habits of consultation encouraged tolerance of the other partner's idiosyncracies. French participants have reported an increasing recognition of the problems of interministerial coordination in Bonn. German policy-makers were largely able to distinguish between the arguments of high principle still often floated by French negotiators and the substantive interests which constrained them.

Co-opting the British: a mismatch of objectives

The record of the 1970s thus reveals an irregular triangle in which the shortest side was Franco-German and the longest Franco-British, and where there was not much scope for the three becoming more equal. Yet there were moments, especially in the latter part of the decade and after the renegotiation episode, when the shape of an equilateral triangle began to appear. In early 1976 'inspired' stories were published in the French press implying that the French government was consider-

ing the merits of a *directoire* or top table of key and major EC governments in a collective guiding role, especially when faced with Mediterranean enlargement, and the possibility of a two-tier Community, thus
resurrecting Gaullist ideas canvassed in 1962 and again in 1969. Both
British and Germans were clearly nervous of the idea; the Italian
government feared that a nominal 'Big Four' would rapidly turn into a
'Club of Three'; and understandably the other member governments,
their status threatened, were vigorous in rejection of any such notion.
But ever since that period the possible emergence of a *directoire* has
been part of the hidden agenda. In a quite contrary vein, occasional
French suggestions have surfaced that such a troublesome partner as
Britain, should be demoted to associate membership of the Community.

The one hard example of the potential triangle emerged in the
discussions on the EMS. Published accounts reveal a story which started
with a conventional Community mode of operation, and moved into a
trilateral phase, but which took its main impetus from a bilateral
Franco-German caucus.[7] After the initiative launched by Roy Jenkins
in the autumn of 1977, Helmut Schmidt decided that the next monetary move should be a new currency arrangement. His plan was unveiled
at the Copenhagen session of the European Council in April 1978 at
which he, Giscard d'Estaing and James Callaghan breakfasted *à trois,*
and a secret group was established of senior officials from each of the
three countries. After several meetings the British representative, Mr
Kenneth Couzens, absented himself, with the result that the plan put to
the Bremen session in June 1978 was largely of Franco-German inspiration. The outcome was the establishment of the EMS, from the central
element of which the British government excluded itself.

Britain's critics were quick to seize on the *prima facie* evidence as
demonstrating yet again a lack of commitment to the Community.
Substantive arguments about the suitability of the EMS for sterling
were seen as excuses not explanations. Other member governments,
whilst they may have resented Franco-German collusion, were sufficiently enthusiastic about the plan, in both form and content, to
applaud it. The Irish even went so far as to decouple the punt from
sterling in return for compensating financial transfers.

There was clearly a striking difference of approach between the
British on the one hand and the French and Germans on the other.
Chancellor Schmidt and President Giscard d'Estaing had both been
Ministers of Finance when the currency snake emerged from the discussion of Economic and Monetary Union. Their reference point was a
shared commitment, initially disappointed in the snake and on which
they had to improve. The British experience, on the other hand, had
been of a botched effort to join the snake. British policy-makers were
less predisposed to look to a Community framework in this economically important and historically sensitive area.

Neither French nor German leaders were engaged in altruism, but there was a complementarity of interests linked to the close inter-dependence of their economies. None of these held good for the British, whose substantive interests were interpreted as pointing in a different direction and for whom, in any case, the symbolism of the EMS raised great political discord within the government's own ranks. Some of those engaged on the French and German sides have comment-ed privately that it quite suited them to create a manageable EMS without the inclusion of volatile sterling. Differences of political style were also evident. M. Clappier and Dr Schulmann were clearly the personal emissaries of the French and German leaders with a remit to move plans forward. Mr Couzens, the British member of the secret triumvirate, was present on a more conditional basis, partly for reasons of constitutional convention and partly because there was no agreed policy line in London. The EMS episode was especially important, because for many of those involved EMS was viewed, rightly or wrong-ly, as a critical stage in the development of the EC as a whole. The achievement was interpreted as a Franco-German advance in which Britain had no part. The apparent cosiness of the relationship between Paris and Bonn should not, however, be overestimated. The fledgling EMS almost fell from the nest with the eruption of French insistence on abolishing Monetary Compensatory Amounts for agricultural prices, although an agreement was finally stitched together to enable the EMS to take wing.

Interpretations of the EMS story were fuelled by the simultaneous controversy over the Community budget. Renegotiation and the agreed Financial Mechanism (adopted in 1976) had not solved the problem of the net contribution from the British economy. Other member govern-ments found that they could not sigh with relief, since first Mr Callaghan's Labour government and then the new Conservative govern-ment robustly led by Mrs Thatcher made it plain that a more effective and comprehensive settlement would have to be found. On the one hand, a British-German community of interest lay in the fact that, as the published calculations eventually demonstrated, the British and German economies between them bore the burden of financing the budget for the whole Community. But their starting-points were differ-ent in that the FRG was much wealthier than Britain, and also benefit-ed from the industrial market, and German receipts were useful to the vocal agricultural sector. The German government preferred to separate budgetary changes from agricultural reform. Any alleviation of the British and, eventually, German burden required a heavier charge on the French economy, so that the French stood to lose both agricultural receipts and a broadly neutral net budgetary outturn. Since all the other member governments benefited from positive outturns, they were bound to be reluctant to accept changes.

The debate was to continue squarely at the centre of the Commun-ity stage until 1984, and it was evident throughout that no solution would be found unless and until all three governments had put together an agreement to which the other member states could rally. Franco-German collusion would not, on this occasion, prove the way ahead, since the British position could not be sidestepped as it had been on the EMS, and because both German and French interests were threatened by the inevitable zero-sum element in the situation. Moreover, the ramifications of the budgetary imbroglio impeded movement on other key dossiers and on the adoption of new initiatives.

New opportunities and old quarrels

By the end of the decade the underlying trends were beginning to move away from a pattern of EC bargaining in which a Franco-German entente could provide the bedrock. The interim solution of Britain's budgetary difficulties deriving from the agreement of May 1980 for the first time delivered to the British not just useful sums of money but recognition by the other member states, notably France and the FRG, of the existence of a structural problem. Of course there were many who hoped to return soon to the *status quo ante* by some magic sleight of hand. But behind the formal governmental negotiating positions emerged an acceptance of the validity of the British case, if not of the sums of money attached to the demands. The German government came closest to explicit agreement by piggy-backing on the British arrangements with its request for some alleviation of the consequent charge on the German economy, which in turn increased France's fiscal burden. Old habits and entrenched interests die hard, but the ground was beginning to shift.

The explanation for this lay less in the persuasiveness of British arguments than in the dawning realisation that some fundamentals of the *acquis communautaire* were becoming both obsolescent and an obstacle to progress on other fronts. Enlargement and the imminent exhaustion of own resources focused minds; movement on both required British consent. The old arrangements would not satisfy either the broad aspirations or the substantive interests of the French and German governments. Changes of government in the two countries made a difference, but, more importantly, French and German thinking was moving towards a major reappraisal of policy. Thus all three governments were simultaneously engaged in questioning some of the fundamentals of EC collaboration.

The German government's instinctive preferences followed two different routes.[8] They made for the high ground of proposals for political and security cooperation outlined in the Genscher–Colombo Plan, a corollary of their entire role in post-war Europe. They also held to the low but important ground of reinforcing the industrial common market. The Genscher–Colombo Plan, covered in Chapter 12, signalled the German concern to enlarge the EC agenda significantly and to reassert common commitments to integration. This symbolism should not be underestimated, especially given the German preference to link progress in the EC to the maintenance of an effective security umbrella. *Sub rosa* some German policy-makers were also beginning to complain about the free riders, those countries which were clearly beneficiaries of Community policies, but whose governments and parliaments were jibbing at NATO plans to modernise theatre nuclear weapons.

At first sight German insistence on the need to reinforce the common market for traded goods might appear a simple restatement of a long-held policy. But the preoccupation also sprang from worries about the downturn in the German economy and fears that other governments, notably the French, might be tempted to impede free movement of goods. To the irritation of both British and French, German thinking has not yet extended this logic to the service and agricultural sectors, in both of which German policies render the market less, not more, common. As far as manufactures were concerned, the Germans found themselves on the side of the angels in the form of EC Treaty commitments and the Commission's approach. This latter was not simply a matter of luck, since the close similarity between Commission and German thinking showed evidence of a cultivated dialogue going back over some 10 years, a factor which repeatedly gives the German government a starting advantage in EC negotiations.

Alongside these developments have evolved the German approaches to the Common Agricultural Policy (no unified approach has ever been evident). While the agricultural constituency remains important, as was shown in 1984 by the insistence on special offset arrangements to accompany milk quotas, its relative bargaining power has diminished in the linked discussions of financial stringency and economic efficiency. Uneasy compromises have still to be struck amongst the different domestic interests and their partisans, but there is more scope now for slotting into British — and increasingly French — concerns over financial discipline, and French worries about effective agricultural exchange rates and price levels. On many of these issues the German government has found itself out of alignment with its French and British opposite numbers.

Meanwhile, French thinking has also been evolving — especially since the spring of 1981 and the change of government.[9] French ministers have been willing to entertain some strengthening of the Community's institutional infrastructure, and the French government's memorandum of October 1981 — a *'relance'* document — pointed to the scope for more majority voting in theory. Practice followed in May 1982 with the majority vote on the agricultural price package to override the threatened British veto, a switch which surprised not only France's EC partners but also many French officials. President Mitterrand built on this new strand of policy in his Strasbourg speech to the European Parliament in May 1984, although it is debatable how literally his words were intended.

French attitudes are also moving on the EC's core policy agenda. For some time there has been a muffled debate about the need to re-examine the effects of the CAP not just on French farmers' ability to compete efficiently but also on the rest of the French economy. The debate has become more open within the socialist party and more legitimised within government circles. Mediterranean enlargement and budgetary constraints have fuelled this. Powerful obstacles remain: it is an area in which old orthodoxies die hard, and the French official line on issues such as subsidised exports to Eastern Europe still tends to favour rigid principles, often even against the evidence. In acute cases, such as lamb and mutton, French governments may still be tempted as they were in 1979–80 to protect a vulnerable constituency. None the less, the ground is moving, not least because agriculture now seems to have slipped down the league table of domestic policy priorities. A very significant opinion poll taken in 1984 (during the European election campaign) showed French public support for EC priority action on other economic and social issues, notably unemployment, to be a long way ahead of support for agriculture.[10]

Over the last three years the two French priorities have been quite different from the German list. The October 1981 memorandum proposed *un espace social européen*, a concept which puzzled other EC partners but reflected the genuine concern of a campaigning socialist government with the issue of unemployment. Perhaps more important-ly the French government produced in 1983 a more vigorous document advocating *un espace industriel européen* inspired by fears of European decline in the face of American and Japanese competition. Again the concept has not been readily understood in London or Bonn — especially in Bonn where reactions have been deeply critical of this attempted *'Colbertisme'*. But the French government has attempted to put to the Commission and partner governments plans for a radical re-thinking of what the Community should do for the sunrise industries. In particular, it has argued that the workings of an unfettered market risk being cumulatively deleterious to both French and Community interests. This insistence resulted partly from long-standing French views and partly from the argument of the socialist left wing that a more systematically protectionist policy should be adopted, if neces-sary on a national rather than a Community basis. This linked together EC dossiers on the internal market, external trade and industrial (especially technological) investment. Although the French government has since been forced to modify its economic policy, the set of issues remains a priority.

In contrast, British thinking has been 'implementationist' rather than reformist, more concerned with adjusting and enforcing the existing range of EC policies than with introducing grand new areas for collab-oration. The importance of this commitment to the existing Treaties was obscured by the budgetary issue. The British government has found itself trapped by a chicken and egg conundrum about whether budgetary improvements should be a result or a precondition of movement on other policies. Critics of British policy have repeatedly castigated the British apparent lack of interest in dossiers other than those with significant financial significance. But the prevailing view in the government insisted on sorting out the budget before contemplating any possible step change. This reflects old political legacies, but it has also been reinforced by the economic and monetary doctrines of current Conservative ministers.

The British government has experienced real difficulty in persuading its EC partners that it is unequivocally supportive of the Common Market and indeed of its reinforcement. Genuine British interest in opening up the service sector has met at best a lukewarm response and often obstruction. But unlike the French and Germans, the British government has shown a less active interest in the symbolic dimension to further develop the Community. Institution-building through redefining constitutional rules is not a British *penchant* and European Union has a misleadingly threatening connotation. In any case, from the British perspective, a system that was seriously flawed on a dossier as crucial as the budget needed modification first, and only then reinforcement. However, recent British thinking has markedly evolved from a series of efforts in 1981–82 to present the British case in terms which would strike stronger chords with its partners towards a more global affirmation of broad Community objectives. Mrs Thatcher's paper, circulated to the Fontainebleau European Council in June 1984, constituted an important recasting of approach. While British policy is less overtly initiatory than either French or German, it has moved on from its erstwhile reactive and defensive mode.

Consultation and coalition-building

Over the last five years or so it has been striking just how dependent negotiations in Brussels have been on bilateral bargaining among the member states and with the Commission. There have always been such consultations, but their significance has increased and their character has altered. The volume of interactions in capitals, whether through embassies, by telephone or in specially convened meetings, has grown apace, not least because the dossiers have in many cases become more complex and networks of contacts have become better established. Views differ about the importance of direct bilateral contacts. Some negotiators prefer to rely on conversations in the margins of plenary EC meetings and claim that these are sufficient. For those whose policy responsibilities require regular and intensive meetings in Brussels, notably in managing regimes for agricultural commodities, this may be an adequate basis for testing out other positions, gathering the relevant information and feeding in elements of their own thinking informally. Where the subject matter has a momentum and rhythm of its own, prior and/or separate consultations may have little added value.

However, many of those involved argue that they can be more effective, more subtle and more productive in negotiation, if, alongside the multi-lateral forum, they improve their channels of communication and the quality of their dialogue with key partners. For the three target countries of this study, this tends to mean in practice the other two and the Commission on most issues, bringing in other governments in particular cases.

In the Franco-German relationship, there is a mutual reinforcement between consultations on bilateral subject matter and bilateral dialogue on EC issues. The resilience of these practices has certainly helped to contain conflict and to resolve problems. The arguments of 1982—83 over whether German technical standards impeded French imports were contained by the opening first of a bilateral dialogue and then of a shared agreement to facilitate further discussions at the EC level. In the very different case of the EMS, any stresses and strains over the relationships between the franc, Deutsche Mark and the system as a whole have so far been resolved, partly because of the symbolic and practical value attached by each partner to keeping the EMS intact. Accepting the economic consequences of political commitment is a key feature of the Franco-German relationship, but it has not come easily, and some German policy-makers would argue that their tolerance of special French pleading has been pushed to the limit. By contrast, the external trade/common market cluster of issues (going beyond the harmonisation of standards) and industrial policy have proved much less amenable to resolution, as is also evident at the 'pure' bilateral level.

The Franco-British relationship within the EC has been marked by contradictions in recent years. Grievances have manifested themselves on relatively small issues, notably sheepmeat and turkeys, which have been interpreted by public opinion on both sides as touchstones. The prevention of easy access for British sheepmeat to the French market was widely viewed in Britain as evidence of French hypocrisy in relation to the CAP, while most French opinion saw the reverse process applied to Breton turkeys as proof that the British were not meeting Treaty obligations. Neither stereotype stands up to careful examination: in both cases substantial domestic interests were at stake, but equally in both cases the level of conflict rose quickly and permeated relations more generally, a quite different phenomenon from the cognate Franco-Italian 'wine wars' which have been waged without seriously damaging the broader political relationships. The damage-limitation reflexes present in the Franco-German relationship were still absent from the Franco-British dialogue of the early 1980s. Indeed, partly in recognition of this, both governments have recently taken active steps to improve the quality, frankness and intensity of the dialogue (see Chapter 8).

Another special feature of the Franco-British relationship within the

EC is that there are probably more significant areas of mutual under-standing than is generally appreciated even within the two governments. Steel and external trade negotiations are both good examples. In the case of steel, the French and British industries have painfully but promptly adjusted to Community disciplines. Policy-makers in both capitals have slowly built up a closer relationship with each other more easily than either has with its German counterpart. This reflects, first, important similarities of substantive interest and, second, efforts by individuals to improve the dialogue in the national capitals as well as in Brussels. Substance and form have reinforced each other.

External trade negotiations offer a rather different case, in which French and German views lie at opposite ends of the debate, with the British tucked in the middle. Given the deep-rooted character of Franco-German divergences on trade issues, the British are, on the face of it, well placed to perform their historical role as 'bridge-builders'. It is an especially interesting case in that it illustrates more clearly than most the potential for a triangular relationship alongside the bilateral dialogues. In some ways the German position is the most comfortable, since it clearly lies within the bounds of EC and especially Commis-sion orthodoxy (a mirror of broader GATT orthodoxy), and carries the support of other member states (the Benelux governments and Den-mark). German policy-makers have not insisted on 'national interests'. British inclinations are to ride with German rhetoric but to favour a harder-headed and more protectionist stance on particular industries — textiles and the series of Multi-Fibre Arrangements (MFAs) being particular cases in point. The French have been explicit *demandeurs* in the sense of wanting to pull against the orthodox line, normally with the support of the Italian government. Both generally in the GATT and in the last MFA round, the French clearly looked to the British for support and received it up to a point.

The dynamics of these textile negotiations have highlighted several interesting features. Discourse between the French and British has been easier in this area than in either of the other two pairs, and has been reflected in bilateral visits, recourse to the telephone, and mutual alert-ing to difficult parts of the package on the table in Brussels. There was some structured bilateral management of awkward issues such as imports from Hong Kong and the Maghreb. But residual suspicions have prevented the dialogue from being as frank as that which characterises either Franco-German or German-British relations on issues where interests similarly converge. There was a feeling in Paris that more and better could have been achieved if these suspicions had been overcome on both sides. Conversely in London, policy-makers were sufficiently keen to maintain a balance between the French and German positions and not to come down too explicitly on the French side. On some issues French and British negotiators did not clearly signal their moves to each other. Moreover, on those elements of the textile package which especially concerned French and German interests in outward processing, the eventual EC outcome followed directly from a bilateral Franco-German trade-off which was greeted with some relief by other EC partners. This episode suggests that for a coalition to 'deliver the goods' requires a careful nurturing of the dialogue and habits of consultation as well as a convergence of interests. On the other hand, on external trade issues, the Franco-British dialogue has reached a qualitative threshold beyond the levels yet achieved in most other sectors.

The integration of British external trade policy with the EC and the relatively rewarding Franco-British relationship have, however, taken a long time to spill over into the broader bilateral relationship or into EC relations as a whole. Somehow trade issues, although resting on a cornerstone of the EC, have occupied a separate and rather autonomous compartment of policy-making in both capitals. Thus the relationship on trade is barely cited by other policy-makers or observers as a counterbalance to the more difficult relationship on other issues.

The EC's budgetary difficulties present a different image. The budget has been a priority issue for all three governments; indeed under the current system, with its various modifications, they are the only three with a negative net financial burden. No durable budgetary arrangements can emerge unless all three actively consent – the issue is too important – and this is beginning to generate a shared (if not fully admitted) sense of 'us the payers' and 'them the beneficiaries'. But, in the absence of wholesale restructuring, the bargaining takes the form of a zero-sum game, a factor not conducive to coalition-formation on any side of the triangle. In all three governments the problems have been compounded by the difficulties of aligning the agricultural and financial dimensions, although they have been more amenable to central direction in London than in Paris or Bonn. Yet gradually bilateral consultations have intensified as the three governments recognised this to be a necessary condition of broader EC agreement. In particular, the reinvigorated Franco-British dialogue paid handsome dividends at the Fontainebleau European Council of 1984, enabling the broader bilateral relationship to blossom. If anything, the Franco-German side of the triangle is currently the weakest in this issue area.

Over the months since Fontainebleau, Community discussions have moved into a new phase of agenda setting and reappraisal, as the EC gears itself for Spanish entry. For all three governments this has involved a reorientation of thinking away from the fixed agenda of the last five years and the established procedures for negotiation. Much of this has been focused in and around the Dooge Committee's deliberations, which await discussion at the June 1985 session of the European Council. Policy in the three capitals has not yet crystallised. On the one hand, both the French and German governments have gone along with the rhetoric of European Union more easily than the British. Equally, the British have thus far been more explicit about precisely **what** modifications to institutional practice they wish to see, including a considerable reinforcement of majority methods compared with previous British policy. The French and German positions are less easy to read, being still couched in apparently maximalist language, while beneath the surface in both capitals more cautious and pragmatic voices can be heard. We should be wary of deducing from the British footnotes to the Dooge Report that they are out of line with what may be the eventual positions of the French and German governments.[11]

Conclusions

Of the three bilateral relationships, the Franco-German has been the most solid. It is therefore difficult to envisage the EC developing further unless it can rally French and German support. Yet the resilience of the relationship should not be overestimated nor should its achievements be over-sentimentalised. Solidarity has very much depended on the generation of tangible gains to both partners in terms of both detailed policy and the character of the EC enterprise. Although other member governments would not generally wish to see a tense relationship between Paris and Bonn, it does not necessarily follow that an intimate and intensive Franco-German relationship excludes or preempts good and 'special' relationships amongst other governments. Significantly there have been some moves to reinforce Benelux cooperation as an antidote to the shortcomings in Community bargaining.

As we have seen, the British government is now engaged in the EC's coalition-building processes, especially through bilateral links with France and the FRG. But it is both theoretically and empirically much more difficult to construct a stable three-way relationship, especially amongst partners of comparable weight and influence. Much of coalition theory would suggest that even-handedness is hard, if not impossible, to attain. Certainly a trilateral relationship requires more complex handling within each government; it demands difficult decisions about reciprocity and burden-sharing; it would need to depend on the qualitative and quantitative investment of all three partners on a sustained basis. But if the Fontainebleau agreement holds firm, an opportunity may exist for enlarging the policy agenda in a way that might accommodate all three partners' other important policy interests.

A further key issue is whether an improved trilateral relationship is likely to develop automatically into an explicit *directoire* — a predominant caucus of the three governments. Such a notion is understandably threatening to other EC partners, although most would also admit to concern about the costs of acrimony in any part of the London—Paris—Bonn triangle. A distinction has to be drawn between a *directoire* of both large and small members on the one hand, and a London—Paris—Bonn triangle excluding the Italians (and potentially the Spaniards) on the other. Fitting the Italians into the process may become a necessity which would in turn require the three countries under study to rethink their bilateral links with Rome. Each has an embryonic dialogue based on recurrent summit meetings and so on, but so far with only a modest rhythm and intensity. Whereas a formal *directoire* would be fundamentally damaging to the Community enterprise, a Community of which 'differentiation' may well become a central feature may require some recasting of the old orthodoxies. Whatever else, in order to achieve current national policy goals it is in Britain's interests to be treated as a full part of the system. To smother French and German voices which have periodically been heard to suggest that Britain is in some respects marginal to the EC core, the British have made a renewed investment in their bilateral relations with Bonn and Paris in particular, prompted partly by a firm desire to dispel any such notions.

At any critical stage in the EC's development, the quality of the relationships amongst the three is vital. Openly to operate *à trois* would be a risky strategy for all and difficult to manage in practice, but to neglect to ensure that the three are pulled together on key issues or tolerant of each other's individual concerns is equally risky. The value of closer alignment of French, German and British approaches would depend ultimately not just on whether it produced a more sustained consensus of the three but crucially on whether it generated ideas for EC action which were agreeable to other member governments.[12]

Notes

1. John Newhouse, *Collision in Brussels* (London, Faber, 1967); and F. Roy Willis, *France, Germany and the New Europe* (London, Oxford University Press, 1968).
2. Loukes Tsoukalis, *The Politics and Economics of European Monetary Integration* (London, Allen and Unwin, 1971).
3. Françoise de la Serre, 'L'Europe communautaire entre le mondialisme et l'entente franco-allemand', in Samy Cohen and Marie-Claude Smouts (eds), *La Politique extérieure de Valéry Giscard d'Estaing* (Paris, Presses de la Fondation Nationale des Sciences Politiques, 1985).
4. Helen Wallace, William Wallace and Carole Webb (eds), *Policy-Making in the European Communities*, 1st ed. (Chichester, Wiley, 1977), Chapter 6.
5. Ibid., Chapter 7.
6. Haig Simonian, *The Privileged Partnership: Franco-German Relations in the European Community 1969–84* (Oxford, Clarendon Press, 1985) which includes an excellent bibliography.
7. Peter Ludlow, *The Making of the European Monetary System* (London, Butterworths European Series, 1982).
8. On the development of German policy see Bernhard May, *Kosten und Nutzen der deutschen EG-Mitgliedschaft* (Bonn, Europa Union Verlag, 1982); and Rudolf Hrbek and Wolfgang Wessels (eds), *Das Interesse der Bundesrepublik Deutschland an EG und EPZ* (Bonn, Europa Union Verlag, 1984).
9. See *L'Europe: les vingt prochaines années* (Paris, Commissariat du Plan, 1980) which shows some evolution of ideas in the Giscardian period; and *Quelle stratégie européenne pour la France dans les années 1980* (Paris, Commissariat du Plan, 1983).

10. Reported in *The Guardian*, 19 March 1984.
11. *Report of the Ad Hoc Committee on Institutional Affairs to the European Council* (chaired by the Irish Senator Dooge), Brussels, March 1985.
12. R. Fisher and M. Ury, *Getting to Yes. How to succeed in negotiation without giving in* (London, Hutchinson, 1982).

10 International Economic Policy Coordination
Nicholas Bayne

The late twentieth century has been marked by international economic consultations of increasing intensity and complexity among the Western industrial democracies, which reflect the extent of interdependence between them. The adaptation, and even the simple maintenance, of the international economic system depends on the consensus that can be achieved among the major participants. In this context each individual country promotes its own interests and objectives by forming or joining coalitions of other like-minded countries, with the aim of generating a movement which will, in due course, determine this consensus. Thus, bilateral relationships among the major countries become not an end in themselves but rather a means: the first and often the most important step in building up such coalitions. When these coalitions are formed, the chosen direction of policy is determined by the first two or three members to come together; those who join in fourth or fifth or subsequent places may exert some marginal influence, but usually have to accept the main lines of the policy as given.

The summit meetings of the seven largest Western industrial democracies provide a regular occasion for reaching and expressing the prevailing consensus on international economic policy. These summits have brought together, annually since 1975, the leaders of the United States, Japan, West Germany, France, Britain, Italy and Canada, together with the President of the European Commission. They have dealt with a fairly consistent range of economic issues — macroeconomic policies, monetary matters, trade, energy and relations with developing countries — augmented in recent years by some political subjects such as hijacking and terrorism, Afghanistan and the stationing of missiles in Europe. Because of their importance in the consensus-forming process, these summits also illuminate the bilateral relations between the main participants as they seek to initiate or influence coalitions on economic subjects, and they are not only a particularly rich source of insights into relations between France and Germany, but are also instructive about relations between these two countries and the United States. Only after analysing these combinations, however, does it become possible to discern Britain's place in the scenario, partly because Britain carries less economic weight than the others but partly also because of different policy priorities. Study of the summits can further be used as a guide to Japanese policy and especially to US–Japan relations. But since that falls outside the scope of this study, Japan's role will not be considered here.

Origins of the summits

The summits were invented in 1975 for a variety of reasons,[2] one of which derived from the management of interdependence. During the 1950s and 1960s, the proliferation of international dealings between the major Western countries in trade, investment and finance, although a great stimulus to economic growth, also reduced the Western governments' autonomy in domestic decision-making. This was acceptable as long as steady growth continued, but when troubles began in the early 1970s, with monetary confusion, oil crisis and recession, tension built up between economic interdependence and national sovereignty which only heads of government seemed able to resolve. Another reason for initiating the summits stemmed from the shift in relative power between the United States, the European countries and Japan. Although the United States remained still by far the largest single actor on the scene, it could no longer, on its own, provide leadership for the system. Some new arrangements were required which would associate the Europeans and Japan with the United States in a role which hitherto the Americans had undertaken alone.

The summits also came about through the personal intervention of a few leaders, notably President Giscard d'Estaing and Chancellor Schmidt. When they were both finance ministers, they became accustomed to working very closely and informally with their American, British and Japanese counterparts in what became known as the Group of Five. When they attained supreme office, within a few months of one another, they concluded that a similar select and personal group, at head of government level, could help to resolve the problems of economic interdependence and of shifts in the balance of power, which went beyond the capacities of officials or other ministers.

So the economic summits, like so much else from the mid-1970s, were born out of the remarkable partnership between President Giscard d'Estaing and Chancellor Schmidt. The links between them were closer than between any other two leaders of modern times — certainly during peacetime — largely due to the ease of communications. As Helmut Schmidt has said, in fact they knew each other's minds so well that they didn't really need to telephone one another, except for confirmation.[3]

One of their objectives was to establish a high-level link between Europe and the United States, especially on economic issues. Earlier attempts to do this, for example Dr Kissinger's 'Year of Europe', had failed. But Giscard and Schmidt saw things differently from their predecessors. Although they recognised the great weight carried by the United States in the system, they believed that the economic summits would enable the Europeans to combine together as a counterbalance which would exert collective influence on the United States in a way acceptable to the Americans themselves. In practice, that is how the summits have worked.

The summits and the Franco-German relationship

While they remained in office, Giscard and Schmidt exerted a powerful influence on the format and tone of the summits. They also acted in concert on various policy issues with the aim of influencing the Americans. At the London summit of 1977, for example, they worked together to achieve a more forthcoming American position in the final stage of the Conference on International Economic Cooperation, and to moderate President Carter's restrictive approach to the export of nuclear technology. At the Bonn summit the following year they combined in urging President Carter to restrain US oil imports and also tried to gain American endorsement and support for the European Monetary System, which Giscard at least saw as the first step to a world monetary system which would also embrace the dollar. Subsequently, at the summits of 1981 and 1982, the French and Germans combined to resist President Reagan's attempt to limit the scope of East–West trade. In the same years they exerted joint pressure on the Americans in North–South relations, for example over attendance at the Cancun summit of 1981 and the global negotiations proposed at the UN.

In retrospect it is striking that there have not been more joint Franco-German policy initiatives in the summit context, even at the height of the Giscard–Schmidt era, since this was a period of intense Franco-German contact on economic issues, with responsible ministers and senior officials meeting at frequent and regular intervals. Nevertheless, on many occasions, France and Germany found themselves on opposite sides in summit discussions; for example on trade issues, international monetary matters, and macroeconomic policy.

This illustrates one unusual aspect of the Franco-German relationship. France and Germany are very closely linked: they are each other's largest trading partner, they have a long common frontier, and so forth. But very often they approach policy issues from opposite directions. The German government, even under Schmidt, promoted the role of the private sector while the French government, even under Giscard, intervened extensively in both industry and finance. The Germans favoured free markets and were the champions of the open trading system; the French felt more at ease in managed markets and advocated 'organised' trade. The French gave priority to exchange-rate stability, as a necessary discipline to promote price stability; the Germans saw things the other way round. So the French and Germans, at the technical level, often found it difficult to agree, and the closeness of the relationship made things harder rather than easier. Even during the Giscard–Schmidt era relations between officials concerned with economic and monetary policies could be quite tense and prickly, while parallel Anglo-German and even Anglo-French relations at that level were more harmonious because they were less substantial.

The political leaders of both France and Germany, from de Gaulle and Adenauer onwards, have seen the adverse consequences of widespread disagreement at the technical level. There is recognition at the top of the overriding common interest between the two countries, and constant pressure on lower levels of the two administrations to overcome their sectoral differences. There was something special about the personal friendship between Giscard and Schmidt, well illustrated by their joint pursuit of the European Monetary System against official scepticism in both countries. But Chancellor Kohl and President Mitterrand have exactly the same perception of common interest and the need for pressure from the top.

One favourite technique of keeping up this pressure is by institutional innovation. Examination of most of the initiatives of the Giscard—Schmidt era shows that these are nearly all concerned with procedures, machinery and institutions, rather than with the substance of policy. This applies to the economic summit, the European Council, even — to a large extent — to the European Monetary System. In this context economic summits serve not only as a channel for France and Germany to exert joint influence upon the United States, but also as an incentive for them to agree among themselves before they sit down with the Americans. Institutional innovation continues although the leaders have changed. For example, President Mitterrand has sought to invigorate the Franco-German relationship by reviving the defence element in the bilateral exchanges.

The Bonn summit of early May 1985 tested the relationship to the limit, because the divergence appeared at the very top — for reasons that will be explained in the next section. It was not French and German officials, but President Mitterrand and Chancellor Kohl who differed over launching the next GATT trade round and attitudes to the US Strategic Defence Initiative. The coolness persisted over the Franco-German bilateral summit a few weeks later; but neither leader could allow the breach to remain unhealed. At the European Council at Milan in late June the return of harmony was symbolised by a further characteristic bout of institutional innovation, this time in the Community context.

This leads to the conclusion that the forces for continuity in the Franco-German relationship are strong enough to survive periods of marked divergence in economic policies. This is partly a consequence of the economic interdependence between the two countries, built up over the decades, and partly a perception of the adverse consequences of serious dispute. The very occasions when the tension over specific policies is strongest — as, for example, when the French franc is realigned against the Deutsche Mark in the EMS — always provoke the recollection of the two countries' underlying shared interests and of the many joint achievements since the war. Whoever may be in power in Paris and Bonn, and whatever may be the economic disputes between the two countries, both sides attach overriding political importance to the ties which bind them together.

The economic summits illustrate another aspect of coalition forming among major powers which is relevant here. Although the summits were invented to provide a context in which French and Germans could combine to bring the Americans along, sometimes the French have used the summit process to form a coalition with the Americans in order to exert joint pressure on the Germans; and sometimes the Germans join with the Americans to exert pressure on the French. The Tokyo summit of 1979 was held at a time when oil prices were soaring and the Western position was in disarray. Before the meeting the French deliberately made common cause with the Americans to advocate targets for oil imports and surveillance of oil markets as the best response to the crisis in order to win over the Germans, who believed everything could best be resolved by reliance on market forces alone. At the summit itself, although Giscard held the Presidency of the European Community, he departed from the agreed European position to achieve the results which he (and the Americans) wanted. There is no clear example of a Franco-American coalition over economic policies during the Mitterrand Presidency. But in the security context the French and Americans worked in parallel in 1983 to stiffen the resolve of Chancellor Kohl's government over the stationing of intermediate-range missiles.

The Germans made common cause with the Americans, to bring along the French, at the first Bonn summit of 1978 over international trade. The summit was held at a critical stage of the GATT multilateral trade negotiations, aimed at reciprocal reductions of tariffs and other trade barriers. The French had been holding back the Community negotiators on a number of key issues, notably agriculture. But at the summit the Germans joined forces with the Americans to put pressure on the French so as to ensure that the negotiations could be brought to a conclusion by the end of the year. At Ottawa in 1981, the first summit attended by President Reagan and President Mitterrand, and again at Versailles the following year, German criticism of President Reagan's economic policies was muted, because of the pressure they exerted on France to change its economic strategy, which the Germans found even more unwelcome. The second Bonn summit of 1985 provided a conspicuous instance of a German/US coalition which failed in its effect. Once again this focused on trade; the Germans hoped the summit would bring the French round to agree a launching date for a new GATT round, strongly advocated by the Americans, but the German leaning towards the Americans was too strong for President Mitterrand, who refused to move.

These coalitions are not fortuitous. They suggest that both the

French and Germans have a conceptual approach both to their own relationship and to that with the United States which is active and innovative, although not always successful. This enables them to envisage various tactical combinations and techniques for ensuring that the consensus on any international economic issue reflects as much as possible of their national aims and interests. These combinations are possible, moreover, because of their perception of basic common interests uniting the three countries. Just as France and Germany will not risk a fundamental dispute between themselves, so will neither risk a fundamental dispute with the United States — even though French public statements may sometimes suggest otherwise. Although President Mitterrand might be exasperated and even occasionally perhaps angry at President Reagan's policies, this would not shake the underlying perception of the West's common interest in resisting the Soviet threat.

Britain's place in the picture
It is now time to consider where Britain fits into this pattern. It must be admitted that fewer summit initiatives have come from Britain than from France, Germany or the United States. Britain was not initially influential in launching the summit process — Prime Minister Wilson backed up President Giscard and Chancellor Schmidt but did not contribute ideas of his own — and in subsequent years, Britain tended to join existing coalitions rather than promote their formation. Successive British governments used the international support provided by the summits to justify domestic economic policies, with considerable success, but they seldom took the lead. The most striking exception was the 'five-point plan' put forward by Mr Callaghan before the Bonn summit in 1978. This covered growth, trade, energy, monetary stability and North—South relations; and its basic principle was that commitments by one country in one area could balance commitments by another country in a different area — an approach adopted by the summit itself. But the key policy commitments were made by the United States, Germany, Japan and France, rather than by Britain.

This analysis would not necessarily hold good outside the context of international economic issues considered by the Seven-Power summits. In security issues, for example, the conclusions might be rather different since, where tight Community discipline applies, all the member states close ranks before tackling the Americans. But this is seldom the case at the economic summits, where the procedures allow the European participants considerable room for manoeuvre, even on issues like international trade which fall under Community competence. Generally, in international economic matters the tradition has been that the French and Germans look to one another before going outside their bilateral relationship. Nor would they necessarily feel that they need to have prior British support before they move to tackle the Americans.

There are some good objective reasons for this situation and limits to what can be done about it. The economic links between France and Germany will always be far stronger than with Britain. The United States will always loom large as a determining force on international and economic monetary issues, in a way that Britain no longer can. Furthermore, it is not a British interest to see relations between France and Germany deteriorate to a point where either turns to Britain as an alternative to each other. Even so, it may be worth considering some ways by which Britain might improve its relative position and move closer to the centre of the coalition-forming process.

The first suggestion is for some institutional innovation in Anglo-French and Anglo-German relations. The Franco-German relationship holds together in time of strain because there is a tight network of links at all levels, which the respective heads of government ensure are maintained. Anglo-French and Anglo-German relations, although not wholly unstructured, are much more informal and more fluid as befits the normal British style. Nevertheless, it is worth considering the advantages of building up a tighter structure and a more formal organisation. This seems to suit the French and the Germans best, in their different ways, and, if the British proposed it, they would regard it as a sign of greater seriousness and deeper commitment. A tighter structure of relations would help to ensure greater continuity — fewer ups and downs — and promote the habit of working together.

Institutional innovation need not be confined to bilateral relations. It can spill over into European Community affairs, with a powerful influence at times. The European Monetary System has become one of the strongest symbols of the close Franco-German relationship, which remains as potent for Mitterrand and Kohl as it was for Giscard and Schmidt. More generally, Britain has an instinctively cautious approach to Community institution building, preferring to make the best use of existing, trusted bodies rather than to create new ones. This approach is not shared by the French, the Germans or even the Italians, who realise that far too many of the policy issues handled by the Community have little public appeal and may even be incomprehensible to all but a few — like Monetary Compensatory Amounts. The building of Community institutions is, however, a far more accessible idea. It can help to remind the populations of the member states of the general aims and aspirations of European unity, even when the governments do not always live up to them. President Mitterrand and Chancellor Kohl regularly launch new ideas for institutional reform in the Community. Their personal involvement gives their ideas heightened political visibility, while, as argued earlier, this joint activity provides valuable cement to their bilateral relationship.

By contrast Britain is seen as slow to offer new ideas for Community institutions and procedures, perhaps because for so long there was the overriding need to get the budget problem settled. Since June 1984, however, the British Government has made up for lost time with its paper 'Europe — the Future' circulated at Fontainebleau and in the run up to Milan, with its proposal for a formal agreement on political co-operation and its detailed suggestions for improvements in decision taking. It was perhaps hardly surprising that other member states were reluctant to see Britain occupying so much high ground. The Germans and French produced their own draft treaty on political cooperation, most of it hastily plundered from the British proposal. In the event, the Milan European Council agreed only to discuss all these issues in an intergovernmental conference.

A second suggestion is to make more use of Britain's close links with the United States, on the basis of a clear conceptual approach such as the French and Germans appear to adopt. When Britain first joined the Community, in the early 1970s, the first priority was to establish its European credentials, and to give no grounds for French accusations that Britain would be a 'Trojan horse' for the Americans. But 12 years on, circumstances have changed and there are no grounds for neglecting the United States in the interests of getting closer to Europe. The French and the Germans, as has been argued already, no longer feel the need of Britain as an intermediary, or even as a supporter, in their dealings with the Americans. Even so, Britain still has advantages not enjoyed by the French and Germans in relations with the Americans, the most important of these being the common language. There have been recent occasions when the British contribution has made all the difference in reaching a transatlantic consensus. At the Versailles summit of 1982, for example, a British formula helped to bridge the gap between the Americans, French and Germans and launched the current practice of consultations on economic policy convergence and exchange-rate stability, and it was a proposal advanced by the British Chancellor of the Exchequer at the IMF meeting in September 1983 that produced agreement between Americans and Europeans on the use to be made of the resources of the Fund.

Since British interests so often lie somewhere between the position of the French or Germans and the position of the Americans, that could provide the basis for a more active role in building up coalitions. France and Germany would take their relations with Britain more seriously if they believed that British ideas had a good chance of being accepted by the United States; and the process could also work in reverse. This would be even more likely to impress the Germans and French were it combined with the more imaginative approach to institution-building, both in bilateral relations and in the European Community, which has already been suggested.

Conclusions

This analysis has paid scant attention to the actual issues involved in international economic relations: protectionism, monetary stability, energy conservation and debt problems. It is not intended to understate the seriousness of the problems in all these areas or to infer that they can easily be resolved. But the basic thesis is that whatever approach is adopted towards them and whatever solutions are found will largely depend on the consensus achieved between the United States, the West European countries and Japan, with each having their contribution to make. The economic summit process has played an important part in promoting this consensus. Summit activity initially was dominated by the United States, France and Germany, so that coalitions formed between these three, in various combinations, determined the outcome. This was not surprising in one way, since all of them carry greater economic weight than Britain, but it did mean that Britain's chance of influencing the content of what was agreed was much reduced. Because the first step towards coalition-building is taken through bilateral contacts, Anglo-French and Anglo-German relations are extremely important in this context. It is therefore worth taking thought and looking deliberately for ways to encourage France and Germany, in some economic issues at least, to consult Britain as readily as they consult one another and to involve Britain in the pattern before they tackle the United States.

Notes

1. The author, who is a member of the British Diplomatic Service, writes here in a personal capacity. The chapter is based in part on research he conducted as a Visiting Fellow at the Royal Institute of International Affairs.
2. See Robert Putnam and Nicholas Bayne, *Hanging Together: the Seven Power Summits* (London, Heinemann for Royal Institute of International Affairs, 1984).
3. *Die Zeit*, 27 May 1983.

11 The High-Tech Triangle
Christopher Layton

Introduction

The governments of Britain, France and Germany are the three key actors in the drama of Europe's high technology, but what business have governments in industrial cooperation at the European level? In the commercial marketplace, where private firms are the principal actors, their main task is to remove barriers and enable a European common market to work. But when governments get into the act through public enterprise funding or monopolies of purchase or production, cross-frontier cooperation has to be promoted actively by themselves. Thus the French and British state electricity grids have linked up through a cross-Channel cable to pool electricity and relieve peak loads. The French and British gas authorities also collaborate. Above all, there is now a range of key high-technology (and generally defence-related) industries — aircraft, electronics, space and nuclear power — which have come to be promoted by the state in every advanced Western country, and where scale has made international collaboration a necessity.

Governments consider these industries to have a high political significance, and their growth — or at least that of the electronic information technology central to them all — has become fundamental to all industrial development. In most, the high cost of research and development requires large-scale finance, production and markets, and public money to compete with the public R and D subsidies of foreign competitors.

In these industries Europe is in the grip of a fundamental contradiction. Because of their importance the French, British, and German governments have sought to protect, support with R and D funding, and generally pamper their own national companies. Yet, during the last 30 years, the main challenge to their survival has come not from the other small European companies and countries, but from Japan and the United States. The giant US multinationals — Boeing in civil aircraft, IBM in computers and now AT and T in telecommunications — already dominate or threaten to dominate world markets.[1] Their continental home market and the huge size of US Federal government spending give them advantages which no European country alone can hope to match.

Learning from the Americans, 'Japan Incorporated' has developed a joint government—industry strategy for electronics which provides a second fearsome challenge. Europe's story, in these sectors, has been a painful learning process as the three key governments and the European Community as a whole have learnt the hard way that economies of scale to compete with their great rivals can only be achieved by a united effort.

In struggling to work together to pool their markets, R and D funding and industrial structures, France, Germany and Britain have, on the face of it, started from different points of view. In France it often appears that governments decide the shape of industry. To a French official European 'policies' mean cross-frontier industrial 'groups', cartels or projects, while his first suggestion in discussion with British and German officials on telecommunications or electronics may be '*parlons avec nos industriels*': that is, you tell Siemens, Plessey or GEC, and we will tell our current favoured company, to get together and find a way of cooperating on new products or projects.

In the Federal Republic of Germany the first reaction from the liberal Ministry of Economics to such interventionist suggestions appears to be one of horror: 'in a social market economy it is not the business of governments to tell industry what to do'. The Germans have genuinely favoured the worldwide opening of markets, despite the protective side-effects of their own meticulous national standards and regulations. In Germany, public support for programmes of industrial development — in electronics, for instance — the initiative for projects has to come from industry.

In Mrs Thatcher's Britain the 'market' is even more in fashion. On the surface, priority is given to getting British Telecom or British Airways to buy or sell competitively, and privatisation takes priority over any long-term strategic view of industry.

Yet these differences are far more apparent than real. Both the British and German governments do provide massive financial support for all these key technologies — in Germany under the philosophical heading of 'support to R and D'. The German Ministry of Economics itself has twice forced companies in the aircraft industry to merge under threat of receiving no more funds. Even Mrs Thatcher is deeply committed to government support to information technology.

The problems of economic philosophy that ostensibly separate the three key governments are more differences of language, industrial culture and local political colour than of long-term substance. When combined with British lack of vision, French self-centredness or German disillusion with the whole affair, they can block progress. But since the three countries provide the bulk of Western Europe's public financial support to the three industrial sectors considered in this chapter, some progress has been made in cases when they *have* agreed.

Aircraft: A fight for survival

The aircraft industry is the outstanding case where a major strategic change in the world scene has been brought about as a direct result of collaboration between the three, but not without a great deal of trial and error.

Since the early 1960s the world aircraft market has been transformed by the massive impact of US space and defence programmes, which have funded vast R and D expenditure in US industry, supplemented by the immense natural advantage of the home continental market for civil aircraft. By 1978, 90 per cent of the world market for civil aircraft was in the hands of the US industry and 70 per cent of the market for civil airliners in the hands of one company – Boeing.[2] All European governments have had to recognise that the costs of developing the largest modern aircraft were too great to be funded and amortised by one European country on its own.

The French and the Germans (whose industry was almost extinguished in 1945) realised this first, and the first European collaborative projects were the Transall and Breguet Atlantic bilateral Franco-German projects of the 1950s, designed by French industry and conceived through bilateral negotiations at industrial and official level. The huge British airframe industry – with the Comet, VC10, Trident and BAC111 on the stocks – was not interested. Rolls Royce supplied the Tyne engines for the Franco-German aircraft, as it did many of the jet and turbine engines used throughout the early post-war world.

Concorde, initiated in 1961, brought a first major cross-Channel partnership, when even the British aircraft industry had to recognise that it could not afford to develop a supersonic airliner on its own. National pride, so potent in the British and French aircraft industries, meant that there were two high-cost production lines for the airframes. Indeed, the project might have had a better press politically in Britain if it had been sold as a purely technological adventure (Europe's moonshot), not a commercial one. In France, where it was always seen primarily as a technological challenge to America, it left the industry strengthened and with its pride enhanced. The historical background was interesting. Bristol-Siddeley's engine partner was SNECMA, descendant of the GNOME-RHONE engine company, created by two Bristol engineers in France after the First World War. Joint work on the Olympus between Bristol and SNECMA continued a tradition of partnership which in the years covered by this study was always more harmonious than the relationship between proud Rolls Royce Derby and the French.

The real foundations, however, for today's collaborative, multinational European industry were laid in the mid-1960s, when both the strengths and the problems of intergovernmental bilateral and trilateral industrial collaboration were exposed. Under the political leadership of Roy Jenkins and Denis Healey, and of men like Alan Greenwood in industry in Britain, and powerful French civil servants like Martre, and Henri Ziegler who led the Breguet company in France, an attempt was made to develop, on a collaborative basis, both a large new civil airliner and a family of military aircraft designed to meet most of the requirements of the next 15 years. The civil airliner was eventually to become the Airbus A300; the military family was the political package of an Advanced Variable Geometry Fighter Aircraft, a range of helicopters and the Jaguar Ground Attack/Trainer.

There is not space here to describe the details of the negotiations of the years 1965 to 1968,[3] but they quickly revealed the problems of seeking to organise, by political means, massive industrial ventures between two proud and nationalistic countries whose industries remain commercial rivals in many other fields. The main problems were: establishing a common view of requirements; ill-matched and changing industrial structures in the partner countries; imbalance between the contributions and potential benefits of the partners; and conflicting ambitions to lead, control and exploit the project commercially.

Establishing requirements was not an easy task. Those for the Airbus swung from an initial concept of a 200-seater up to a much larger aircraft at one time demanded by Lufthansa, to settle finally at the 300-seater aircraft of today. But the requirement based on an international market was much healthier than the narrow design for a single airline (British Airways) which stifled sales of the Hawker Siddeley Trident in the same decade. It was the first step in Airbus's subsequent success.

More difficult was the haggling over military requirements, between air staffs whose views were as fundamentally different as those of Britain and France. The difficulties showed either that Dassault was right ('aircraft should be dreamed up by designers, not committees'), or that Europe needed far more effective staff integration of its defence requirements.

Conflicting ambitions were, however, the major problem. At political and top official level the need for some balance or equality between the partners was fully recognised. One senior French civil servant even argued, at the time, that the two governments should reach an overall strategy agreement: Britain should lead on aeroengines, France on missiles; Britain on large civil aircraft, France on certain military aircraft. The trouble was that even the weaker industrialists in the two countries were not always willing to accept another's commercial leadership, while the more ambitious ones who were sceptical of Europe caused more serious upheavals. In the event, the civil servants tried to stitch a bundle of projects into a balanced partnership, through a package of projects, with the result that a large part of the package quickly tended to come apart at the seams.

On the French side, it was Dassault whose determined individuality and self-confidence quickly upset the military project, causing the cancellation of the Franco-British Variable Geometry aircraft and thrusting the British into the arms of the Germans and Italians, so that the trilateral Multi-Role Combat Aircraft or Tornado became Europe's largest-ever military aircraft development during the subsequent decade. Dassault's determination to keep design leadership has re-emerged in 1984—85 as the major obstacle to a pan-European successor combat aircraft between these three partners, plus France and Spain (see Chapter 13).

On the British side, it was Rolls Royce Derby which played the role of over-mighty subject. The initial agreement on the Airbus gave design leadership to Hawker-Siddeley, who had designed the wing which has made the A-300 a success. The engine was to be built by France's SNECMA and Bristol Siddeley Engines, carrying on a partnership which dates back to 1923. SNECMA would have led, but the engine would have been the Pratt and Whitney JT8D built under licence. To Rolls Royce this was both insult and injury. An American-designed engine would power the new European airliner, and it would be built by Bristol Siddeley Engines, Rolls Royce's British rival.

A pre-emptive strike was required. By this time (1966) Tony Wedgwood Benn had taken over responsibility for aircraft at the Ministry of Technology. He had a ready ear for pleas from Derby to back a takeover by Rolls Royce of Bristol Siddeley Engines, in order to establish a single 'national champion' aeroengine company. Hence, Bristol Siddeley Engines was taken over by Rolls Royce, the JT8D project was killed and so was the partnership with SNECMA. The Airbus engine, it was agreed, was to be the RB207, a version of Rolls Royce's new RB211. Leadership on the airframe reverted to France. As Sir Denning Pearson, then Managing Director of Rolls Royce, put it to the author in an expressive outburst of Derby hubris: 'We shall have Europe *and* America!'

It was not long before the bubble burst. Rolls Royce soon found itself incapable of developing two versions of an advanced engine. It lost interest in the Airbus, and the British government, urged by sceptical civil servants, withdrew from the Airbus project. Soon after, Rolls Royce went bankrupt, dragging Lockheed into trouble in its wake. Rolls Royce survived, but it has never found a place in the Airbus, the most successful European civil aircraft in history, and its reliance on the American aircraft market has not paid off.

After these disasters, the situation of the European civil aircraft industry was saved by the Germans. Anxious to revive their aircraft industry and determined to do it by the European route, the German government, which had joined the Airbus project in 1967, not only continued to fund its own share of the project, but in 1968 invested £30 million in Hawker-Siddeley's development work on the vital wing. The Germans saw not only the technical value of the British work, but the strategic industrial importance of keeping Britain in the project.

Ten years later, when the energy crisis and the growth of the world market had vindicated the economical Airbus as a product, boosting its sales to some 400 aircraft, that vision was rewarded. There was a market opportunity for a new smaller version (the A-310). Boeing saw it too and invited both British Aerospace and (separately) Airbus Industry to join its venture. Both said 'no', seeing that a partnership with Boeing was like embracing an octopus and would have meant the control of their commercial and development strategy from Seattle. Despite lobbying by Rolls Royce, which wanted to get its engine into Boeing's 757 and 767, British Aerospace joined Airbus Industry instead, and the new aircraft was launched as a European project.

This was the second important milestone in the history of European aircraft collaboration. Now at last all three major industries were partners in a permanent commercial organisation whose aim was the development not of a single project, but of a family of aircraft.

What observations can be made about this history and what lessons learned? First, the achievements were largely the result of bilateral or trilateral contacts and negotiations between both officials and industrialists. Both were indispensable, with the initiative coming sometimes from one, sometimes from the other. The whole pattern of collaborative projects, civil and military, would not have developed without the political decisions that this was the way to go, or without patient and imaginative efforts by officials to achieve the goal. But as Dassault and Rolls Royce showed, without industrial support as well, nothing could be achieved. The second lesson is that a real strategic response to world competition in such sectors cannot be fully effective until all three countries play their part. Airbus is now a single commercial force in the world market which can challenge Boeing, but British Airways has been the launching market for Boeing's rival 757, which indeed might never have been launched without the Rolls Royce lobby which got it into British Airways.

The world commercial prospects for Airbus may have been helped by its having an effective US engine; this certainly helped to get its one American order, from Eastern Airlines. It is Rolls Royce, as we have seen, which has suffered from its early lack of interest in the Airbus market: it has remained excluded from its natural major market for large civil aircraft — Europe.

A third reflection is that the 'leadership' of projects, the subject of intense early struggles, was greatly overrated in importance. The British and Germans ultimately had the sense to concede that France would 'lead' Airbus Industry, that is, appoint the managing director, assemble the aircraft, and thus satisfy French pride, and they have lost little by it. What matters is the work, role and profit each has in the projects concerned. What also matters, however, is the quality and commercial criteria of management. The best marketing director Airbus Industry ever had was a Dutchman, Dan Krook from Fokker. If it is to survive into the 1990s, Airbus Industry will have to take further steps towards open, modern management.

All these elements have brought home the importance of the decision taken by the three governments to launch a new member of the Airbus family, the 150-seater A320. Its launch gives Airbus Industry the chance to develop into a permanent, major aircraft enterprise, offering a family of aircraft to world airlines.

Rolls Royce, moreover, now in partnership with Pratt and Whitney and its MRCA partners, MTU and FIAT, on a new engine, has a fresh chance to become a major supplier to the new aircraft. A pattern is emerging of two major civil airframe groups, one in the United States (Boeing) and one in Europe (Airbus Industry), supplied by two transatlantic engine groups, GE-SNECMA, and Pratt and Whitney/Rolls Royce, with MTU and FIAT as junior partners.

The French, German and British governments, and their relationships, hold the key to the future of the European aircraft industry. French pride, tenacity and determination to stand up to the Americans are primarily responsible for the success of the Airbus and its survival through the lean years of British doubt. The French have been great Europeans when the tricolor has been hoisted above the result. German patience, money, European conviction and willingness to accept French or British leadership have been essential too. As for the British, there would be no Airbus and no MRCA without British industrial technology. But Britain has been caught in the past between its own immense inheritance (and its even larger opinion of it) and its diminishing means. The result has sometimes been vacillation and a short-term view. Hopefully, even in a time of economic troubles, all three governments have, with the A320, mustered the resources and the vision to push ahead.

Information technology: a Community strategy

Nationalism and the computer revolution

For some 20 years, it has been apparent that electronic and computer technology held the key to the industrial future; for most of that time, it has been clear that Europe lagged disastrously behind the United States whose continental market and federal government programmes gave huge advantages of scale to multinationals like IBM and now AT and T.

A historian might therefore expect France, Germany and Britain — and the Community as a whole — to have developed major common strategies or programmes for this sector. The reality is different. Because a large part of the market is commercial and private, governments have not played the predominant role that they have in the aircraft sector. Because small new companies — especially American ones — have constantly proved successful, despite the dominance of IBM, the arguments for building a countervailing industrial colossus have been plausibly challenged by those who argued that individual European companies and countries could seek out profitable niches of their own.

On the surface, technological changes have been so great that tempting new opportunities have frequently emerged despite scale problems, whilst second-line American partners have been constantly available to offer new bilateral partnerships to Europeans unable to agree amongst themselves.

Against this background, the dominant political reality of the years 1963—85 has been not development of European strategies but the emergence of national programmes in France, Germany and Britain to support the three national companies (ICL, CII-Honeywell Bull and Siemens) each of which, at one time or other, has had links with American or Japanese firms. Thanks to abundant public money and procurement support, computing in these countries has survived.

The overall picture of the European computer industry today, however, is catastrophic, considering its potential and compared with the single-minded achievements of the other late arrival, Japan. The three 'national champion' large computing companies have each at times won between 30 and 50 per cent of their home market. None has seriously penetrated other European markets, so none has achieved economies of scale comparable to those enjoyed by IBM. All have piled up heavy losses at key points during the period; all have therefore retired hurt from the attempt to compete on their own in the market for large computers — the French falling back on importing Honeywell machines; ICL and Siemens on importing and selling Japanese products.

In microelectronic components, the key 'high-tech' raw material of industry as a whole, Europe imports over 60 per cent of its integrated circuits and all the most advanced information technology products. The trade deficit for the EC as a whole has grown from under US $1 billion in 1978 to over US $15 billion in 1984. As old industries decline, information technology is one of the few areas where new jobs are rapidly being created. It employs some 2 million in Europe today, but if Europe had a dynamic industry and a positive trade balance, it could directly employ at least another million, quite apart from the countless other jobs in other parts of industry that would be indirectly created as a result of increased competitiveness. The outlook, if past trends continue, is bleak.

The shortcomings of purely national solutions were apparent to the farsighted as long ago as 1962, when Siemens, Olivetti, Bull and ICT held talks to explore the possibility of some kind of collaboration. But the talks soon broke down at industrial level. Some wanted market-sharing; some technical collaboration; none was prepared to merge its computer business; there were fears over who would lead; and there was no overall strategic view. Olivetti sold its computer business to the General Electric Company of the US and fell back (sensibly) on peripherals; Bull too sold out to GEC (USA) in the first of the dramatic changes in alliance which have occurred in France; Siemens decided to base its computers on the RCA's technology; ICT in its insular way went on alone.

In the mid-1960s, as governments surveyed the wreckage and became aware of the importance of computing, each of the three key governments developed national support programmes: the British for ICL, the Germans for Siemens, and the French in their *Plan Calcul* for a new company, CII. None the less the pressures to achieve greater scale remained importunate and found their first practical expression in the early 1970s in the bilateral Franco-German link which gave birth to Unidata.[4] To both the industrialists and the governments concerned it seemed, and indeed was, the only possible way to create a European IBM, a major data-processing company covering the entire range of conventional computers and occupying a large share of the European and world markets. The companies agreed to develop a new joint range of computers and to market them together. The governments agreed to combine their national support programmes and procurement policies behind the group.

It soon became apparent to the industrialists, however, that to be competitive and efficient they had to go further and merge under a single management. However, the French government considered a merger to be unacceptable for, despite its backing for Unidata, it had never imagined a complete 'pooling of sovereignty' in this key sector, especially since Siemens started off with a larger market share than CII. Despite proposals that there be a French managing director and equal partnership, in terms of shareholding, in the new group, the French felt the reality of Siemens' size would tell.

At this the lobbyist Jean Brulet, the French managing director of Honeywell-Bull, controlled by Honeywell US, seized his opportunity. He persuaded the French government that Honeywell-Bull and CII should merge under 51 per cent French ownership and join with Honeywell US in a worldwide arrangement to market and share products. This deal, the American lobby argued, would combine both French 'control' and access to advanced technology. The solution reflected the lack of conviction in France's European policy at that time and mirrored the combined forces of Giscardian Atlanticism and Gaullist nationalism which then held power together.

The lack of political consultation with Bonn before this sudden switch of alliances was remarkable: so was the lack of contact between the French government and the partner industrialists, Siemens and Philips. The rupture embittered relations with Bonn and with Munich (the Siemens headquarters) for some years. After two years of attempting to go it alone, Siemens was pushed into the arms of the Japanese, and became a distributor of Fujitsu large computers. CII-HB was eventually nationalised in the early 1980s and absorbed by the French telecommunications administration. Telephone revenues were a convenient way to pay for its mounting losses.

EC: foundations for a strategy

It was left to the EC to pick up the pieces after the collapse of the Unidata experiment — offering, as it did with some tenacity, a framework in which collaboration, and even the building of an eventual strategy, could go on.

The 1974 Resolution of the Council of Ministers on data-processing[5] — adopted when hopes of Unidata were high — had called for 'common projects of Community interest' and eventually a 'medium-term programme concerning the application, development and production of data-processing systems'. The collapse of Unidata knocked the stuffing out of these euphoric ambitions, but a few useful applications projects were agreed by the Council in 1975 and 1976,[6] and in 1977 the Commission proposed a 'four-year programme for the development of informatics', which carefully avoided the contested field of medium-to-large computers, and proposed a Community programme of support for developments in the burgeoning new markets of peripherals, microcomputers and applications. The Germans and French quickly killed off the '*perinformatique*' plan. Chastened by the Unidata experience, and aware that this was a sector in which small companies could do well, they preferred to put resources into national support plans. A cut-down 4-year programme worth some £15 million (25 million écu) finally emerged from the Council in 1979.[7] It offered a credible framework for collaboration in markets and standards and some useful joint projects in applications which proved that the Community could do useful work, but provided no strategic answer.

Nevertheless, a new Franco-German willingness to work together had begun to emerge in the key sector of microelectronics. Here America's dominance had been massive since the space programme of the late 1960s and 1970s, and a formidable new Japanese challenge had been launched with their Very Large Scale Integration (VLSI) programme in 1976. In 1976–77, at meetings of the senior national officials responsible for microelectronics, the French made it clear that they were prepared for a European programme to balance their new American ties in this sector. On the German side, there was also an official and political will to act.

The discussions in the Community soon seemed to generate a meeting of minds. The Commission and governments invited top managers from all the key European companies in microelectronics to joint meetings. A technical group rapidly agreed on objectives for what would have been a European VLSI programme to match the Japanese. But when it came to implementation, the understanding fell apart. The largest companies — Philips and Siemens — were cautious about sharing knowhow on new product developments with weaker partners, and at that time were more concerned to buy into the US industry (Philips and Sygmatics) or otherwise acquire American technology (Siemens deal with Intel) than to do collaborative deals in Europe. They had yet to learn the bitter lesson that such deals may temporarily narrow a technology gap, but will not close it. Like the national aid programmes, these deals kept Europe running along behind the leaders, but did not bring profit or innovative market leadership.

French and German officials, who at that time had a real desire and will to collaborate, were never fully on the same wavelength. They seemed to have learned different lessons from the Unidata tragedy. The French, while concerned that their then 'national champion', Thomson, should remain an independent company, declared that they were willing to tell their industry they would get no more national aid unless they joined in a common programme – if other governments would do the same. The Germans, whose aid and attitudes to industry were far less authoritarian and who knew of Siemens' coolness, were not prepared to do this, but would have been prepared to switch significant national aid to a merged semiconductor company set up by Thomson, Plessey and AEG Telefunken. The French were unenthusiastic about this. Philips, lacking national aid, wanted Community money, but the Commission lacked leverage, since at that time both the French and the Germans saw the scheme as mainly funded by national funds coordinated together. The ambition and the goals of a 500 million écu (£300 million) development programme to match the Japanese were there, the will to mobilise such disparate forces was not. Thus, the talks collapsed, and the French government in particular turned to arranging partnerships for the manufacture of current technology US microchips in France.

In the somewhat soured aftermath of these disappointments, an attempt was made to promote bilateral cooperation on 'individual projects' between the key countries. The Germans, who were constructing a new cyclo-synchrotron facility in Berlin to develop and test X-ray lithography, invited others to participate. The French suggested deals on work concerning new materials. Nothing came of all this, and it was left to the Commission to find a way forward.

This way forward was found first on a modest but genuinely strategic level with the programme on microelectronic technology conceived in 1979–80 and agreed by the Council in November 1981. The main industrial companies had been unwilling to share work on developing new products, although they were aware that their ability to do this depended critically on the existence, in Europe, of manufacturing equipment and technology and computer-aided design techniques as advanced as those in the USA and Japan. Lacking these, they responded favourably when the Commission invited them to form a working group to draw up a programme. The resulting 30 million écu (£20 million) programme eventually adopted by the Council was far more modest than the US $210 million Pentagon programme launched in parallel with the same objectives, as America's response to the Japanese challenge, and Community delays in decision-making wasted a year. But at last, at least a first strategic step was taken.

Meanwhile other changes were taking place. Since 1979 Viscount Davignon, the Commissioner for Industry, had been stimulating a new, high-level political awareness of the crucial importance of information technology. The leaders of the largest European electronic companies had at last realised that their backs were to the wall. When Davignon brought together the heads of the 12 largest European electronics companies, in new 'round table' discussions, he found a greater willingness to act than when the lower-level heads of their semi-conductor enterprises had met the Commission two years before. They were shocked, in particular, by the Japanese 'fifth generation computer' programmes, which aimed credibly not just to catch up with the Americans but to overtake them and command world markets in a new computer age where intelligent computers could become the friendly tools of everyman. Fifteen years after the Japanese first announced their fantastic 'Plan for the Information Society', European governments had at last also become aware that, if Europe missed out on the new information revolution, its overall industrial competitiveness would inexorably decline.

All this has given birth to the ESPRIT programme, the EC's first serious attempt to grapple strategically with the need to promote a major new industry as a source of jobs and wealth. ESPRIT (European Strategic Programme for Information Technology), like the earlier more modest microelectronics programme, carefully avoided getting involved in current product development where competitive company interests arise. It is a long-term programme of technology development, designed, like the Japanese fifth generation computer programme, to transform the capability of European industry, so that companies can, by the late 1980s and 1990s, competitively seize new markets by their own endeavours.

The programme has an even broader scope than the Japanese fifth generation computer programme, for Europe has more ground to make up. It covers not merely the new generation computing and software techniques, but the whole range of microelectronics technology and the two key future areas of application, office automation and computer-aided manufacturing and robotics.

The key to the hopes formed round it has been industrial support and the agreement expressed, not only in the determined support of the heads of the 12 companies, but in the high level of staff sent by them to formulate the programme in a task force of working groups. The groups arrived rapidly at a consensus on what should be done. The 1,500 million écu (£1,000 million) programme (of which half was to be paid by the Community and half from industry) passed through the Community's decision-making processes at record speed — a mere five months. Meanwhile, even before implementation, major companies began to work together: ICL, Siemens and CII in particular have agreed to set up a joint laboratory.

With the ESPRIT programme, the Community has proved that it can be the focus for the gestation of a great, complex endeavour, although it has still to prove that it has the political and industrial strength and imagination to carry the project out successfully.

There is, however, another major level where the need for joint action is imperative: that of markets and standards. It is most apparent in the huge electronics-related area of telecommunications, where national markets are still largely closed. Protectionism has cushioned both national administrations and industry. Yet the world market share of European industry is falling, and the new digital networks are placing strong new pressures on the administrations to harmonise their systems so that they can integrate.

This is an area where the Commission has laboured on and off for years to bring about some opening of markets and greater harmonisation. There are plenty of regular contacts between the national telecommunication administrations, particularly between those of Britain, Germany and France. Such bilateral contacts, and those between the administrations in the framework of CEPT (the European Committee on Posts and Telecommunications) and with the Commission, sparked off, in 1979, the creation of a new network of systems engineers with a small 'nucleus' in Darmstadt, who were given the task of 'harmonising' the characteristics of the new Integrated Services Digital Networks (ISDNs) which the PTs (Postes et Télécommunications) would build. Such contacts gave birth, without involvement of the Commission, to EUTELSAT, the users' organisation of PTs which guides the use of the European telecommunications satellite.

In 1984 there were real signs that a political impetus for this was at last coming from the Community governments. The successful model of ESPRIT encouraged the Commission to mobilise industry and the PTs to elaborate a major joint long-term research programme (RACE) for the technologies needed to introduce an integrated broadband telecommunications network by 1995.[10] The governments declared a new willingness to open telecommunication markets within the broad framework of a genuine common market, to be completed by 1992. Nevertheless, the contacts between the PTs have so far been largely concerned with the interrelating of the separate national systems. The inertia and the philosophical differences resisting a move towards a more ambitious European strategy and marketplace remain immense. It took five years, for instance (from 1979 to 1984) to overcome a French veto on a Council recommendation to the telecommunications administrations to liberalise the market for attachments to the network and a first 10 per cent of the administrators' purchases of equipment.[11]

The French feared market opening would open the door to the Japanese and Americans and would not be accompanied by effective measures to protect and promote European industrial groupings. So long as there is no Community protection France prefers bilateral deals which can lead to industrial cooperation in an enlarged protected market. Typical was the 1984 Franco-German deal to develop a radio telephone system together and invite tenders from the two countries. Also in 1984 the French proposed a more ambitious deal with the British on telephone exchanges which was obstructed by the Thatcher government and British Telecom's far greater interest in privatisation and in BT's buying in the cheapest short-term market than in an industrial strategy to beat AT and T and the Japanese.

In Germany, while the Economics Ministry talks and applies pressure for its market ideology, industrial strategy tends to be developed by Siemens and the Bundespost. Decisive progress in European telecommunications will be achieved only if the Commission and the CEPT can somehow establish a framework of standards and market opening within which the major telecommunications administrations (including the Italians) and their industries can make strategic deals.

To achieve this, two major questions will have to be answered. How far are the British and Germans prepared to go to meet the French demand for a protected European market? On the face of it, one might expect governments which protect their national markets today to be prepared to accept a protected European market as a first step to liberalisation. In practice, the Germans in particular have so far found it easier to pay lip service to liberalisation in the GATT while maintaining some national protection in practice.

The second question is how far the three governments are prepared to go to promote a competitive Europe-wide structure for the telecommunications industry through the development of pan-European consortia or groups which might effectively supply several major telecommunications administrations. In computers, France and Germany gave up after the failure of Unidata: only IBM now straddles and supplies the whole European market. Is this to be repeated in telecommunications, with IT and T and AT and T (linked to Philips and Olivetti) the only Europe-wide suppliers? On the face of it there is not much sign that Mrs Thatcher's government would be prepared to support a radical European departure. But perhaps the Reagan Administration's astonishing attempts to restrict the export of technology will tip the scales.

Launching Europe into space: three plus ESA

Europe divided
If the development of a strategy for aircraft or information technology has been largely the work of bilateral and trilateral collaboration between the French, British and German governments and industry, European space policy has involved a quite different combination of bilateral Franco-German collaboration and pan-European organisations.

The first phase of European space policy (between 1960 and 1973) was innovative but confused. It began when the British, seeking a European use for their Blue Streak rocket, invited the other Europeans to create the European Launcher Development Organisation (ELDO). Six nations responded and the result was the development of a three-stage launcher — Blue Streak as stage one, a French rocket as stage two, a German stage three, and an Italian stage four.

In the meantime, Europe's scientific 'mafia' had persuaded governments to set up the European Space Research Organisation (ESRO), much as the physicists had persuaded them to support CERN, Europe's high energy physics laboratory, in Geneva. ESRO, which mainly used American launchers, had little commercial or political motivation; ELDO, a spin-off from Britain's fading aspiration to nuclear independence, had no useful payload to carry on its rockets when they did struggle into the air from their Australian launching-pad.

In the second half of the 1960s, a fundamental difference of approach separated the British from the French, and increasingly the Germans. The French, conscious of the worldwide commercial potential (and still more the political potential) of the new telecommunications satellites, were determined not to leave this new technology as an American monopoly. The British, by contrast, increasingly lost interest in the launcher programme they had initiated: 'Why not buy launchers commercially off the shelf from the United States?', they asked. It took them some time to realise the importance of the new telecommunications satellites.

As in so many other fields, when the British hesitated, the French activated the Franco-German partnership where contact between officials was close and an overall political will existed to get something done. Pre-empting hesitant discussions in CETS, the Committee of the European Telecommunications Services, they agreed and implemented the launching of a Franco-German satellite, Symphonie, in 1970, using the ELDO launcher and ESRO's telemetry facilities. Although it was not much use commercially, it did lead the way, disconcert the British, and precipitate a constructive solution to Europe's space muddle in 1972; by that time Britain had joined the EC and the Heath government, including an imaginative minister responsible for space policy (Michael Heseltine), was seeking to play a constructive part.

1973: a constructive programme

Phase Two in Europe's space endeavours dates indeed from the European Space Conference in 1973, which resolved some of these differences, established a *modus vivendi* over others, merged the two space organisations into one, and agreed a new programme[12] which was an ingenious compromise between a common programme and *à la carte* partnerships. It was primarily brought about by means of at least three factors: a strong Franco-German understanding at the official and ministerial level which succeeded in finding a way round grave differences; a new and constructive British attitude at the political and official levels; and skilful Belgian chairmanship.

The need to merge the two space organisations had been apparent for years. Now, after a period of collaboration between the two organisations in the same building, the resistances of the smaller neutrals (such as Sweden), uneasy at involvement in a launcher organisation, were overcome, and a single European Space Agency (ESA) was created.

Hesitations were partly overcome by a new and skilful blend between the ESRO style, in which all projects were part of a single common programme jointly financed according to an agreed scale, and the ELDO style, where each piece of work was carried out and financed on a purely national basis. In the ESA, each major project was carried out jointly, under the Agency's management, but nations could choose what share of the investment and proportionate amount of work, they would take up in each project.

The fact that all projects were grouped in a common programme all managed by ESA allowed the Agency to develop a common industrial strategy of encouraging two or three major transnational consortia to build up across Europe. The mix of projects, however, took account of the major participants' fundamental differences in priority while bringing in as many partners as possible to enable a broad European commitment behind each project. Thus a plan to develop a new-generation European launcher — Ariane — was built round French capability (derived from the French *force de frappe*) and had the largest financial contribution from France. Germany, which shared the French view of the project's strategic importance, and Italy shared the remaining cost. Britain did not participate.

On the other hand, the Germans, whose policies had always sought to balance their European loyalties with transatlantic ties, were the major European partner in Spacelab, the manned space laboratory launched by the American space shuttle in November 1983. Here other European countries, such as Britain and Italy, participated on a smaller scale. The British took the lead in MARECS, the Marine European Communications Satellite, to be used as forerunner of the European contribution to a worldwide navigation system for shipping. All countries joined in a joint European experimental Orbital Telecommunications Satellite (OTS), precursor of an operational European Communications Satellite (ECS), which was to bring Europe back into the central commercial business of the space age. The five-year programme, which cost some US $400 million per year, and its successor have proved remarkably successful. Europe has achieved commercial competence in telecommunications satellites and, with MARECS and ECS, batch production of seven satellites at a level of technology and cost comparable to the United States. The Ariane launcher, too, has been a success. It is the only launcher in the world to be optimised for the launch of geostationary satellites suitable for telecommunications purposes. Now operational, it has been handed over to a joint Franco-German company, which has been price-competitive and successful in winning launching business for telecommunications satellites from customers as diverse as Intelsat, India, Brazil and the Arab League. The results of the European contribution to Spacelab have not yet been evaluated, but it will at least give Europe a toehold in the next fatefully important phase of space technology — space manufacturing.

The work of the 1970s, built round the Council meeting of 1973, transformed Europe from an uncohesive force to a serious potential competitor in the space age.

The seeds of decay

None the less, even while ESA's programmes were moving towards a successful conclusion, the seeds of decay were being sown and were taking root.

With the excitements of its gestation and birth over, the level of ESA's Council meetings quietly declined; instead of meetings at ministerial level, the political senior role was happily pre-empted by senior officials. The birth of ESA and of the first and second programmes had been truly political acts, in which Europe's needs and the creative tensions between countries had been resolved by statesmanship: a statesmanship in which intensive dialogue at official and ministerial level — especially between the three key countries — had been crystallised by the innovative proposals and creative diplomacy of an international organisation. The Belgian chairman of the European Space Conference in 1973 played the same concilatory role as does the chairman of the EC Council of Ministers. The ESRO/ELDO secretariat under Sir Hermann Bondi played the same innovative technical and political role as the Commission at its best.

By the late 1970s, however, ESA was developing into a mere technical organisation implementing agreed programmes, its Council calcifying into a bureaucratic body lacking the vision to look ahead and initiate new strategies. At the same time, as Europe acquired the capability to compete in world markets, pressures and government policies developed to hand commercial exploitation back to national private industries. The logic of adopting a commercial company structure was soon demonstrated by Ariane's success in world markets. The dangers of 'going national' were demonstrated, by contrast, in the market for telecommunications satellites, where separate German, French and British enterprises failed to get a single order outside the home countries. The ESA-promoted consortia did not collapse altogether, and have made important bids for international business, but they have lacked adequate political backing. While the USA has obtained many orders for satellites outside Europe, the Europeans, lacking economies of scale, joint marketing, joint political pressure and joint investment in low-cost export finance, have obtained only two. The European governments have deliberately decided not to allow ESA to back joint European bids for such orders. At the same time, even within Europe, governments have been turning to national or bilateral arrangements to meet domestic needs.

In the field of telecommunications, the European telecommunications administrations do work together in EUTELSAT, which manages and makes use of the new ECS satellites launched by ESA. But the French, claiming in 1979 that European discussions and initiatives were going too slowly, have launched their own incompatible telecommunications satellite, Telecom I. On the positive side, they made use of the ESA's industrial work by purchasing the satellite from a member of an ESA multinational consortium (MATRA) and in effect purchasing an eighth of the batch of ESA satellites developed during the 1970s. But on the user side. Telecom I undoubtedly blocked the way for a completely integrated European system of satellite communication, making use of ECS. A working relationship between Telecom I and ECS has been established; but it does not provide the same coverage as an integrated European system. In the liberalised British market several groups have made plans to buy national satellites from British industry.

Meanwhile, in the new area of television direct-transmission satellites, no effective European user organisation or requirement has been defined. With ESA weak and rudderless, the French and Germans took a bilateral initiative in 1980 to launch a Franco-German direct-transmission TV satellite. This time (in contrast to 1972, when the bilateral Symphonie was followed by an overall European programme), Europe split: the British gathered the remaining interested Europeans together within ESA to back L-Sat, which will also make channels available for direct TV.

A programme for 2001

As Europe now considers its space endeavours for the last decades of the twentieth century, a gap in communication and attitude between the French and Germans, on the one hand, and the British, on the other, has reopened. The needs are formidable. Implementation of telecommunications satellites and their replacements in the 1980s could be a business worth US $10 billion for satellites alone, and perhaps ten times as much for related investments (launchers, aerials, networks, etc.). By the end of the century, manned space laboratories could be commonplace; a new high technology space manufacturing industry will be born. Earth resources satellites could create growing markets throughout the next 20 years. Solar power stations in space, beaming energy to earth by laser, still face big technical problems but by the end of the century these should be nearer resolution, offering new solutions for the world's energy supplies.

A Europe whose traditional industries are in decline surely cannot opt out of the new space age, leaving the running to the USA, Russia, Japan, China, and others too? There are signs that Europe is beginning to respond to the challenge. Early in 1984 the three key European governments responded in a coordinated way to the new US proposals for collaboration on future space projects including a manned space station. President Mitterrand also tried to activate both the Bonn—Paris relationship and the Community with new proposals of his own. In June 1984 first steps towards a new programme were taken in ESA, when it was agreed to develop studies for a new heavier-duty version of Ariane and a manned space module. Space strategy clearly has a place in the new phase of European development launched at the Fontaine-bleau meeting of the European Council in June 1984.

Conclusions

The aircraft industry seems to have provided a unique example of bi-lateral and trilateral collaboration. The external challenge was dramatic, the scale of the problems was immense, and the capacity to develop large aircraft and engines was concentrated mainly in two countries. More to the point, perhaps, the industry, in the three principal coun-tries, remains under tight government control: a control which officials want to keep. Since it has been the government which has controlled the major market, defence, it has been possible for a few ministers and officials to decide the structure of the industry.

However, one of the industry's successes has been the creation, under committed personal leadership, of a permanent European struc-ture, Airbus Industry, which has in some measure acquired a life of its own in a wider marketplace. Airbus Industry has a simple task — to compete with Boeing to produce a family of aircraft. If London, Paris and Bonn continue to back it, it can succeed.

In space, the equality between the three countries, so evident in the aircraft industry, does not exist. France, with its consistent strategies and political concept of the importance of space industries, and Ger-many, with its powerful industrial base and concern to develop links with both France and the United States, make by far the largest finan-cial contributions. Their strength has tempted both to fall back on national or bilateral initiatives. The smaller contributors, in this case including Britain, have lately tended to back the ESA programmes (at least in communications satellites) and to fall back on *ad hoc* American industrial partners from time to time. ESA's ingenious *à la carte* struc-ture has managed to hold this disparate group together.

Although much has been achieved, the verdict must be 'not yet good enough', for within the last four years bilateral moves have contributed to disintegration. If a new phase of European space development is to go forward, the three countries must share long-term political commit-ment and objectives with France playing the European game and the British dropping their hesitations on space policy and sharing in the leadership.

As for information technology, why have the governments accepted a Community role in this field? Partly perhaps because bilateralism failed; partly because the Community has developed a modest credibility in this sector and has learnt to refrain from intervening in industrial structures and supporting products where companies are in competition with one another. Above all, IT products serve a vast commercial market, and many companies are present in this effervescent game. Now that the share of defence in the market is less than 10 per cent, a broad organisation with responsibilities for building up a market seems appropriate as does the long-term concept of support for future technology embodied in ESPRIT — based as it is on industrial consensus-building round long-term strategic goals.

Of course, specific political decisions in such programmes depend, above all, on support and agreement at both industrial and political levels round the triangle. Just possibly, too, in a sector such as telecommunications, where there is a public market, the three governments will one day be able to give some encouragement to the formation of cross-frontier industrial groups. Their past experiences, however, suggest that their most useful contribution would be to step out of the way and encourage the industrialists to find their own partners.

The slow and painful struggles of the Community in the telecommunications field are a reminder that, where governments wholly control the market and there is an almost incestuous relationship with the industry (as in aircraft), the Community has great difficulty in acting as a whole, and bilateral and trilateral actions may be needed. The trouble is that, in this sector, a Europe-wide network and a European-scale market-place are needed. Some new combination of effective bilateral or trilateral inspiration and action between the main PTTs, and a larger Community/CEPT framework for all this, needs to be found.

Throughout this chapter the creative tension between bilateral or trilateral collaboration and the wider European Community has been evident. Understanding and even joint action between the three key governments is essential to any European action, but it must take place in the wider context of a European market and Community. At its best the three, plus the Commission, can provide the engine for European progress. When their relationships flag, the Community flags too.

The confused, hesitant progress of Europeans in bringing together their key industries to confront external challenges and combine their strength leaves one chary of drawing institutional conclusions, although not human ones. The successes have generally been the result of long and patient efforts to build up common interests, of developing habits of contact and collaboration between officials and industrialists, and of imaginative political and industrial leadership at important times. They require the three countries to be in broad support of a given policy and to be prepared to compromise and adapt to carry it out. The benefits of tenacity and strategic vision (Airbus and Ariane are the best examples) are remarkable; but the unfulfilled potential of European industrial collaboration is even more immense.

EUREKA, the scheme to promote European technology put forward by the French in 1985 as a colourful political riposte to President Reagan's Strategic Defence Initiative, reflects the tension between the three and the Community. The French left out defence and invited 17 European countries, including the neutrals, to participate. They made it crystal clear that they do not want the Commission to manage the scheme. Yet 80 per cent of the technical areas first suggested by France for collaboration in EUREKA are already covered by the Community's major long-term R and D programme, ESPRIT. What is one to make of this?

Even in the sectors covered by ESPRIT, there is scope for supplementary 'front-end' industrial projects to develop products for the market-place, like the big project between Philips and Siemens to develop a megabyte chip. The French and German governments are prepared to spend money on such bilateral projects, but not through the Community. Yet it is just such marketable products which need the market and goodwill of the whole Community.

Notes

1. See *Fortune International 500* (Time Life Inc., August 1985).
2. See *The European Aerospace Industry: Situations and Statistics*, CEC(78) 32/98 (Brussels, EEC Commission, July 1978) and in subsequent years.
3. For background see Ronald Miller and David Sawers, *The technical development of modern aviation* (London, Routledge & Kegan Paul, 1968).
4. Georges Hamel, *Renversement des Alliances: L'histoire d'Unidata* (Paris).
5. Council resolution concerning a common policy for data-processing (15 July 1974), *Official Journal of the European Communities*, 20 July 1974.
6. Council decision concerning a series of common projects in informatics, *OJC* L223, 22 July 1976.
7. Council decisions concerning a series of projects in informatics (portability, support for the use of informatics, high speed data transmission), *OJC* L255, 27 September 1977.
8. Council decisions concerning a pluriannual programme in the field of informatics, *OJC* L231, 13 September 1979.
9. Council decision of February 1984 concerning a European programme of research and development in the field of information technology (ESPRIT), *OJC* L67, 9 March 1984.
10. Council recommendations of 12 November 1984, concerning the implementation of harmonisation in the field of telecommunications and the first phase of opening of public markets, *OJC* L298, 16 November 1984.
11. Communication from the Commission to the Council on R and D in advanced communications technologies in Europe (RACE), Com(85) 113 Final, 25 March 1985.
12. European Space Agency: *Four year programme of research and development*, 1972.
13. European Space Agency: *Four year programme of research and development*, 1985.

12 Foreign Policy: the Management of Distinctive Interests
William Wallace

In foreign policy, as in other fields, the shape of the Paris—London—Bonn triangular relationship has altered considerably over the past 20 years, and, now as in the 1960s and 1970s, has been perceived differently by each national capital. Each of the three governments has clung to distinctive views of its foreign policy interests and of international order; convergence among these views has been slow and limited, and affected as much by changes in the external environment as by mutual consultation. There is no self-evident harmony of interests and understandings between France and Germany on the major issues of foreign policy. Indeed, on many issues, it has been easier to find common ground between London and Bonn, or even between London and Paris, than between Paris and Bonn. To the extent that foreign policy differences have been more successfully managed between Paris and Bonn than between Paris and London, that success must be attributed to the efforts made on both sides to mitigate conflict — or to the underlying commitment to collaborate in spite of their differences.

We are thus examining a pattern of asymmetrical relations, rather than a set of relatively stable or balanced bilateral links. The balance among the three governments has changed radically over time. In the early 1960s, Germany could safely be treated by both Britain and France as a junior partner in the transatlantic dialogue; in foreign policy outside the North Atlantic area the Federal Republic was only a marginal actor with a very limited role, while in Eastern Europe it was inhibited both by memories of the Second World War and by its preoccupation with the division of Germany. By the early 1980s, however, the FRG was clearly the United States' most important European partner, and the most vital European *interlocuteur* for the Soviet Union. While Britain and France retained some elements of their global responsibilities and interests, the relative weakness of their economies and of their industrial bases limited their ambitions and forced them to rely extensively on the additional weight which German support could provide for their diplomacy, their international relations, and their armaments industries.

For all three countries, foreign policy, defence and security have been closely linked, although France has drawn different conclusions from the linkage than have Britain and Germany. The argument of this chapter is thus closely interwoven with Chapter 13. The need for American protection against the Soviet threat, and the problems of representing distinctive European and national interests to Washington, were dominant themes of all three foreign policies in the 1950s; time and again since then, the question of relations with the United States has shaped and reshaped relations among them. France has been the most active partner throughout, seeking both to challenge the accepted doctrines of British and German foreign policy and to harness the resources of its neighbours to its own foreign policy objectives. For Britain and France, questions of status and prestige have been significant factors; for West Germany, the competition for recognition and status with East Germany and the slow recovery of international acceptance and respectability have set tighter bounds to its ambitions.

For convenience and clarity of exposition, this chapter focuses on three time periods and three issue areas. Rather than attempt to squeeze the foreign policies of the three major European states over the past 30 years into such a narrow compass, we examine the alignment and approach of each to major issues in the early 1960s, the early 1970s, and the early 1980s. Relations with the United States, it has already been argued, have been a constant preoccupation for all three governments. Second only to that have been relations with the Soviet Union and its East European allies, responses to 'the Soviet threat' as each has perceived it and the possibilities for developing a more constructive dialogue. Extra-European interests – the Middle East, Africa and Latin America – have reflected both distinctive historical and colonial ties as much as contemporary concerns and, increasingly, the question of how far each European government is willing to follow American leadership in responding to crises in the Third World.

Fouchet, Berlin and the Atlantic community

It is not easy to disentangle the thrust of French foreign policy between 1958 and 1963 from the personal strategy of General de Gaulle, its dominating guide and interpreter. De Gaulle's perception of foreign policy, of its association with nationhood and national pride and with rank and status, made the relationship with the United States peculiarly complex. As the dominant military and economic power in the international system America provided the standard against which to measure France's status, the foil for French efforts to demonstrate that status, and the most immediately visible threat to the independence and autonomy which de Gaulle considered intrinsic to the preservation of French power and status. Until the completion of the withdrawal from Algeria, the strength of the French challenge to American domination was moderated to an extent by a cautious acceptance of the unwiseness of taking on too many foreign policy tasks at once. But the developments of 1963–66, from the veto on British entry to the EC in January 1963 to the withdrawal from the NATO integrated organisation in July 1966, were foreshadowed in de Gaulle's memorandum to Eisenhower and Macmillan in September 1958, in which he proposed the creation of a three-power *directoire*, which 'would make joint decisions in all political questions affecting global security', adding that 'the French Government . . . will make all further development of its present participation in NATO contingent' upon acceptance by the 'Anglo-Saxons' of this proposal.[1]

Preoccupation with France's international power and standing permeated the whole Gaullist approach to foreign policy and to specific relationships. The relationship with Germany was, of course, a central factor in French perceptions of the balance of national power — as noted further below. De Gaulle's interpretation of the Cuban missile crisis and its outcome as demonstrating the establishment of American strategic and political dominance thus led his government, from 1963 on, to lay more emphasis on opposing American power than Soviet; the threat perceived to French independence from the United States was more compelling.[2] The Soviet Union, struggling to maintain its position as a major power, had greater attraction for France. From the Gaullist perspective, there were mutual interests to be explored: in supporting each other's international standing, in providing a counterbalance to a reviving West Germany and a limit to American predominance. From 1964 onwards, therefore, the French government actively pursued special relationships with the Soviet Union and the Eastern European countries, with a succession of visits in both directions and a series of declaratory statements by President de Gaulle.

French policy towards the Middle East was refracted through its North African preoccupations and through the pro-Israeli sentiments of its domestic public. France had collaborated much more wholeheartedly than Britain with Israel in the attempt to topple Nasser's radical Egyptian regime in 1956, hoping thereby to stem the flow of outside assistance to the Algerian rebels. Close links with Israel were established under the Fourth Republic, sustained by the personal links between the Israeli political élite and French political leaders, and maintained through the early years of the Fifth Republic. France was, in particular, a major source of armaments for Israel; the world reputation of the Mirage fighter aircraft was established by Israeli pilots in the 1967 Six-Day War.

For the British government, in contrast, the period between 1958 and 1963 was dominated by the special relationship with the United States. The aberration of the Suez episode had only reconfirmed to the British political élite the overriding importance of the link with the United States. In the imagery of the 'Three Circles' concept which then governed British assumptions about their country's place in the world, the 'circle' which linked Britain to the United States was the only one which brought Britain a clear accession of power and prestige, without imposing too heavy a cost. Harold Macmillan's recognition of the need, in the aftermath of Suez, to adjust Britain's foreign policy objectives in line with its reduced capacities led his government to increase the pace of decolonisation in Africa, and to reassess its relations with the European continent — a process which culminated in the first application to join the EC, in July 1961. However, the relationship with the United States remained the first priority; it was successfully re-established after the strains of the Suez affair, and sustained through the change of presidency in 1960 by the rapport which Macmillan built up with the new Kennedy Administration.

Britain's approach to the Soviet Union was governed partly by its relationship with the United States and partly by its sense of its position as a power claiming global status. Gaullist France pursued an active policy towards the Soviet Union in order to strengthen its claim to be accepted as a power of the first rank. From 1958 on, Macmillan's Britain pursued an active policy towards the Soviet Union in order to maintain its position as a major power, taking initiatives and seeking to soften the sharp edges of US—Soviet relations to demonstrate to its partners — and to its domestic public — that Britain still had 'a seat at the top table'. Macmillan successfully played on his image as a world statesman in the 1959 General Election, making much of his conversations in Washington and Moscow, which laid the ground for the abortive East—West summit meeting in Paris in May 1960. The high point of British diplomacy between the superpowers was the achievement of the Partial Nuclear Test Ban Treaty of 1963, the conclusion of which the British government could plausibly claim to have assisted.

In Middle East policy, British sympathies with Israel were tempered by the breadth of its interests in the Arab world, in particular by its ties to Jordan and Iraq. In spite of the Suez setback, Britain retained a degree of influence in Middle East politics which France had lost with the Second World War. British forces remained in Aden until 1967 and in the Gulf until 1970 and British companies played a major role in the development of Middle East oil.

Federal Germany was still feeling its way back to an independent foreign policy in this period, thus its approach to international issues was dominated by its twin concerns for security and for the maintenance of the principle of a united Germany. Unavoidably, therefore, relations with the United States were paramount. The Federal Republic needed American protection and support — protection against the Soviet threat, support for reunification. But such a dependent relationship was not always as comfortable as the less evidently unequal partnership between Britain and the United States. In the mid-1950s West German efforts to commit American public opinion to the defence of Germany as a central factor in the defence of the West succeeded in building a close and mutually satisfying relationship. But successive crises over Berlin from 1958 on made for a more ambivalent relationship. Adenauer did not succeed in transferring the good personal relations his administration had established with the Eisenhower Administration to that of President Kennedy. The (to the Germans) moderate and cautious response of the United States to the erection of the Berlin Wall in 1961, thus effectively accepting the Soviet imposition of its own solution to the German problem, raised further doubts.[3]

German approaches to the Soviet Union were similarly governed by the overriding preoccupation with East Germany. With little prospect of any Soviet willingness to accept moves towards reunification except on terms which were humiliating to the Federal Republic and unacceptable to its Western partners and protectors, there was little room for active diplomacy. Recognition of the continuing bitterness of memories of the Second World War provided a further inhibition. As to the Middle East, the German government had as yet few interests to pursue and little standing to pursue them; the extreme delicacy of its relations with Israel, to which West Germany was making 'reparations', made for considerable caution in German approaches to the Arab world.

On the crucial relationship with the United States the German leadership thus occupied a position between the confident partnership to which the British declared their commitment and the combative competitiveness of the French. For each of them, their perception of each other's availability as alternative partners and sources of support was a factor in their relations with the United States. There *were* alternative patterns, which repeatedly emerged as options both for Britain and for Germany. Although France was sufficiently committed to its distinctive strategy not to waver back towards 'Atlanticism', shifts in policy either by Britain or by West Germany would have substantially affected the French view of North Atlantic and European collaboration. A more sympathetic British reaction to the French proposals for a *directoire* in September 1958, for example, would have tempered Gaullist suspicion of the 'Anglo-Saxons' and perhaps laid the basis for a renewed Franco-British understanding. But the British image of France, as an unstable political system bogged down in internal conflicts and the Algerian war, was too strong for such a response to be practical in terms of domestic politics. Memories of Suez, where the acceptance of collaboration with France had led to the most significant setback to British foreign policy since the Second World War, reinforced preconceptions established during that war and in the difficult years which followed.

The diplomatic game about the future shape of European-American relations, in which these three countries were the key European players, was played thereafter according to the rules of the evolving Franco-American relationship, in which considerations of foreign policy, defence and economic advantage intertwined. De Gaulle's ideas on European political union were outlined first to Adenauer in their bilateral meeting of July 1960: they encapsulated the French aim of building a 'European Europe' capable of dealing with the United States on an equal footing. The Fouchet Plan, as it was called, provided a model for European collaboration in foreign policy, in deliberate contrast to the Atlantic collaboration encapsulated in NATO. The Atlantic alternative, set out most explicitly as the Fouchet Plan negotiations were collapsing in President Kennedy's Independence Day speech of July 1962, was for a Europe which included Britain working as a loyal partner of the United States. There were those within both the British and the German governments who wished to avoid the necessity of choosing between these two models, and also some who denied that they were incompatible. But the perceived necessities of British dependence on the USA for nuclear delivery systems led to an agreement at Nassau which de Gaulle read as reconfirmation of the British preference for Atlantic over European connections. There followed, in quick succession, the French veto on British entry to the EC, the Franco-German Treaty, and the Bundestag's addition to that Treaty of a preamble which explicitly rejected the French model of transatlantic relations and reaffirmed the German commitment to the United States.

A number of aspects of this brief history should be noted. First, foreign policy was central to the French approach to bilateral and multilateral relations within Western Europe, in a sense never entirely shared by the British or the Germans. For example, British negotiators for Community entry between 1961 and 1963 approached the EC as an economic and commercial arrangement, protesting to their party and their domestic public that membership need not fundamentally affect Britain's relations with the United States and the Commonwealth. Adenauer and his party had of course a far better sense of the political significance of European economic cooperation than their British colleagues, but they had no illusions that closer European collaboration could replace the American security guarantee.

Second, the French need to bridge the gap between their wide foreign policy objectives and the limited resources available to them required them to find like-minded partners. The Treaty of Rome amongst other things successfully harnessed German economic resources to French political objectives in Africa through the creation of the European Development Fund. The Fouchet Plan represented the same ambition on a broader scale — since, after that failed, so did the Franco-German Treaty. West Germany appeared more easily available as a partner than Britain because its still limited international acceptability and its consequently confined foreign policy objectives made it a potential auxiliary rather than a rival. Nevertheless, there were some potential points of common interest with Britain, most particularly in the field of nuclear deterrence and in the preoccupation with standing and status, which were never explored.

Third, the Franco-German Treaty was centrally concerned with foreign policy collaboration — and with defence collaboration — in accordance with this French strategic view. The Treaty committed the two governments to consult each other: '*avant toute décision, sur toutes les questions importantes de politique étrangère, en vue de parvenir, autant que possible, à une position analogue*' (II:1). The French pursuit of reconciliation with Germany had included, from 1958 on, a conscious association of France with Germany's immediate foreign policy concerns. While Britain — preoccupied with superpower relations and with the reduction of tension between them — was searching for an accommodation over Berlin, France combined a refusal to support Germany's long-term aims of reunification with staunch and explicit support for the German position on Berlin, earning the reputation in Bonn of a reliable though difficult ally, as reconciliation and co-operation in other fields advanced in parallel. French policy towards Germany and towards the Soviet Union were indeed far more self-consciously linked than were these two dimensions of British foreign policy, good relations with each being seen as strengthening France's position *vis-à-vis* both. The pragmatic style of British foreign policy did not make for such deliberate linkages, or such a clear view of strategic aims and tactical advantages.

Ostpolitik, Anglo-French entente, and the Year of Europe
Changes of government in all three countries in 1969—70 led to significant changes in the orientation of their foreign policies. Most of these changes resulted from domestic pressures or external developments; few resulted from the relationship between the three themselves. The most striking example of policy shifts related to intra-European objectives and consultations was the reorientation of the priorities of the Heath government from transatlantic ties towards Western Europe, a move which accompanied and assisted the Anglo-French dialogue of 1971—73. The European priority had been a matter of personal conviction for Mr Heath over a number of years: for him, the centrality of Anglo-French relations — and of foreign policy issues in cementing those relations — were lessons of bitter experience. For Pompidou, in turning from the partnership with Germany towards Britain, foreign policy issues were of more direct importance. The pursuit of *Ostpolitik* turned the Federal Republic, in the perception of the French political élite, from a reliable junior partner to an unreliable and independent ally competing for influence in Moscow. Worse, it reopened French fears of Germany, with a resurgent German economy facing an economically shaky France, and the old spectre of Germany 'turning towards the East' rearing before the more fevered Parisian imaginations. Pompidou's turn towards Britain, as a necessary counterbalance to the Franco-German relationship, was not undertaken solely for foreign policy reasons; but a certain convergence of British and French approaches to the transatlantic relationship and to East—West relations (if less clearly on the Middle East) both assisted the entente and was a necessary accompaniment to it.

French policy towards the Middle East had executed a rapid *volte-face* in 1967, in the wake of the Six-Day War. The Pompidou Administration inherited and extended this shift of policy to mount an aggressive and successful campaign in the early 1970s to capture Arab markets for French armaments and capital goods. But it was two events in 1968 which had the fullest impact on French foreign policy: the 'events' of May 1968 in France, which weakened its economy, heightened domestic inflation, and led to the devaluation of the franc in 1969; and the Soviet invasion of Czechoslovakia in August. The first emphasised the disappointment of Gaullist hopes of creating a strong French economy with a high rate of capital formation, which would be capable of matching German competition, and required the French government to turn more deliberately towards Britain as a counterweight. The second put an end to Gaullist illusions about the future development of East–West relations and the dispensability of the Atlantic Alliance. As the German government began to move away from acceptance of American leadership and protection in relations with the East towards a more independent and active policy, the French government was moving in the opposite direction. Regular Franco-German consultations on foreign policy, established under the 1963 Treaty and firmly adhered to throughout this period, did not serve to prevent misunderstandings or to allay suspicions of German motives. Not for the last time, most officials, politicians and commentators in Paris appear not to have heard German attempts to explain and justify their forward policy. To some German officials, the French reaction suggested a belief that a Franco-Soviet special relationship was good for the stability of Europe, but a German-Soviet dialogue dangerous.

The *Ostpolitik* was itself the dominant foreign policy priority of the Brandt government from the transition from the CDU–SPD grand coalition to the SPD–FDP coalition in 1969 onwards. That in its turn carried implications for the relationship with the United States: of a greater degree of autonomy of action than its predecessor governments had dared to display, and a greater willingness to risk disapproval in Washington in the pursuit of German objectives.[4] German leaders had drawn rather different conclusions from the invasion of Czechoslovakia than had their French counterparts: namely, that it was necessary to deal direct with Moscow and its insecurities, rather than attempt to cultivate better relations with East European countries, and that the invasion made active diplomacy towards Moscow more necessary rather than less. The forthcoming nature of the response from Moscow disturbed many French foreign policy-makers as much as it disturbed officials in Washington. Mistrust of German motives and of German susceptibility to manipulation by Soviet initiatives was strong in Paris, and was further strengthened by the poor personal relations between Brandt and Pompidou and by French suspicions about such leading Brandt advisers as Egon Bahr.

When leader of the opposition, Mr Heath had set out a more Euro-centric vision of British foreign policy in his 1968 Godkin lectures.[5] The secondary preoccupations of British foreign policy still revolved more around East of Suez than around Eastern Europe; indeed the Conservatives in opposition committed themselves to reopening the issue of a military role East of Suez, after the Labour government's decision for a gradual withdrawal between 1967 and 1970. In the approach to France, however, it was the sense of a European rather than an Atlanticist priority which counted; and for the French it was the 'concept', the attitude, which mattered as much as any specific actions taken. The Labour government's commitment to the Atlantic Alliance and the transatlantic partnership had naturally inclined it to look to Germany as the main European partner and to see France as the main obstacle and opponent. Thus after the second French veto on the British application for EC membership in November 1967, the government pursued the goal of continuing consultations on European and international issues — as well as on 'military, technological and monetary' questions — through a revival of the machinery of Western European Union (WEU), in which it might look to the support of Italy, the Benelux countries and Germany against France.[6] Thus, too, the Labour government's response to American pressure for a greater European military commitment to the Atlantic Alliance and the defence of Western Europe was to propose the creation of the Euro-group, in 1969, in which Britain and Germany played the leading roles and in which France declined to join.

Relations between the three countries on foreign policy issues at the end of the 1960s were thus beginning to be caught up in proposals for more regular and multilateral consultations. They were also caught up with the changing balance of power and influence among them, with rising French concern about German economic and political strength feeding back into its approaches to Britain and to the United States at the same time that rising German self-confidence and the success of the *Ostpolitik* were feeding a sense of independence from American tutelage. It is thus difficult to disentangle developments in each government's foreign policy towards third countries from developments in their relations with each other; the two were inextricably linked, each affecting the evolution of the other.

It was, for example, a British proposal for a special meeting of WEU foreign ministers on the Middle East (on which British and German views differed substantially from French) in February 1969, which provoked the French decision to boycott the WEU. But this extension of France's 'empty chair' policy had much more to do with the intricate manoeuvrings over Britain's candidacy to the EEC than with Middle East policy itself. Similarly, the ideas floated by President de Gaulle to the British Ambassador in Paris, Sir Christopher Soames, two weeks earlier (the 'Soames Affair', as it came to be called), had focused primarily on the future of the Atlantic Alliance and the shape of European cooperation. But its motivation, in retrospect, seems to have been primarily a recognition of the need to forge a closer relationship between a weakened France and Britain, to help maintain a balance of influence within Europe with Germany; and the British response, in turning first to the Germans to report on the French proposals, demonstrated both the depth of British mistrust for the French and the automatic assumption of the shared British and German commitment to Atlantic cooperation as an overriding priority.[7]

The French President's insistence, at the Hague Summit of December 1969, on reviving the Fouchet proposals of 1961 for consultations between European governments on foreign policy was therefore not simply a gesture towards his Gaullist inheritance. The collapse of the Fouchet Plan had, after all, been followed by the creation of the bilateral framework of the Elysée Treaty, through which de Gaulle had hoped to harness German resources to French ends. The balance of the 'triptych' which the French proposed at the Hague summit included not only the completion of the Common Agricultural Policy through agreement on mechanisms for common funding, and the proposals for Economic and Monetary Union through which some hoped to lock the French economy together with its stronger German counterpart, but also the commitment in principle to accept Britain as a member of the Community. Political cooperation could thus serve as a framework for balancing Britain against Germany, as foreign policy priorities shifted − provided that Britain's priorities *were* shifting towards a course convergent with that of France.[8]

European Political Cooperation (EPC) began to get under way in the autumn of 1970, with Britain not yet a participant. The first two ministerial meetings, in November 1970 and May 1971, saw detailed but fruitless 'exchanges of views' between France and its five partners on the situation in the Middle East, and substantial discussion on West European reactions to the repeated lobbying of the Soviet Union for a conference on European security − about which the German government was more enthusiastic than the French. Differences of view between France and its partners over the appropriate European response to the Nixon 'shocks' of August 1971 and the accompanying call for a redefinition of the transatlantic relationship played a large part in the postponement until October of the expanded West European summit originally planned for March 1972.

Yet the 1972 European summit marked a high point of convergence among the three countries on transatlantic and East−West issues, even if not on the Middle East, on which the French position remained very different from that of either Britain or Germany. Both the British and German governments had gradually adopted a more independent stance in their relations with the United States. President Pompidou, in his opening 'declaration', spelled out his definition of a 'European identity' in a far less antagonistic way:

> Our relations to that great country, the economically most powerful in the world, with which eight of us are allied in the Atlantic Pact, are so close that it would be an absurd idea to create Europe *against* it. But it is precisely this closeness of relations which means that the European personality must maintain itself vis-à-vis the United States . . .[9]

All three countries had now accepted the desirability of a Conference on Security and Cooperation in Europe (the CSCE, as it became), and Britain then joining the Political Cooperation machinery in advance of its formal membership of the EC the 'Nine' found in the CSCE process a rationale and proving-ground for political cooperation. Extensive bilateral consultations between Britain and France, as well as between France and Germany, preceded and accompanied these developments.

In the course of 1973—74 this convergence of views on foreign policy disintegrated. The pressures exerted by Dr Kissinger's declaration of a 'Year of Europe' were contained — at least initially — through the machinery of EPC. The French proposal that a clearer definition of Europe's 'identity' in the international system must precede a European response to the American challenge to redefine the Atlantic relationship enabled their British and German partners to temporise. But the shock of the October 1973 Middle East War brought out the still divergent assumptions which underlay their approaches to the major issues of foreign policy. Instinctively, the British government rallied to reassure the United States of its commitment to the Alliance, despite some hesitations about its handling of the Middle East crisis. Equally instinctively, the French government's suspicion of American hegemony erupted in a vigorous resistance, founded partly upon its by now established commitment to a distinctive Middle East policy. The German government was neither happy with the United States' unilateral actions over the Middle East (which included extensive use of its bases in Germany as staging posts and sources of resupply) nor prepared to follow France into an open confrontation with the guarantor of its security.

As on other occasions, personal factors played their part in the attitudes and interactions of the three governments. The illness of Pompidou and the central role played in the winter of 1973—74 by his Foreign Minister, Michel Jobert, sharpened the anti-American tone of French diplomacy. The fissures which opened between French and German approaches — to the proposal for an International Energy Agency, for example — were widened by an atmosphere of mutual distrust on *Ost-* and *Westpolitik* at the top. In the spring of 1974 personalities changed both in Paris and in Bonn, but without substantial changes in the composition of the ruling coalition in either capital. Schmidt and Giscard had worked closely together on international economic issues as Finance Ministers. They differed in a number of ways in their approach to Atlantic and East—West relations, although in both areas their differences were less than those of their predecessors. More importantly, they understood each other, respected each other's judgement, and were determined to cooperate in spite of their differences.

For Britain the high point of the 1972 Heath—Pompidou conversations had never overcome substantial differences between British and French perceptions of their international role and priorities. Nor had it lasted long enough to establish a degree of consensus or of mutual understanding among a wider group of politicians and officials within both governments before the crises of 1973 overwhelmed it. The change of government in Britain in March 1974 was far sharper than in either Paris or Bonn. It brought to the prime ministership and the Foreign Office instinctive Atlanticists, at the head of a party profoundly ambivalent about the European connection. James Callaghan's closest personal rapport, as Foreign Secretary, was with Henry Kissinger rather than with any of his Continental colleagues. The enthusiasm with which the British Diplomatic Service took to European Political Cooperation as it developed, and Mr Callaghan's own increasing commitment to it from the time of the Cyprus crisis in the summer of 1974, was offset by the sustained but unsuccessful British demand for a separate seat from the European Community delegation at the 1976 Paris Conference on International Economic Cooperation — a Giscardian initiative, which received cautious German support, to mark out a distinctive European role in North—South relations. On specific issues, within CIEC as it proceeded as much as within the Euro-Arab Dialogue (another French initiative, launched in the winter of 1973—74), British and German responses were often much closer to each other than either were to the French.[10] What was lacking between London and Bonn, and far more between London and Paris, was a sense of mutual commitment — and, more, of mutual respect — not primarily on foreign policy issues as such, but on domestic and international economic policy and on the European Community, and this hung over the whole relationship.

The growth of multilateralism

The development of EPC, which mushroomed in the second half of the 1970s, brought representatives of all three foreign ministries together on an increasingly intensive basis and across a broadening agenda. The Franco-German Treaty of 1963 had declared (1:11) that *'les hauts fonctionnaires des deux ministères des Affaires étrangères . . . se rencontreront chaque mois alternativement à Paris et à Bonn pour faire le point des problèmes en cours et préparer la réunion des ministres'*. Over a decade, in spite of divergent policies, these regular exchanges had established a certain rapport between the two ministries. British ministers and officials had exchanged views and information almost as intensively with their German counterparts on East—West issues through the NATO machinery, but there had been no similar link with

Paris. From now onwards 'the Nine' became a convenient forum for bilateral and trilateral exchanges between the three 'serious' European powers, as the French were inclined to put it — even though the French and German political directors have continued to maintain their separate treaty-bound monthly meetings on top of their other exchanges.

The British and German Foreign Offices rapidly established an easy and close partnership within EPC, most evidently in confidential discussions in 1976—77, when British and German proposals for strengthening and extending the mechanisms for cooperation met with firm resistance from the Quai d'Orsay. Between the British and French diplomatic services the prevailing relationship was a blend of mutual respect for quality and professionalism and of a rivalry which came close to a sense of hereditary enmity. Suspicion of each other's motives was rarely far below the surface, even when working relations were good; their respective embassies in London and Paris both suffered from a tendency to see themselves as embattled outposts encamped within a hostile power, rather than as representatives of a close ally. Conversations in the Quai d'Orsay in the mid-1970s did not indicate a great respect for the quality of German diplomats or diplomacy, and suggested deep undertones of distrust on East—West relations. But French recognition of the necessity of harnessing German economic strength to French objectives was matched by German tolerance of French activism, and an awareness that French initiatives could also be harnessed to German ends. Perceptions both in Paris and in Bonn that Britain's economic difficulties reduced its standing and its usefulness as a partner in foreign policy were reflected in a growing preoccupation in London with the consequences of economic decline. There was little point in the British government proposing a European initiative in handling relations with Portugal, a British official privately explained in 1976; it would come down in the end to asking the Germans to pay, so it was more tactful to leave relations to be handled as the Germans thought best.

But the style and the atmosphere of relations on foreign policy — as on other issues — was set from the top. The close relationship between Giscard and Schmidt was strengthened by a degree of convergence in their international outlooks, above all towards the crucial relationship with the United States. Giscard did not share the instinctive anti-Americanism of the Gaullist heritage. He was more concerned to establish France as a major partner with the United States in managing and maintaining the global order, although he was still domestically constrained in admitting the closeness of the relationship by the Gaullists within his coalition and the Communists in opposition. Schmidt and his party became progressively more disillusioned with the quality of American political leadership as the 1970s progressed, and consequently more concerned to provide a vigorous European voice in Washington.

The increasing self-confidence of German diplomacy — in marked contrast to Britain — reflected the passing of the 'war-guilt' generation out of German politics, the admission of the Federal Republic to the UN in 1973 (and the parallel expansion of German representation and interests in the Third World), the successful completion of the first objectives of the *Ostpolitik*, and the underlying strength of the German economy under conditions of global economic crisis.

Giscard d'Estaing's most important international initiative in the first years of his presidency — the proposal in 1975 to establish regular and informal seven-power summits on international economic issues — registered and symbolised this shift. The proposal had, from the outset, the full support of Helmut Schmidt, who had been with Giscard a fellow participant in the informal and confidential gatherings of finance ministers from which the initiative sprang. Indeed, its rationale rested on the combination of French and German economic weight to counterbalance the predominant influence of the United States. Britain was included, as a necessary fourth participant; but 'it is hard to detect any UK influence on the conduct of the summits before the London meeting of 1977 comparable to that of the Germans as well as the French'.[11] The Four-Power Guadeloupe summit of December 1978 was a strikingly Franco-German initiative, assuming that the dialogue with the United States had to be made direct, and that the relationship between the United States and Britain could be taken for granted. Zbigniew Brzezinski recalls that 'Schmidt said it made him feel "uneasy" that President Carter, Giscard and he never met together in informal, top-level discussions of political-strategic issues . . .'[12] From the perspective of the Elysée and the Kanzleramt, a British government preoccupied with its own economic problems and uncertain about its international strategy — above all, of how far it saw itself as operating within a European framework — had become to some extent a marginal actor.

Preoccupation in all three capitals with problems of international energy markets, domestic and international economic management, and the interaction between political, economic and security factors in their relations both with the United States and with the Soviet Union lowered the boundaries between foreign policy — strictly defined — and other dimensions of external relations. Paradoxically, these different dimensions were coming to be managed multilaterally in relatively distinct compartments: in the different 'baskets' of the CSCE; in the distinction between the economic agenda of the seven-power summits and the security issues of Guadeloupe; in the boundary between the external economic relations of the European Community, and the foreign policy collaboration of EPC. Yet relations in one issue area spilled over into others, for good or bad; as, for example, transatlantic arguments over the exportation of nuclear fuels or the development of the neutron bomb contributed to Bonn's declining respect for the quality of American leadership as a whole. The imperatives of French domestic politics, in which the orthodoxy of Gaullist doctrine proved too strong for Giscard to question, kept French defence policy apart to some extent; but behind the scenes Giscardian practice moved some distance closer to NATO, to the satisfaction of France's German and American partners. The British Labour government attempted similarly to separate its cautious approach to the EEC from its enthusiastic participation in EPC: a distinction which was never accepted in Paris and not sympathetically received in Bonn, where Schmidt's strong perception of his Labour colleagues as unwilling to stand up to obstructive elements within their own party on Europe or on economic management lent an air of progressive disenchantment.

Afghanistan, Iran, Poland and after

The pattern of relations which obtained between the three capitals by the end of the 1970s was thus very different from that which had obtained some 20 years before. Working relations between the three foreign ministries were now extremely close and the Germans were no longer a junior partner. Bilateral summits between London and Bonn, and London and Paris, supplementing the well established link between Paris and Bonn, had intensified bilateral contacts between diplomats at lower levels; the frequency of meetings was virtually the same on all sides of the triangle. The three Foreign Ministers, their political directors and other senior officials saw each other almost every week, in the context of EC Council meetings, Political Cooperation meetings, bilateral summits, four-power conversations on Berlin (which provided convenient cover for discussing wider issues with the Americans on a confidential basis), seven-power summits, and so on. Information was exchanged relatively freely, and discussions between men who knew each other well were relatively open. From this, and from a shared concern for the direction of American policy and the deteriorating atmosphere of East–West relations, emerged a substantial degree of convergence on the major issues of foreign policy.

The asymmetries in the triangle arose from the distinctive inhibitions under which each operated. British diplomacy, uniformly praised in the Auswärtiges Amt and the Quai d'Orsay for its competence and its openness to consultation, was held back by the constraints of domestic 'anti-Europeanism' and by the perception which its partners held of the absence of political commitment. The change of government in 1979 brought to the post of foreign secretary an experienced minister well-known and widely respected in Paris and Bonn, but in both those capitals respect for Lord Carrington was tempered by awareness of the distinction between his personal commitment and the more ambivalent approaches of his colleagues. Carrington's position and reputation lent British diplomatic efforts increased weight both within EPC and as a representative European voice in Washington and Moscow — particularly during the difficult months after the invasion of Afghanistan in December 1979, which witnessed West European governments following the United States in imposing sanctions on Iran and setting out a distinctive position on the Middle East in the Venice Declaration, and again during the British presidency of the Community and of EPC during the second half of 1981. But the commitment to quiet and useful progress in informal cooperation, demonstrated in the acceptance of 'the London Report' in October 1981, was counterbalanced by a marked unwillingness to be seen by the British Parliament or public as clearly committed. The close and easy relations between the British and German foreign ministries, and between Carrington and Genscher, should logically have made the British Genscher's natural partner in his ambitious proposal for a 'European Act', 'reaffirming' the commitment to 'a common foreign policy' and to 'the coordination of security policy and the adoption of common European positions in this sphere'. But British representations focused on potential domestic difficulties, in arguing that an 'Act' would be less difficult than a treaty and a solemn declaration easier than either in parliamentary terms; thus, the initiative went forward as the Genscher—Colombo Plan, to meet a cautious response from Britain as well as from France.[13]

French inhibitions revolved above all round their continuing ambivalence towards Germany's international role, and their uncomfortable awareness of their dependence on German cooperation. The certainties of Gaullist foreign policy had rested upon assumptions of an American commitment to European security, and a German acceptance of the American security guarantee, both of which were now rapidly weakening; and the painful reconsideration of French priorities which this situation necessitated erupted from time to time in outbursts of Parisian hysteria about the direction of German policy. In 1979—80, and again in 1981—2, the French élite were preoccupied with 'the German problem' and with 'the threat of a new Rapallo' — of the Federal Republic turning to the East and preferring the prospect of reunification to the maintenance of Western solidarity. Mutual confidence between Giscard and Schmidt helped the two governments through the confusions of the first six months of 1980, with Giscard's ill-judged and unilateral decision to meet President Brezhnev in Warsaw failing to re-establish France's old position as the Soviet Union's preferred *interlocuteur* in Western Europe. Less well-established understandings between the new Mitterrand administration and its German counterpart led to a short-lived crisis in Franco-German relations after the imposition of martial law in Poland in December 1981, with wild accusations about German intentions being voiced in *Le Monde* and in French political circles, and with Chancellor Schmidt travelling at short notice to Paris in January 1982 to iron out differences.

French attacks on the Federal Republic for its failure to support the United States sufficiently firmly under conditions of East—West tension, repeated at intervals from 1981 to the change of German government in 1983, tell us much about their perceived dependence on Germany for their security and for their freedom of manoeuvre in foreign policy. Such tensions indicate not only that there remain considerable differences of approach to foreign policy between the two countries and to the respective roles that they should play in transatlantic and East—West relations, but also that the sense of mutual dependence — of the necessity of maintaining the closest possible relations with Germany, as the first priority of French foreign policy — is now deeply rooted in Paris. As Chapter 13 will argue, French willingness to reopen a dialogue on defence policy between the two countries in 1982, and President Mitterrand's vigorous and politically valuable support for Chancellor Schmidt on the need to accept American intermediate nuclear missiles in Germany, were indicative of French adjustment to a more assertive and self-confident Germany. As seen from Paris, a German government which was no longer subservient either to American or to French pressures required a more vigorous and visible demonstration of French support for shared interests in order to maintain German support for the vital interests of France.[14]

German inhibitions were those of its past and of its strategic vulnerability. By the early 1980s the passage of time had weakened the inhibitions which flowed from the Second World War. What remained, alongside the self-confidence which stemmed from its economic strength and regained political respectability, was a tolerance within the German élite of French neuroses, and an acceptance that it was still convenient to follow France in initiatives on global diplomacy — although not on Eastern Europe or on transatlantic relations — rather than to exercise its economic strength too visibly for political ends. For 'out-of-area' support for international peacekeeping and global security, the Germans accepted a passive role: giving increased economic assistance to Turkey and to Pakistan in the wake of the Afghanistan invasion; providing (with the rest of the EPC governments) the multilateral framework for the commitment of forces from four West European governments to the peacekeeping force in Sinai; and keeping abreast of the consultations between Britain, France, Italy and the United States over their forces in Lebanon in 1982—83. But the atmosphere within the German political and official élites towards collaboration in foreign policy with France and Britain was remarkably relaxed: understanding towards their difficult friends in Paris, a little disappointed with their easier partners in London, concerned to explain the aims and the limits of their own *Ostpolitik* and to encourage joint efforts to maximise the European influence in Washington.

Under the pressures of the successive international crises of 1980—81, the three Foreign Ministries worked together extremely closely on a trilateral basis, operating as an informal European *directoire* in responding to American concerns and demands. During the course of 1980 there were a number of very secret meetings of senior officials and even of ministers, some on a trilateral basis, some with the Americans as the fourth partner, growing out of the framework of the Berlin Group and to some extent using that group as cover. The extreme secrecy was above all to protect them from Italian and Dutch displeasure, far more than from the Soviet Union or from their own domestic publics. When news of one of these meetings leaked out in July 1981, Lord Carrington was forced to divert his return journey from Moscow (where he had been representing views agreed informally among the four) via Rome in order to soothe the offended susceptibilities of Italian political opinion. When the Reagan Administation came into office in 1981 its officials were strongly impressed by the concerted representations of Western European governments, as foreign ministers from Britain, France, Germany and Italy visited Washington in succession. The change of administration in France in 1981 temporarily lessened the instinct for collaboration, as the Mitterrand Administration marked out an independent line on the Middle East and on Central America. But the transformation of approaches, the assumption of solidarity even when interests differed, was vividly demonstrated on the invasion of the Falkland Islands by Argentina in April 1982, when the French and German governments led their West European partners in public support for Britain. (The effectiveness of this demonstration, it must be added, was somewhat lessened by the rapidity of hints from Paris that the British government should make concessions in its negotiations on the Community budget in return, and by the failure of the British to keep Paris and Bonn as fully informed as Washington of their approach to negotiations with Argentina.)

The intensity of interactions among ministers and officials undoubtedly worked for a convergence of views among the three governments. The Mitterrand Administration's brief essay in independence in its approaches to Israel and to Lebanon shrank back towards the lines of the 1980 Venice Declaration, influenced by the tight constraints on European freedom of manoeuvre as well as by the pressures of its partners and the advantages — and acquired reflexes — of working together. The British government's shift towards a more flexible approach to East—West relations, particularly towards Eastern Europe, in 1983—84 owed something to the persuasiveness of German Christian Democrats, outweighing through the closeness and the frequency of political and ministerial conversations instinctive Conservative sympathies for the perspectives of Washington.

The closeness and effectiveness of exchanges among politicians and officials, each new government being socialised after a brief interlude into the developing sense of solidarity, was all the more remarkable in that substantial differences of interest and outlook continued to exist between the three countries, above all in the unintegrated (and often uninformed) nature of their public debates on foreign policy. French enthusiasms and economic interests were turned much more towards the Middle East, Africa and the Third World; West German trade, and its political and security interests, were focused most strongly on Western and Eastern Europe; Britain retained strong economic and emotional links with North America. Personal relations aside, misunderstandings and mistrust between the three, still evident beneath the surface on some issues, related rather more to each other's domestic politics and the pressures which these exerted on government than to the government itself or its political leaders: French concerns about Greens and anti-nuclear sentiment in Germany; French and German concerns about the insularity of British public opinion; and German and British concerns about the echoes of Gaullist rhetoric in France. If Britain was still in some respects less close to Paris in 1984 than was Bonn, that partly reflected the shorter timespan of its involvement in such intensive interchanges, 12 years of such diplomatic consultations and only 8 years of bilateral summitry, as against 21 between Paris and Bonn. It partly reflected, too, the continuing importance of geography and of political perceptions of geography, with French and German opinion convinced that they were condemned to cooperate by virtue of the inseparable character of their concerns for security, and with Britain still basically hesitant about the depth and priority of its Continental commitment. But that is the subject of the next chapter.

Notes

1. The full text of this memorandum was published in *Atlantic Community Quarterly* (March 1966), pp. 457–8.
2. On this, see Edward A. Kolodziej, *French International Policy under de Gaulle and Pompidou* (New York, Ithaca, Cornell University Press, 1974), especially pp. 90–2.
3. Alfred Grosser, *The Western Alliance* (London, Macmillan, 1978), pp. 108–10.
4. Angela Stent, *From Embargo to Ostpolitik, the Political Economy of West German-Soviet relations, 1955–80* (Cambridge University Press, 1981), p. 162.
5. Edward Heath, *Old World, New Horizons: Britain, the Common Market and the Atlantic Alliance* (Oxford University Press, 1970).
6. Kolodziej, op.cit., pp. 386–8.
7. Uwe Kitzinger, *Diplomacy and Persuasion: How Britain joined the Common Market* (London, Thames and Hudson, 1973), pp. 46–8; Maurice Couve de Murville, *Une Politique Etrangère* (Paris, Plon, 1971), pp. 427–9; see also the two articles by Alan Campbell on 'Anglo-French relations a decade ago: a new assessment' in *International Affairs*, Spring and Summer 1982.
8. For the Fouchet Plan and the development of European Political Cooperation, see William Wallace, 'Political Cooperation: integration through intergovernmentalism' in Helen Wallace *et al.*, *Policy-Making in the European Community* (Chichester and New York, Wiley, 1983); Philippe de Schouteete, *La Coopération Politique Européene* (Brussels, Labor, 1980).
9. Translation following Alfred Grosser in *The Western Alliance*, op.cit., p. 264.

10. On the Euro-Arab Dialogue, see Jacques Bourrinet, *Le Dialogue Euro-Arabe* (Paris, Economica, 1979); on the management of the Cyprus crisis and the development of Political Cooperation during this period, see David Allen *et al., European Political Cooperation: Towards a foreign policy for Western Europe* (London, Butterworth, 1982), especially Chapter 8.

11. Robert D. Putnam and Nicholas Bayne, *Hanging Together: the Seven-Power Summits* (London, Heinemann, 1984), p. 24.

12. *Power and Principle* (London, Weidenfeld and Nicolson, 1983), p. 294.

13. On British, French and German approaches to EPC during this period, see relevant chapters in Christopher Hill (ed.), *National Foreign Policies and European Political Cooperation* (London, Allen and Unwin, 1983); on the Genscher—Colombo proposals, see Wallace, op.cit.

14. Much of the information in this and the following paragraphs draws upon extensive interviews in the three capitals in 1982—83.

13 Defence: the Defence of Sovereignty, or the Defence of Germany?
William Wallace

Geography, history and political ideology intertwine in the pattern of relations on defence and security policy among Britain, France and the Federal Republic of Germany. The post-war division of Germany, and of East and West through the middle of Germany, left the West German state with an acute sense of insecurity; half of its population living within 100 miles of the fortified border with the GDR, strung out from north to south in a truncated country without strategic depth, visibly dependent for defence upon the German and allied forces in their midst. For strategic depth and Low supply lines with a degree of security, the Countries were far too close to the East–West border, and France constituted the safest route for re-supply and for reserves. Conversely, for France West Germany constituted the 'glacis' through which an invader would have to break before he reached the borders of France, the ground which *had* to be defended if France was to remain secure; although for 30 years after the signature of the North Atlantic Treaty, there remained an underlying dualism in the French perspective as to whether the threat to its vulnerable northern frontier came more from the Warsaw Pact or from the dangerous neighbour which Germany had been from 1870 to 1945. For both countries, the United States was thus a key partner: the guarantor of West Germany's security (and good behaviour) and, after Germany iteself, the main supplier of the conventional forces which maintained the 'forward defence' of German territory and blocked the route to France.

For Britain, the defence of the North Atlantic, of the 'western approaches' to Britain as well as of the Channel and the North Sea was the most immediate and tangible security concern. The commitment in the 1954 WEU Treaty to maintain substantial land and air forces on the European continent marked a decisive break; before then the 'expeditionary forces' which British governments had despatched across the Channel at the outset of both World Wars had not led to any acceptance of a peacetime or permanent continental commitment. Hitherto it had been the Channel ports and the Low Countries which had been the focus of Britain's continental concerns. Although the defence of the North German plain has now become one of its major contributions to the Alliance, it has not been absorbed into popular consciousness or historical tradition; it lacks the immediacy of the Alsace-Lorraine border for France, or the sense of the 'zonal border' for the Federal Republic. Since the Second World War the United States, again, has been the key partner for the maritime defence of Britain, and this has evolved into an essentially bilateral partnership, in which the small West German navy has come to play an auxiliary role and the French navy, increasingly concentrated in the Mediterranean from the early 1960s, has played almost no part at all.

Historical perspective is partly subjective — the selection out of conflicting traditions and different time periods of symbolic events which reinforce, or undermine, current preferences. Some British politicians and military officers in the early 1980s still saw the Second World War as the appropriate central frame of reference in Anglo-French relations: the wartime alliance in which British forces, together with the Free French, sustained French resistance to Germany and played a large part in the liberation of France. From the French perspective, even the wartime alliance had ambivalent undertones. General de Gaulle guarded until his death the recollection of the Anglo-American partnership paying insufficient attention to French priorities. Although almost no-one in Britain remembered Mers-el-Kébir, where in 1940 British ships shelled and sank part of the French Mediterranean fleet after its Vichyite commanders refused to give guarantees that they would keep it out of German hands at all costs, it remained a vivid memory within the French navy a generation later, and an obstacle to trust still repeatedly mentioned to British visitors 40 years after the event.

The bitterness of the German defeat and the German occupation of France remains an underlying point of reference in the Franco-German relationship, which surfaces from time to time in outbursts of Parisian invective against alleged deficiencies in German civil liberties or commitment to the Western Alliance, or against threatened revivals of German nationalism. Yet the depth of that bitterness, during the war, was tempered by a degree of both official and unofficial mutual collaboration, and tempered a little more by the reciprocal French occupation of south-western Germany and by the common experience of post-war deprivation and economic reconstruction. For many French and German politicians, officials and officers the most important historical frame of reference is the period from 1950 to 1963, the years of reconciliation: of economic recovery, of German rearmament and of French acceptance of its historical enemy as an ally. These were, of course, the years when British attention was most firmly fixed outside Europe, on the Atlantic partnership and on the political and military responsibilities East of Suez.

Setting the post-war pattern

Both Britain and France played ambivalent roles in the controversy which followed American demands for a German contribution to the defence of Western Europe after the outbreak of the Korean War. The imaginative French proposal to establish a European Defence Community in 1950 was predicated upon a countervailing British military commitment to provide reassurance against the potential threat from a rearmed Germany. The eventual defeat of those proposals by the French Assembly in 1954 owed in its turn something to the unwillingness of the British government to make that commitment. The following month Anthony Eden, then British Prime Minister, at last made the historic commitment to 'continue to maintain on the mainland of Europe, including Germany, the effective strength of the United Kingdom forces which are now assigned to SACEUR — four divisions and the Tactical Air Force'.[1] This commitment given, a treaty for 'Western European Union' was rapidly signed, linking Britain and France (together with Italy and the Benelux countries) to West Germany within the context of NATO, and providing a framework for monitoring the rebuilding of the West German armed forces and armaments industry.

For a brief period between the end of the first Indo-China war and the outbreak of the Algerian revolt, French military attention focused primarily on the European theatre. British preoccupations remained predominantly extra-European throughout the 1950s. The 1956 intervention in Suez resulted from the momentary coincidence of different British and French objectives in the Middle East and North Africa, and its aftermath saw the British turn back to their transatlantic and Commonwealth ties which were briefly damaged during the Suez crisis. Only three years after Anthony Eden's pledge, the 1957 British defence review announced a 30 per cent reduction in UK forces in Germany, much greater emphasis on nuclear deterrence, and maintenance and further development of the chain of bases East of Suez.[2] For the British, the Suez intervention was a mistake to be forgotten; France, with a succession of weak governments struggling to contain the Algerian conflict and hold the Fourth Republic together, was not a realistic alternative partner to the United States.

For the French, the British behaviour during and after the Suez invasion was a betrayal. French resentment at their exclusion from the privileged Anglo-American relationship was heightened by the resumption of close cooperation between Washington and London on nuclear matters, signified by the 1958 amendments to the US Atomic Energy Act of 1954, which appeared to place France by implication in a subordinate capacity. General de Gaulle's proposal, on the establishment of the Fifth Republic in 1958, to resurrect the post-war *directoire* of the western 'Big Three', must be seen against this background. France, like Britain, needed an ally to help bridge the gap between its international aspirations and the resources available to sustain them. The

USA and Britain had most to offer, if either or both were prepared to accept France as a partner. From the British perspective, however, France had little to offer in return: its technology less well advanced than Britain's, its government still unproven, its forces bogged down in North Africa. Given French aims and needs, the British refusal necessitated more vigorous pursuit of an alternative partnership with Germany.[3]

For West Germany, the period from 1955 to 1963 was one of rebuilding its armed forces and establishing its place in the Alliance. It found itself doing so against the backdrop of rapid changes in Alliance strategy, with both the British and the American governments switching their emphasis towards nuclear deterrence and reducing their forces in Germany. Questions of nuclear weapons — of which it was denied possession under the WEU Treaty — and the exclusiveness of the Anglo-American relationship thus played an important part in the evolution of German perspectives; and Adenauer and Franz-Josef Strauss, West Germany's Defence Minister from 1957 to 1962, similarly turned to France as an alternative partner. Anglo-German relations in defence matters were poor, and poorly handled, through much of this period: the British resented the slow pace of German rearmament, while the German economy raced ahead, and expressed this in arguments over support costs for British forces in Germany; this was matched by German resentment at British insistence on its special nuclear status and British dalliance with proposals for disengagement in central Europe.[4]

Franco-German bilateral conversations on nuclear and conventional weapons took place on a number of occasions during 1957, in self-conscious counterbalance to the Anglo-American duopoly. On his accession to power, General de Gaulle vigorously reasserted French control over its armaments programme. But the logic of Franco-German cooperation in resisting Anglo-American domination of the Alliance and of its strategy ensured that consultations continued. The limiting factor in this cooperation on the German side was the recognition that the American commitment to European defence must remain paramount; while on the French side the contradictions between sovereignty and alliance, and between Germany as a threat and as a partner, provided parallel inhibitions.[5]

The reorientation of British foreign policy which accompanied the first application to join the EEC, submitted in August 1961, almost reopened the question of defence priorities. Slow economic growth and pressures on public expenditure were forcing painful cuts in military procurement, particularly in the development of new weapons; Blue Streak, the liquid-fuel rocket intended to provide the second-generation British deterrent, was cancelled in 1960. In spite of its extensive — and expensive — capabilities in research and development, Britain was failing to keep abreast of the United States in civil or military technology;

France, successfully rebuilding its defence industry, now seemed to some to offer an alternative partnership. An agreement for the joint development of a supersonic civil transport aircraft (Concorde) was signed in 1961. 'In the summer of 1962 certain members of the Macmillan cabinet turned their attention to the possibility of collaboration with France on ballistic missiles and perhaps warheads.'[6] Because Peter Thorneycroft, British Minister of Defence, and Julian Amery, the Minister of Aviation, were both in favour of closer relations with continental Europe and a lessened dependence on the United States, a number of conversations took place on the potential for an *'entente nucléaire'*. But they were interrupted by the crisis in Britain's Atlantic partnership provoked by the cancellation of the Skybolt stand-off missile, which the British had agreed to purchase in place of Blue Streak. The crisis was concluded with the Nassau Agreement of December 1962 under which Polaris was offered on generous (and exclusive) terms. De Gaulle's response to this reaffirmation of the Anglo-American partnership included the French veto on Britain's EC application in January 1963, and the conclusion in June 1963 of the Elysée Treaty, in which defence cooperation with Germany played a central part.

For Germany the choice of partners was much less between Britain and France than between the United States and France; the link with Britain was seen as a secondary dimension of the transatlantic connection. The Bundestag's addition of an Atlanticist preamble to the Elysée Treaty killed Gaullist interest in its defence provisions. But France could neither supply the conventional nor the nuclear security which loyalty to the United States ensured for Germany. The loss of American strategic invulnerability, however, and the development of the doctrine of flexible response had shaken German confidence in the American strategic guarantee, setting off the series of discussions and demands which ended in the proposals for an Atlantic 'Multilateral Force' (MLF) of nuclear weapons platforms, presented to a NATO Council meeting in June 1962. A British government which was attentive to German insecurities and anxious to build a closer relationship with Bonn, might have acted as a broker between Bonn and Washington on the issue of sharing control of nuclear strategy and nuclear weapons, but British attention was oriented outside Europe. British ministers and officials vigorously resisted American attempts to link the Nassau Agreement to the MLF proposal; and the later Atlantic Nuclear Force (ANF) proposal of 1964–65 reflected the domestic preoccupations of Britain's new Labour government rather than any sympathy for German concerns. Only after the French withdrawal from the NATO integrated organisation, in 1966, and the parallel establishment of the Nuclear Planning Group, with full German participation, did Britain and Germany develop a fruitful partnership as the United States' main *interlocuteurs* in the Alliance.

The pattern of the 1960s

Defence and security policy may be broadly divided into three categories: strategy and security policy, including the balance between nuclear and conventional defence, and attitudes to arms control, to alliance partners and potential threats; defence and armed forces, including structure, tactics and training; and procurement. Conveniently, these represent the three commissions of the Franco-German defence dialogue, which began in February 1982, and to which we shall return later.

In the early 1960s the patterns of convergence and divergence among London, Paris and Bonn on all three of these dimensions were confused. Britain and France both laid heavy stress on nuclear deterrence as a strategy — but Britain saw it in the context of an integrated alliance, while France (in some ways with greater logic) insisted on the incompatibility of integration and independent deterrence. Unlike France and Germany, Britain had opted for smaller professional armed forces, and had placed a high priority on the maritime role; France, like Britain, attached continuing priority to extra-European commitments, and was already paying less attention than Britain to the conventional defence of Germany. German forces and equipment were only now reaching full strength, and as such outweighed the British and French contributions to the defence of the central front, setting the framework for rising demands for the German weight in the Alliance to be better recognised in its strategic discussions and command structure.

The German armaments industry was still in the process of reconstruction and was faced with an overextended British arms industry and a still expanding French industry. During the first 10 years after Germany's accession to NATO the German armed forces procured over a quarter of their equipment from the United States, manufacturing a proportion of American equipment under licence in Germany. Both British and French aircraft lost out to the F-104 Starfighter in the crucial choice of a supersonic aircraft in 1957 — partly on technical grounds, but partly also on the political grounds of reinforcing the American link and providing some compensation for the American military presence in Germany. Determined French salesmanship, closely linked to the cultivation of political relations, ensured, however, that, from the outset, France was virtually Germany's second most important military supplier, leaving Britain and Italy well behind as sources of procurement and as collaborators until the later 1960s.[7]

Collaboration in arms procurement was on the NATO agenda from the early 1950s, under American leadership; and rivalry between Britain and France was apparent in its earliest initiatives. The French government withdrew from the NATO project for a ground-support aircraft in 1957, when an Italian prototype (with a British engine) was chosen in preference to a French design; the resulting Fiat G-91 was completed as a bilateral Italian-German project. The choice of a French rather than a

British design for a common maritime patrol aircraft, in 1958, led in turn to British withdrawal, and the Atlantique continued into production as a French-led consortium with German, Dutch and Belgian participation. In parallel to this came the first bilateral Franco-German project, the Transall transport aircraft, a successful collaboration between French design leadership and German cost- and production-sharing. This set a pattern of complementary advantage, narrowing the gap between French ambitions and the financial resources available to meet them, while enabling the Germans to buy into new technology and advanced design.[8]

If the German arms industry was still rebuilding its expertise, and the French industry successfully re-establishing itself, the British industry was already in crisis at the beginning of the 1960s. Overexpansion during the rearmament 'boom' of the 1950s, fragmentation of companies, proliferation of competing designs and failure to capture export markets in the face of strong American competition forced a series of reorganisations, cancellations, and attempts at collaboration from 1960 on. On taking office in 1964, the Labour government found itself faced with an unsustainable burden of military projects in process of development. Its response was to turn towards France. The Martel air-to-surface missile project, agreed in 1964, was followed by a complicated package of balanced advantages and shared production, including three military helicopters, the Jaguar strike/trainer, and an Advanced Variable Geometry Aircraft (the AFVG). From the British side these agreements were made not as part of a deliberate or strategic turn towards European collaboration in procurement, but as a series of pragmatic responses to immediate needs, not fully supported by the industrial companies involved. The French administration claimed at the time the 'conscious aim of protecting the future of their aircraft industry by linking it to the British',[9] in order to build an effective counterweight to the Americans. But *their* industrial companies were not of one mind, and the political impetus which carried France out of the integrated structure of NATO in 1966 also cut across this technical commitment to collaboration.

In June 1967, in the midst of Harold Wilson's exploratory visits to continental capitals to promote a renewed British application to the EC and his associated proposals for a 'European technological community', the French government cancelled the AFVG. The resistance of Dassault to collaboration on any basis except acceptance of its own superiority was not insignificant in this; its approach to collaboration was clearly demonstrated, after its amalgamation with Bréguet, in its vigorous efforts to sell the Mirage jet in third markets in competition with Jaguar (for which Bréguet had been the French partner). Consequently, the British government turned decisively towards Germany, agreeing in 1968 a collaborative project for a Multi-Role Combat Aircraft (MRCA, later Tornado, with Italy as the third partner) as the main fighting aircraft of both air forces for the 1980s. Other bilateral and trilateral projects (with Italy, or with the Netherlands) followed. The misunderstandings and suspicions engendered between 1964 and 1968 left behind a legacy of bitterness and rivalry between the British and French aircraft industries and procurement executives which persisted on both sides of the Channel through the next 15 years. Continuation of the three helicopter projects (Lynx, Puma and Gazelle) and of Jaguar maintained a degree of collaboration, but not without repeated British claims of French sharp commercial practice or French charges of British inefficiency.

Franco-German collaboration on missile development, which began with the agreement on Milan and Hot in 1965 and Roland in 1966, went much more smoothly. Once again, the two partners were complementary rather than competitive. The Germans were willing to accept French design and technical leadership, and were later glad to let the French government take the lead in overseas sales. Indeed, with mutual disillusion in London and Paris over Anglo-French collaboration, both governments were competing to woo the Germans: the French with a more deliberate and determined strategy, explicitly linking arms collaboration to political relations from then on. One limiting factor in Bonn's response, from 1964, was the rising American pressure for 'offset' purchases of military equipment as an indirect contribution to the cost of maintaining US troops in Germany.[10] The pattern of arms collaboration thus established was missing one dimension. Anglo-French rivalry blocked any trilateral projects between the three countries, leaving Anglo-German or Franco-German collaboration as the only choices for Bonn.

The progressive withdrawal of France from the integrated structure of NATO between 1963 and 1966 completed this asymmetrical pattern. French insistence that nuclear strategy and the control of nuclear weapons were central to the concept of national independence closed the possibility of consultation in that sphere. At the high point of Gaullist security policy in 1967—68, the doctrince of defence *à tous azimuts* effectively denied the Soviet threat to Western Europe and assumed a neutral posture for France.[11] Britain and West Germany, in contrast, were coming closer together in discussions of strategy, through their common membership of the Nuclear Planning Group which was established in 1966 after the collapse of successive proposals for shared control of nuclear weapons, with Britain and West Germany as the United States' key European *interlocuteurs*.

The Anglo-German connection in defence policy was closer between 1968 and 1970 than at any point in the previous decade — and perhaps closer than for most of the decade following. Personal relations between the two Defence Ministers, Denis Healey and Helmut Schmidt, were excellent and of long standing. Collaboration in military procurement was proceeding. The succession of arguments over offset arrangements, in which British governments had weighed in alongside the US administration in demanding compensation for maintaining their forces in Germany, had reached its height in 1966–67 and were now subsiding. Shared concern over American distraction with Vietnam and impatience with what Senator Mansfield and others saw as Europe's reluctance to provide for its own defence led to the Anglo-German initiative to establish the Eurogroup, in 1968, and to the Eurogroup's European Defence Improvement Programme in 1970. For the British Labour government, anxious to demonstrate its new-found commitment to European cooperation, the Eurogroup initiative was also important as a demonstrative gesture, as was its parallel initiative to promote consultations on foreign policy through WEU, where again it met with German support and French obstruction.

Cooperation and contact between British and Fench armed forces were sharply reduced by the French withdrawal from NATO. Military links between Britain and France thus declined and remained intermittent and formal – even excessively formal – until the early 1980s. British and German officers, in contrast, served together within the NATO military command. German tank crews trained in Britain and British forces exercised in north Germany, developing, in the latter case, sophisticated liaison methods for recompensing their German hosts for the unavoidable damage they caused.

If Anglo-French military links withered, Franco-German links were less sharply affected. Geography, history and ideology again intervened to maintain the connection through even the 'purist' period of Gaullist defence policy. German officials and military staff were anxious to maintain a French conventional contribution to Germany, even under less tight obligations; withdrawal of French forces would have marked a more definitive French break with the Western Alliance. French interests in maintaining forces in Germany were mixed, and included a concern to retain a symbolic influence over German security, which would underline France's continuing responsibilities as one of the four powers responsible for Berlin. Formally the French were willing to revert to the status of occupying forces, recognising that a return to that status carried clear political undertones about French tutelage over Germany. The negotiations which led to the 'Ailleret Accords' between France and NATO and between France and Germany were hard-fought, with French participants indicating their equanimity over withdrawal and their unwillingness to accept any binding obligations.

In reality, both governments recognised the necessity of mutual military cooperation. German insecurity would have been greatly increased by a French move towards overt neutrality. German forces needed the geographical depth and the potential reinforcements; while NATO supply lines through France were formally closed, a number of German supply bases remained throughout. For France, now outside the multilateral links of NATO, the bilateral link became more significant. As French officers and defence officials modified their approach to European defence in the early 1970s, the link with Germany became also a 'back door' into NATO — an entrée into conversations about the common defence without any irrevocable commitments. The high point of Gaullist doctrine had passed with the invasion of Czechoslovakia in August 1968, with its reassertion of the dominance of military blocs and of a Soviet threat to European stability. From then on French strategic and military ideas edged slowly and silently back towards their Alliance partners, so far as the limits imposed by domestic political assumptions would allow. Agreement on a further Franco-German collaborative project, to produce a shared ground attack/trainer aircraft (the Alphajet) in 1970, symbolised this mutual commitment to go on working together in spite of the wide differences on strategy and security policy. It symbolised, too, the French drive for arms collaboration and exports, and the continuing need for German assistance in funding French procurement.

The pattern maintained — and modified, 1969—79

The 'defence card' lay to hand for any British government which wished to demonstrate its commitment to European cooperation or to closer relations with its major continental neighbours. With Germany after 1954 the 'card' represented the commitment of land and air forces to forward defence; with France it represented the potential commitment to cooperation in nuclear weapons and in arms procurement. The progressive withdrawal of British forces from East of Suez, finally agreed in late 1967, made the commitment to the central front the prime task of Britain's land and air forces. Denis Healey played on the symbolic importance of this commitment in 1968—70 in and through the Eurogroup and through bilateral conversations.

It was not open to a Labour government to play the defence card with France, in the face of substantial dissent on nuclear deterrence — and on the British deterrent — within its own party. After the bruising experience of negotiating joint procurement, attitudes within the Ministry of Defence to France as a potential partner were as cautious (even suspicious) as within the Foreign and Commonwealth Office. During the French electoral campaign which followed President de Gaulle's resignation in early 1969, M. Pompidou 'hinted that the future of common European defence lay in agreement between France and Britain; this was followed after the election by an indication of interest in Anglo-French nuclear collaboration on the part of Jacques Chaban-Delmas, the new Prime Minister'.[12] Unofficial soundings from both sides led to a visit to London from General Fourquet, President Pompidou's new Chief of Staff, in November 1969. Although there was a useful technological complementarity between British expertise in warhead design and French advances in missile propulsion and development, the political gap between Britain's continuing commitment to

NATO and to the USA and France's insistence on independence was too wide to be bridged.

The Conservative government which succeeded Harold Wilson's administration in June 1970 had fewer domestic inhibitions about nuclear issues, or about collaboration with France. Edward Heath, the new Prime Minister, had referred in his Godkin lectures at Harvard in 1967 to the long-term logic of 'an eventual European defence system', which 'in my view . . . might also include a nuclear force based on the existing British and French forces which could be held in trusteeship for Europe as a whole'.[13] During the British government's negotiations to join the European Community, between 1970 and 1972, in which Anglo-French conversations were crucial to success, there were a number of further informal discussions, and some limited public soundings.[14] But the political bargain between Heath and Pompidou was achieved without either side wishing to introduce defence deliberately into the balance. Domestic political inhibitions on the French side were too great to allow a compromise to be struck between a more self-consciously European orientation of British defence policy and a French move towards association with the Nuclear Planning Group and the integrated structure of the Alliance.

There were a number of uncomfortable contradictions between France's insistence on independence and national integrity in defence policy and its foreign policy stance as a close partner of Germany and a committed 'European' power. The Gaullist concept of a two-stage battle, in which French forces would test the intentions of an antagonist on the territorial 'approaches' to France before resorting to strategic nuclear weapons to defend the 'national sanctuary', was hard to reconcile with a political commitment to Franco-German partnership. Its implications were made still less acceptable to the German government by the development of French tactical nuclear weapons, announced by General Fourquet in 1969 as a post-Gaullist adjustment towards a strategy of flexible response. 'Pluton' tactical nuclear weapons were to be stationed in France, close to the German border, to be used on West German territory in accordance with independent French commands; their limited range underlined that their targets would also fall within West Germany.

Under Pompidou and Brandt relations between Paris and Bonn were strained by other considerations, notably French mistrust of the implications of the *Ostpolitik*. Under Schmidt and Giscard d'Estaing, from 1974, the ambiguities of French defence policy cut across a stronger mutual commitment. The response of President Giscard and of his chief of staff, General Méry, was to float, in a number of speeches in the spring and summer of 1976, the new concept of an 'extended sanctuary' for French deterrence, which would include (unspecified) contiguous European territory.[15] There were other, domestic, pressures for this attempt to revise French defence doctrines, including discontent from within the armed services at the downgrading of their conventional role, and a degree of professional scepticism within both the general staff and the diplomatic service about the Gaullist rationale. But there were also strong domestic political counterforces. The new approach was sharply attacked both from the right and the left; the socialist party, indeed, was in the process of acceding to the Gaullist consensus as the Giscardians attempted to edge away from it. The shifting balance of French defence expenditure from nuclear forces to conventional, in the second half of the 1970s, was thus not matched by any explicit shift in strategy or in the political parameters of French national defence.

The gap which therefore opened up between doctrine and practice, and between political rhetoric and the preferences and assumptions of the military, led to a certain *engrenage* between French military commanders and the NATO structure which, given its extreme political sensitivity in French domestic politics, became in the late 1970s one of the most carefully suppressed aspects of European defence cooperation. Informal contacts, observer status in Alliance discussions and joint training naturally brought the French closer to the Germans than to the British. French forces were in south-western Germany, British in northern; the non-official character of French cooperation with other forces naturally placed a greater emphasis on bilateral, rather than multilateral, collaboration. British and German land, naval and air forces worked together with Dutch, Belgian and American forces within the NATO structure. French troops relied far more on *ad hoc* links, deliberately established on a bilateral basis.

After the clutch of new cooperative ventures in the 1960s, joint procurement during the 1970s was much more a matter of development and production — and of learning the habits of working together — than of further initiatives. Competition for markets had become acute even before the oil price increases of 1973 as, under Pompidou, the French drive for arms exports became a major factor in France's economic strategy and foreign policy. French and British salesmen competed for orders in the Middle East and elsewhere, sometimes with different variants of joint projects. In contrast, the Franco-German Euromissile consortium worked well together, with the French taking the lead in sales to third markets and with a build-up of mutual confidence as the partnership progressed. Anglo-German cooperation on the Tornado (MRCA) through the Panavia consortium (with Italy) was of a different order: working at the leading edge of technological advance to produce a multi-role swing-wing aircraft, the success of the technological partnership was weighed down by the steady increase of development and production costs, which rose to dominate British and German procurement budgets at the beginning of the 1980s.

One incident in the competition for exports helped to push France back towards the idea of multilateral cooperation on a European basis.

The 'arms sale of the century', represented by the commitment of the four governments of Belgium, the Netherlands, Denmark and Norway to jointly purchase a Starfighter replacement, resolved into a Franco-American battle. A tentative British approach to offer a Jaguar—Tornado package was vigorously attacked by Dassault representatives, determined to promote the Mirage. The intensity of the competition between French and American interests unbalanced both the Belgian and the Dutch governments; French attempts to insist on a preference for the Mirage as the 'European' alternative aroused considerable irritation in Bonn and in London as well as in Brussels and The Hague.[16] The June 1975 decision in favour of the American F-16 set off an agonising reappraisal in Paris, which included a reconsideration of the desirability of remaining entirely outside the Eurogroup structure. The following year saw the establishment of the Independent European Programme Group ('Independent' in deference to the imperatives of French domestic politics) which brought British, French and German procurement officials together, along with their European partners, to consider future equipment requirements and ways in which to collaborate in meeting them. Trilateral conversations among the three major European arms producers were eased by the existence of this forum; confidential trilateral meetings on procurement issues began to follow towards the end of the 1970s.

Perhaps the most significant development in the course of the 1970s was a *non*-event: the absence of any wider political or military consequences flowing from the close working relationships between British and German forces and defence hierarchies. At the working level, co-operation remained extremely close. German ships (as well as Dutch) worked up from British naval bases, army units trained together, and defence and foreign ministry officials conferred and exchanged information regularly on topics which ranged from East—West relations to arms control. Bilateral staff talks supplemented the daily exchanges between military hierarchies through the multilateral structure of NATO. Yet at the political level there was no greater sense of mutual dependence or trust in 1979 than in 1970. The sense of distance which flowed from the Labour government's hesitant approach to the EC, the adverse German image of Britain as being preoccupied with domestic economic weakness, poor personal relations between political leaders and mutual disenchantment between the Labour Party and the SPD, the reluctance of British ministers after Denis Healey to place public political emphasis on the continental commitment all combined to deprive Britain of political credit for that commitment. Convergence between the French and German governments, in attitudes to the United States and to the continued pursuit of détente, made for an image of collaboration on defence and security policy which belied the ambiguities both of the French commitment to the defence of Germany and of French attitudes towards partnership with Germany in defence and foreign policy. At the four-power Guadeloupe summit in December 1978 the French President played a full part in discussions on NATO's nuclear strategy and on the modernisation of its theatre nuclear forces. His German colleague saw France as a valued and reliable partner, without seeking to press France to accept any of the proposed deployment of long-range theatre nuclear weapons which Schmidt insisted West Germany's neighbours must share. The contrast in attitudes and expectations from Bonn was evident: the British were expected to demonstrate their commitment to the common defence by accepting Cruise missiles without any apparent positive spin-off in Anglo-German relations; the French were excused on domestic political grounds without any apparent adverse consequences.

Yet from the perspective of Bonn the French position *was* shifting, and shifting in a way which reassured German preoccupations. The close cooperation between Giscard and Schmidt, and between the administrative machines in Paris and Bonn, made for improvements in mutual understanding and commitment which went well beyond the assumptions of the French domestic debate. By the end of the 1970s, orthodox Gaullists were sufficiently alarmed by the drift to attack the careful ambiguities of Giscardian rhetoric — the shift from insistence on 'European defence' (without American domination) to 'the defence of Europe' (within the framework of the Alliance). General Buis and Alexandre Sanguinetti refloated the idea of Franco-German nuclear cooperation in the summer of 1979, primarily to underline that a strategic doctrine of '*sanctuaire élargie*' was logically compatible only with the integration of French and German defence, and that in turn was acceptable only if West Germany was prepared to leave NATO.[17] In the spring of 1980 the defence commission of the UDF, the President's party, came out in favour of a European pillar within the Atlantic Alliance, stressing that France must be prepared to consider Europe as its theatre of operations, together with its allies, and arguing also for reopening '*le problème nucléaire*' with Britain.[18]

The intense secrecy which surrounded French defence policy, as well as the extensive use of ambiguous terminology, makes it difficult for observers to grasp the exact nature of confidential discussions. The pressures affecting French defence policy were, however, evident: the difficulties of containing the divergent demands of nuclear deterrence, intervention forces for France's continuing role in Africa, and the conventional contribution to European defence within the constraints of the defence budget; the running-down of collaborative arms production and of export orders for French armaments; strategic concerns about East—West relations, the need to reassure the Americans and above all to hold the West Germans firm to the principles of European solidarity in the face of a resurgent peace movement and of increasing pressure from the East. Successive hints from within the French administration were dropped to London, from the arrival of Mrs Thatcher's government in 1979 on, about the possibilities of an Anglo-French understanding on the Polaris replacement. But it is unlikely that these represented a settled view within the French administration; the blocked nature of the French domestic debate would not have encouraged British officials to take them further, even if the assumption of continuing Anglo-American cooperation had not been so overriding.

It was understood both in Paris and in Bonn that the question of French defence commitments could not be reopened in public until after the French presidential elections of May 1981; but it is clear that both President and Chancellor had agreed that a more open dialogue on European defence would follow Giscard's re-election. Meanwhile, the two heads of government made public efforts to reinforce each other's mutual commitment, against the counter-pulls of domestic dissent. The state visit of President Giscard d'Estaing to Germany in July 1980, which included a joint parade of French and German forces and a joint inspection of French forces in Germany, was used to demonstrate how closely the two countries 'stand together on defence questions' — as Chancellor Schmidt put it in their final press conference.[19] The debate within France, still characterised 'by a sort of theological conformity, even of intellectual terrorism', limiting the acceptability of questioning the Gaullist creed, was lagging behind evolving realities.[20]

The Franco-German dialogue

The rapid deterioration of the international climate from the beginning of 1980 onwards pushed the three governments (and indeed others) together on defence as on foreign policy, in response to American pressure as much as to Soviet. In defence terms, American expectations focused on the demand for a progressive annual increase of 3 per cent in the defence budgets of its allies, and on the deployment of long-range theatre nuclear forces (TNF) in Germany, Italy, the Low Countries and Britain. The European response, concerted first and foremost among the three capitals, combined a determined attempt to reassure the United States on their contribution to the common defence with continued efforts to keep open the possibilities of East—West negotiations and — until the last moment — of the other, arms reduction, element of the 'twin-track' decision on TNF deployment. Yet while trilateral consultations intensified on foreign and security matters, within the framework and 'the margins' of wider multilateral organisations, as well as on questions of arms procurement, the pattern of consultation on matters of strategy, tactics and military cooperation remained firmly bilateral: on a routine basis between Britain and Germany; on a new and intensive basis between France and Germany; and on a limited and more formal basis between Britain and France.

Both for Paris and for London, the relationship with Bonn was the key. The Federal Republic remained the focus of European security, its centrality increased by the uncertainties engendered by the upsurge of domestic dissent on defence and foreign policy and by its determination to maintain its links with the GDR as East–West tensions rose. The link between Bonn and Washington — much more now than the link between London and Washington — was crucial to the maintenance of the American commitment to European defence. The West German procurement budget was now much higher than either the British or the French, funding an industrial base as technologically advanced in many sectors as anything its partners had to offer.

French concern about the drift of German public opinion, and about the spectre of reunification which politicians and policy-makers in Paris saw rising behind German musings about 'national identity' and behind the priority all parties gave to maintaining a dialogue with the East, made the formulation of an active German policy appear imperative. The contradictions between the underlying trends of French defence policy and the language of the domestic debate grew more acute in 1981–82. After the narrow and unexpected socialist victory in the presidential elections, President Mitterrand appointed Charles Hernu, the architect of the Socialist Party's accession to the Gaullist consensus, as his Defence Minister; and he in turn announced a shift of resources away from conventional defence to the independent nuclear forces. Yet at the same time Mitterrand and Cheysson, the new Foreign Minister, were insisting that France was America's most reliable ally in Europe, and were publicly supporting the deployment of TNF missiles in European NATO states as necessary to the maintenance of Alliance solidarity. The most significant, and symbolic, political gesture was made by President Mitterrand in January 1983 when he vigorously supported the deployment of Pershing II and Cruise missiles in his speech to the Bundestag on the twentieth anniversary of the Franco-German treaty, supporting Chancellor Kohl against the doubts of the SPD.

The French and German governments were thus drawn towards each other as much by mutual uncertainty as by mutual commitment. The French were deeply worried about the re-emergence of neutralist and anti-American elements in the German political debate and about its potential implications for the German-American shield which protected the approaches to France's north-eastern border. The Germans were worried about a further weakening of the French conventional capability to reinforce the central front. The basis for bilateral dialogue lay to hand in the preliminary discussions between Giscard and Schmidt, and in the inoperative defence clauses of the 1963 Elysée Treaty. At the six-monthly Franco-German summit in February 1982 the two heads of government agreed to launch a defence dialogue, with senior officials grouped in three commissions under the supervision of their ministers and of the heads of government themselves.

The dialogue began under conditions of intense secrecy, largely concealed from the French public and political debate. It covered a wide agenda in its regular meetings, with both sides determined to influence perceptions and priorities within the other government. It is hard to assess how far French arguments had, by 1984, influenced German approaches to Western strategy and German perceptions of the Soviet threat — partly because French concerns were in many ways exaggerated, trying to convert their German colleagues to views they already held. German concerns were more concrete: to gain a firmer commitment to the conventional defence of Germany; to establish a framework for consultation on the deployment and potential use of French nuclear weapons; and to reopen the question of the role of French territory and French supply lines in European defence. The presentation and shape of the new *Force d'Action Rapide* (FAR), as it emerged in final form in late 1983, differed significantly from the kite-flying of a year earlier in its orientation towards the reinforcement of the central front — in response, German officials claimed, to consistent pressure within the dialogue substantially modifying the priorities of socialist defence policy set out two years before. Sceptical Germans noted that there was as yet no *definite* commitment to the defence of Germany, and that the improvement of French forces and equipment was as yet only a promise. But the sense of movement, of recognition of mutual commitment, was there. German officials who had, over the years, acquired the habit of patience and discretion in their defence relations with France took some satisfaction from M. Hernu's altered rhetoric, claiming that 'the FAR makes concrete our "alliance within the alliance" with the FRG', as evidence of a resumed *engrenage* between France and the common defence.[21]

Britain stood aside from this intensifying Franco-German relationship. It felt no need to reinforce its relationships with Germany: they were already close, they worked quietly and well, and seemed to British ministers and officials not to require any new political emphasis. The Conservative government which came to office in 1979 was less hesitant about European economic cooperation than its Labour predecessor, but differed little from its predecessor in the Atlantic orientation of its defence policy. At the Anglo-French Conference in Bordeaux in September 1980 Mrs Thatcher declared 'that Britain stands ready at any time to develop fuller and closer defence collaboration with France' — a statement which accompanying 'informed sources' suggested was intended to include 'room for working with France on the patrolling and targeting of both countries' nuclear submarine forces'.[22] However, little effort was made on either side against the weight of bureaucratic and political inhibitions in Paris and in London to follow this up. British reactions to the Franco-German defence dialogue were largely sceptical; among those few officials who were aware of its existence it was seen more as another French effort to bring political pressure to bear on Bonn to agree to new projects for joint procurement than as a development of major political importance.

Discretion and secrecy still characterised a number of aspects of each bilateral relationship. Attempts to assess the pattern and extent of military exchanges between the three countries' armed services in 1982—83 revealed a common perception in Bonn and in London that each country's bilateral exchanges with the French were less extensive than the other's; French officials were unwilling to talk about the subject at all, although indications suggested little difference in reality between such links with its partners. Politico-military conversations among the three capitals proceeded at the same rate and with a similar degree of trust and confidentiality. The differences lay at the political level where the visibility of the Franco-German bilateral relationship and the willingness of both sides to invest it with symbolic significance contrasted with the low-key approach to *both* relationships from London. Personalities, as well as political assumptions, do count, in defence as much as in other fields of intergovernmental politics: the replacement of the reserved John Nott by the more flamboyant Michael Heseltine in January 1983 made a positive impact on relations with Bonn, although continuing scepticism about a European dimension to Atlantic defence still limited British attention to the bilateral links with Bonn and Paris.

The hiatus in arms collaboration which continued through the early 1980s demonstrated the limits to which political commitment could overcome technical, industrial and service interests. In 1979 Giscard and Schmidt committed themselves publicly to the development of a common main battle tank, overriding entrenched objections in the way they had successfully done in establishing the EMS two years before. Efforts to agree on a joint concept and design struggled on for three years against the scepticism of German industrial and service representatives, and the unwillingness of French participants to accept German technological leadership, before the determined opposition of the Bundestag defence committee persuaded the heads of government that the project was dead. Thus the sole outcome of intense pressures for new initiatives on Franco-German arms collaboration was an agreement to produce a joint anti-tank helicopter. The developing debate on a future European fighter aircraft, under active discussion in 1984—85, illustrated the continuing vigour of Anglo-French industrial rivalry, with Germany as the prize to be won. Both Dassault and British Aerospace claimed superiority for their designs and experimental aircraft, and both companies briefed the press extensively against each other. British hopes for German preference rested partly on the experience of the Panavia/Tornado consortium, French on the political weight attached to defence cooperation within the closer Franco-German partnership. In early 1985 the press in each of the three countries was resounding with charges of sharp practice and unreasonable demands against their partners, including much criticism within the German press of Dassault's demands for design leadership and a dominant share in the consortium.

The revival of debate on European defence cooperation in 1984 demonstrated how far the Franco-German relationship had now become the focus of German concerns, in spite of (or partly because of) the anomalies and contradictions of French defence policy. Britain had become an important third partner, to be caught up — in so far as it was willing — in any new Franco-German initiatives. But its reluctance to pursue an active policy towards its Continental partners, its continuing transatlantic orientation, the weakness of its political commitment, in spite of the strength of its military contribution, had all reduced its standing. The proposal to revive Western European Union as a forum for European defence cooperation, with the German government coming in early 1984 to support (while modifying) a long-held French objective, was justified by a senior German official as having the advantages of '2 plus 5': that is, of providing a multilateral framework for the core Franco-German dialogue.[23] That dialogue was at the centre of European defence and security partly — as was argued at the outset — for reasons of geography and history. But it had also become the centre of the European defence debate because its French and German participants had worked to make it so, overcoming their differences and mutual suspicions. Their British partners, after the initial turn towards a European defence priority in the late 1960s, had failed to sustain their effort or their political commitment, and had thus become a subsidiary factor, rather than the coping-stone in the arch which might have built a triangular relationship. It remained unclear, however, how far the French government would go in translating its rhetoric into the hard commitments which its less deferential German partner was now likely to demand; and also whether the 'fourth dimension' of American pressures on their three major West European allies would push them further together or apart.

Notes

1. Quoted in Edward Fursdon, *The European Defence Community: a History* (London, Macmillan, 1980), p. 321.

2. On the 1957 defence review, see William Wallace, 'Defence without Tears?' in Vernon Bogdanor and Robert Skidelsky (eds), *The Age of Affluence: Britain in the 1950s* (London, Macmillan, 1970).

3. Andrew Pierre, *Nuclear Politics: the British Experience with an Independent Strategic Force, 1939–70* (Oxford University Press, 1972), Chapter 6; Lothar Ruehl, *La Politique Militaire de la Cinquième Republique* (Paris, Fondation Nationale des Sciences Politiques, 1976), Chapter 4.

4. Donald C. Watt, *Britain Looks to Germany* (London, Wolff, 1965); Catherine M. Kelleher, *Germany and the Politics of Nuclear Weapons* (New York, Columbia University Press, 1975), Chapter 5.

5. Wilfrid L. Kohl, *French Nuclear Diplomacy* (Princeton, N.J., Princeton University Press, 1971), Chapter 1; Kelleher, op.cit.

6. Pierre, op.cit., p. 222.

7. Kelleher, op.cit., p. 102.

8. On early attempts at collaboration in procurement, see the series of six papers on *Defence, Technology and the Atlantic Alliance* (London, International Institute for Strategic Studies, 1967).

9. John Calman, *European Cooperation in Defence Technology: the Political Aspect*, IISS series, no. 1, p. 9.

10. On the offset argument, see Gregory F. Treverton, *The Dollar Drain and American Forces in Germany* (Ohio University Press, 1978).

11. Ruehl, op.cit., Chapters 9 and 10.

12. Pierre, op.cit., p. 297.

13. Edward Heath, *Old World, New Horizons: Britain, the Common Market and the Atlantic Alliance* (Oxford University Press, 1970), p. 73.

14. See, for example, Ian Smart, *Future Conditional: the Prospect for Anglo-French Nuclear Collaboration*, Adelphi Paper no. 78 (London, International Institute for Strategic Studies, 1971).

15. Their major speeches were reprinted in *Defense Nationale*, June and July 1976.

16. Ingemar Dorfer, *Arms Deal* (New York, Praeger, 1983).

17. *Nouvel Observateur*, 20 August 1979 and 10 September 1979.

18. *Le Monde*, 26 April 1980. For background, see David S. Yost, 'The French Defence Debate', *Survival*, January/February 1981, pp. 19–28.

19. *The Times*, 12 July 1980.

20. The quotation is from the president of the UDF Defence Commission, J-M. Daillet, writing in *Le Monde*, 16 July 1980. François de Rose, one of the most active proponents of revisionism in French defence policy, used exactly the same language in *Le Monde*, 21 May 1981, in which he attacked orthodox Gaullism as 'uniquemont fondée sur la sanctuarisation du territoire, autrement dit la neutralité . . .'.

21. *Le Monde*, 5 November 1983, cited in David S. Yost, *France and Conventional Defense in Central Europe* (Marina del Rey, California, European American Institute for Security Research, 1984) which provides an excellent survey of these developments in French policy. Other information on the Franco-German dialogue is drawn from interviews in Bonn and Paris in 1982–84.

22. *The Times*, 22 September 1980.

23. On the WEU initiative, see William Wallace, 'European Defence Cooperation: the reopening debate', *Survival*, November/December 1984. For a dissenting German opinion from an SPD member of the Bundestag defence committee, arguing that the British commitment is more valuable to Germany than the uncertain dialogue with France, see Hermann Scheer, 'Der Zerfall wäre programmiert', *Der Spiegel*, no. 8, 1985, pp. 112–13.

14 Conclusion
Roger Morgan

Any attempt to draw conclusions from the evidence of this study must try to bring the needs of future policy together with the lessons of past experience.

As far as the needs of the future are concerned, it is now accepted more widely and more strongly than ever in London, Paris and Bonn that the three countries must work to overcome elements of rivalry and conflicting purpose which still divide them, and cooperate more closely for the survival and prosperity of Europe. It has long been a concern of British policy — sometimes effectively pursued, sometimes not — to develop London's links with Paris and Bonn into something approaching the intimate partnership prevailing between these two, so that the triangle becomes more evenly balanced. In Paris, also, there have been successive efforts to woo London, as well as Bonn, for attempts to shape the European Community, or the Western Alliance, according to a common design inspired by France. Although it has been a relatively new experience to find leading German spokesmen openly stressing the vital role of this group of countries, this theme is now prominent in German thinking; for instance, Chancellor Kohl's foreign policy adviser, Helmut Teltschik, argues in a paper of March 1985 that progress towards more effective European cooperation 'will depend primarily on three governments: the French, the British and the German'.[1]

It is clear that the three, who between them represent two-thirds of the EC's economic strength, hold Europe's future in their hands in a way that other member states do not: although it is not necessarily true that anything jointly agreed by London, Paris and Bonn can be carried out, it is certainly true that nothing decisive can happen in the Community — whether in institutional reform or changes in the balance of policies — unless they *do* agree. The same applies to any attempt at creating a more cohesive and effective West European entity in the defence field, through WEU or otherwise. The pressures of the 1980s, whether in economic affairs, East—West relations, or 'West—West' relations, are forcing the three capitals even more strongly towards cooperation, and they are increasingly persuaded of the need to upgrade their common interests and overcome conflicts.

As for the experience of the past, on which endeavours for the future must build, the analytical sections of this study have indicated many sorts of strengths and weaknesses in the relationships between the three countries. Each relationship is indeed *sui generis* (partly because the same is true of the countries involved in it) and each relationship is, moreover, made up of a great variety of different strands. Two countries which are in close agreement on some areas of policy — defence, for instance — may disagree seriously on trade or industrial policies. Some important sections of a national governmental machine may communicate easily with their counterparts in another capital — as the British Treasury and the French Finance Ministry appear to do — while the foreign ministries of the same two countries still tend to regard each other as deadly rivals.

The record shows that each of the contrasting explanations for a 'good' bilateral relationship — personal confidence between leaders, the attempt to avert conflicts by elaborate bureaucratic mechanisms, or the compatibility of long-term or short-term interests — may in certain cases be the valid one, or that the 'mix' of different factors may vary from case to case.

The record also shows relationships between capitals changing perceptibly over a period of time, and that even good relations need to be carefully tended if they are to continue to flourish. Perhaps the most important single lesson to be learned from the Franco-German relationship is that the close agreement between these two countries has been based not so much on any objectively predetermined harmony of interests as on the political decision, sustained at the highest levels over a long period, that the relationship required constant private nurturing and public demonstrations in order to be effective. When, for instance, Bonn and Paris found themselves, in May 1985, in serious public discord on at least three important issues — the correct timing of a new round of international trade talks, the implications of Washington's Strategic Defence Initiative, and the level of EC grain prices — they both gave urgent priority to reconciling their conflicts at or before the next in the frequent series of Franco-German summits. The example of what can be achieved with this kind of conscious political purpose should be pondered by those who argue, like British officials for instance, that Britain and Germany 'get along well together without trying too hard to do so'.

If more conscious effort — in making political capital from objective aspects of cooperation, or gearing information and cultural policies more deliberately to long-term political goals — could benefit bilateral relationships, the same applies to the design of working for a better triangular one. When we turn from the management of short-term policy differences to changes which might provide a better basis for avoiding or coping with differences in the long term, several lines of action suggest themselves.

First, the lines of communication between the higher levels of national political systems could be opened further, and more effort could be given to attempting to foresee which issues will require the attention of national leaders and which will not. There are times when it is necessary for the heads of government to be involved in resolving specific issues — like the Franco-German differences of May 1985, mentioned above — but on other occasions their time could be saved for more important long-term considerations if particular problems could be foreseen and resolved at lower levels.

Second, and following from this, there is a strong case for a substantial increase in civil service exchanges between the three countries. The existing cooperation in the training of civil servants discussed in this study is a good beginning, but there is room for a much wider system of exchanges at the working level, to familiarise junior officials with the administrative practices of the other countries and to prepare them to cope with the problems which will certainly face them later, as a result of the inescapable interdependence of the modern world.

Third, the parliamentary dimension of bilateral relationships should be augmented. The working encounters between parliamentarians, and above all between specialist parliamentary committees, mentioned in Chapter 7, provide a basis for cooperation which should be extended. In some cases, the parliamentarians of today will be the ministers of tomorrow; in all cases, the experience of contacts will help parliamentarians to carry out their function of mediating between the concerns of their electors and those of the world of politics, whether national or European.

Fourth, more efforts should be made to communicate to the public — especially through the mass media — the views and analyses of expert bodies concerned with relations between France, Britain, and Germany. Such 'élite' gatherings as the Anglo-German Königswinter conferences, the meetings of the Franco-British Council or the Franco-German Institute, or the research and other specialist activities which underlie them, have too little impact both on the political and administrative decision-makers of the three countries, and on the public as a whole.

Fifth, there is a great need for an expansion in the teaching of the languages, history and contemporary aspects of each of the three countries at all levels of their educational systems. The limitations in this area have been indicated in Chapters 4 and 5. However, it is clear that greater knowledge and understanding would provide a firmer basis for managing the problems which will inevitably arise even between countries as closely involved with each other as Britain, France and Germany.

One of the fundamental lessons of this study is that the three countries are deeply interdependent in a large number of ways. The challenge that faces them is that of how to devise methods for the management of this interdependence, and how to pool their substantial resources for common purposes.

Notes
1. 'The Future of the European Community', unpublished paper by Helmut
   Teltschik, Foreign Affairs Adviser to Bundeskanzler Kohl, March 1985.

Appendix: the Text of the Franco-German Treaty of Cooperation[1]

Franco-German Treaty
signed in Paris on 22nd January 1963

Joint Declaration

The Chancellor of the Federal Republic of Germany, Dr. Konrad Adenauer, and the President of the French Republic, General de Gaulle,

At the close of the conference held in Paris on 21st and 22nd January 1963 and attended on the German side by the Federal Minister of Foreign Affairs, the Federal Minister of Defence and the Federal Minister for Family and Youth Affairs, and on the French side by the Prime Minister, the Foreign Minister, the Armed Forces Minister and the Minister of Education,

Convinced that the reconciliation of the German people and the French people, ending a centuries-old rivalry, constitutes a historic event which profoundly transforms the relations between the two peoples,

Conscious of the solidarity uniting the two peoples from the point of view of both their security and their economic and cultural development,

Aware in particular that youth has recognised this solidarity and is called upon to play a decisive part in the consolidation of Franco-German friendship,

Recognising that increased co-operation between the two countries constitutes an indispensable stage on the way to a united Europe, which is the aim of the two peoples:

Have agreed to the organisation and principles of co-operation between the two States as set out in the treaty signed today.

Done at Paris on 22nd January 1963 in duplicate in the German and French languages.

The Chancellor
of the Federal Republic of Germany
Adenauer

The President
of the French Republic
C. de Gaulle

The Treaty

Pursuant to the joint declaration of the Chancellor of the Federal Republic of Germany and the President of the French Republic, dated 22nd January 1963, on the organisation and principles of co-operation between the two States, the following provisions have been agreed to:

I. Organisation

1. The Heads of State and Government shall give the necessary directives as required and shall follow regularly the implementation of the programme hereinafter laid down. To this end, they shall meet as and whenever required, and, in principle, at least twice a year.

2. The Foreign Ministers shall ensure the execution of the programme as a whole. They shall meet at least once every three months. Without prejudicing the contacts normally established through embassies, the senior officials of the two Foreign Ministries in charge of political, economic, and cultural affairs respectively, shall meet each month alternately in Bonn and Paris to review the state of affairs on hand and prepare the meeting of Ministers. Furthermore, the diplomatic missions and the consulates of the two countries, as well as their permanent delegations to international organisations, shall make all necessary contacts regarding problems of common interest.

3. Regular meetings shall take place between the responsible authorities of the two countries in the fields of defence, education and youth. They shall in no way impair the functioning of already existing bodies — Franco-German Cultural Commission, Permanent Group of General Staffs — whose activities shall, on the contrary, be developed. The Foreign Ministers shall be represented at these meetings to ensure the overall co-ordination of co-operation.

    (*a*)   The Defence and Armed Forces Ministers shall meet at least once every three months. Likewise the French Minister of Education shall meet at similar intervals the person who shall be designated on the German side to follow the execution of the programme of co-operation on the cultural plane.

    (*b*)   The Chiefs of Staff of the two countries shall meet at least once every two months; should they be unable to attend, they shall be replaced by their responsible representatives.

    (*c*)   The Federal Minister for Family and Youth Affairs or his representative shall meet the French High Commissioner for Youth and Sports at least once every two months.

4. In each of the two countries an inter-ministerial commission shall be charged with following the problems of co-operation. It shall be presided over by a senior official of the Foreign Ministry and shall include representatives of all departments concerned. Its rôle shall be to co-ordinate the action of the departments concerned and to report periodically to its government on the state of Franco-German co-operation. It shall also have the task of presenting any appropriate suggestions for the execution of the programme of co-operation and its possible extension to new fields.

II. Programme

A. Foreign Affairs

1. The two Governments shall consult each other, prior to any decision, on all important questions of foreign policy and in the first place on questions of common interest, with a view to reaching, as far as possible, an analogous position. This consultation shall bear, among others, on the following subjects:

- problems relating to the European Communities and to European political co-operation,
- East—West relations both on the political and economic planes,
- matters dealt with in the North Atlantic Treaty Organisation and the various international organisations and in which both Governments are interested, notably in the Council of Europe, Western European Union, the Organisation for Economic Co-operation and Development, the United Nations and its specialised agencies.

2. The collaboration already established in the field of information shall be continued and developed between the services concerned in Bonn and Paris and between the missions in third countries.

3. With regard to development aid, the two Governments shall systematically compare their programmes with a view to maintaining close co-ordination. They shall study the possibility of undertaking joint projects. Several ministerial departments being competent for these questions on the German side as on the French side, it shall be the task of the two Foreign Ministries to determine in common the practical bases of this collaboration.

4. The two Governments shall study jointly the means of reinforcing their co-operation within the framework of the Common Market, in other important sectors of economic policy, such as agriculture and forestry policy, energy, problems of communications and transport and of industrial development, as well as the policy of export credits.

B. Defence

I. In this field the following objectives shall be pursued:

1. In the field of strategy and tactics the competent authorities of the two countries shall endeavour mutually to approximate their doctrines with a view to reaching common concepts. Franco-German institutes of operational research shall be set up.

2. Exchanges of personnel between the armed forces shall be increased: such exchanges shall in particular concern instructors and students of the general staff colleges; they may include the temporary detachment of entire units. In order to facilitate these exchanges an effort shall be made on both sides concerning practical language teaching to the trainees.

3. With regard to armaments the two Governments shall endeavour to organise work in common beginning at the stage of drawing up suitable armament projects and of preparing plans to finance them.

To this end mixed commissions shall survey current research undertaken on such projects in the two countries and shall carry out a comparative examination of them. These commissions shall submit proposals to the ministers who shall examine them at their quarterly meetings and shall give the necessary directives for implementation.

II. The governments shall study the conditions on which Franco-German collaboration can be established in the field of civil defence.

C. Education and Youth

As regards education and youth, the proposals contained in the French and German memoranda of 19th September and 8th November 1962 shall be studied according to the procedures set out above.

1. In the field of education efforts shall be concentrated mainly on the following points:

(a) Language instruction

The two governments recognise the vital importance for Franco-German co-operation attaching to knowledge in each of the two countries of the other country's language. They shall therefore strive to take concrete measures to increase the number of German pupils learning French and the number of French pupils learning German.

The Federal Government shall examine with the Laender governments, who are competent in this respect, how arrangements can be made which will permit the achievement of this aim.

It appears appropriate to arrange, in all establishments of higher education, for practical instruction of the German language in France and of the French language in Germany, open to all students.

(b) The problem of equivalences

The competent authorities in both countries shall be invited to speed up the adoption of regulations concerning the equivalence of terms of study, examinations, university degrees and diplomas.

(c) Co-operation on scientific research

Research organisations and scientific institutions shall develop their contacts, beginning with more comprehensive mutual information; co-ordinated research programmes shall be set up in branches of science where this is feasible.

2. Young people in the two countries shall be given every opportunity to strengthen the bonds between them and to increase their mutual understanding. In particular, collective exchanges shall be further developed.

A body for developing these opportunities and promoting the exchanges, shall be set up by the two countries, headed by an autonomous Board. This body shall have at its disposal a joint Franco-German fund to be used for meetings and exchanges between the two countries of school-children, students, young artisans and workmen.

III. Final Provisions

1. The necessary directives shall be issued in each country immediately to implement the above. At each of their meetings the Foreign Ministers shall review the progress made.

2. The two Governments shall keep the governments of the other member States of the European Communities informed of the development of Franco-German co-operation.

3. Apart from the clauses concerning defence, this Treaty shall also apply to Land Berlin, provided that the Government of the Federal Republic of Germany has not made a contrary declaration to the Government of the French Republic within three months from the date of entry into force of this Treaty.

4. The two governments may make such adjustments as may appear desirable for carrying out this Treaty.

5. The present Treaty shall enter into force on the date on which each of the two contracting parties shall have informed the other party that its constitutional requirements for such entry into force have been fulfilled.

Done at Paris on 22nd January 1963 in duplicate, in the German and French languages, both texts being equally authentic.

The Chancellor of
the Federal Republic of Germany
Adenauer

The Minister of Foreign Affairs
of the Federal Republic of Germany
Schröder

The President of the French Republic
C. de Gaulle

The French Prime Minister
Pompidou

The French Foreign Minister
M. Couve de Murville

Preamble to the Act
of Ratification of the Franco-German Treaty by the Bundestag

Convinced that the Treaty concluded on 22nd January 1963 between the Federal Republic of Germany and the French Republic will intensify and develop the reconciliation and friendship between the German and the French peoples,

Stating that this Treaty does not affect the rights and obligations resulting from multilateral treaties concluded by the Federal Republic of Germany.

Resolved to serve by the application of this Treaty the great aims to which the Federal Republic of Germany, in concert with the other States allied to her, has aspired, for years, and which determine her policy, to wit, the preservation and consolidation of the unity of the free nations and in particular of a close partnership between Europe and the United States of America, the realisation of the right of self-determination for the German people, and the restoration of German unity, collective defence within the framework of the North Atlantic Alliance, and the integration of the armed forces of the States bound together in that Alliance, the unification of Europe by following the course adopted by the establishment of the European Communities, with the inclusion of Great Britain and other States wishing to accede, and the further strengthening of those Communities, the elimination of trade barriers by negotiations between the European Economic Community, Great Britain, and the United States of America as well as other States within the framework of the General Agreement on Tariffs and Trade,

Conscious that a Franco-German co-operation inspired by such aims will benefit all nations and serve the peace of the world and will thereby also promote the welfare of the German and French peoples,

The Bundestag enacts the following Law:

1. Assembly of the Western European Union, *Proceedings, 9th Ordinary Session*, 1st Part, June 1963, I: Assembly Documents, Paris, 1963, The Text of the Franco-German Treaty of Cooperation, pp. 129–32.

Bibliography

This bibliography is mainly limited to books of general importance. References to more specialised works, and to articles and other sources relevant to specific sections in this book, will be found in the notes to the chapter or chapters in question.

Many articles on aspects of the subject will be found in the daily and weekly press and in a variety of journals, including in particular the following: *Allemagnes d'Aujourd'hui; Documents; Dokumente; Europa-Archiv; Foreign Affairs; International Affairs; International Relations; Journal of Common Market Studies; Politique Etrangère; Revue d'Allemagne; Survival; West European Politics; The World Today.*

For a comprehensive list of books and articles on Franco-German relations (and many other related issues) see Dieter Menyesch and Bérénich Manach, *France-Allemagne. Relations internationales et interdépendances bilatérales. Une bibliographie 1963—1982* (München, New York, London, Paris, Saur, 1984).

The following bibliography is divided into four sections: general and historical studies; cultural, media and public opinion issues; economic and industrial aspects; foreign and defence policies and the European Community.

General and historical studies

Aberbach, J.D., Putnam, R.A. and Rockman, B.A., *Bureaucrats and Politicians in Western Democracies* (Cambridge, Mass., and London, Harvard University Press, 1981).

Baring, A., *Machtwechsel: Die Ära Brandt-Scheel* (Stuttgart, Deutsche Verlags-Anstalt, 1982).

Birnbaum, P., *The Heights of Power. An Essay on the Power Elite in France*, English translation (Chicago, University of Chicago Press, 1982).

Birrenbach, K., *Meine Sondermissionen. Rückschau auf zwei Jahrzehnte bundesdeutscher Aussenpolitik* (Düsseldorf, Econ Verlag, 1984).

Breitenstein, R. (ed.), *Pillars of Partnership* (London, Oswald Wolff, 1978).

Cobb, R., *French and Germans, Germans and French* (Hanover, New Hampshire, and London, University Press of New England, 1983).

Cohen, S., *Les Conseillers du Président, de Charles de Gaulle à Valéry Giscard d'Estaing* (Paris, Presses Universitaires de France, 1980).

Frank, P., *Entschlüsselte Botschaft* (Stuttgart, Deutsche Verlags-Anstalt, 1981).

Fursdon, E., *The European Defence Community: A History* (London, Macmillan, 1980).

Grosser, A. (ed.), *Les Politiques Extérieures Européennes dans la Crise* Travaux et recherches de Science Politique no.43, (Paris, Presses de la Fondation Nationale des Sciences Politiques, 1976).

Grosser, A., *The Western Alliance* (London, Macmillan, 1978).

Guttsman, W.L., *The British Political Elite* (London, McGibbon & Kee, 1968).

Howorth, J. and Cerny, P.G. (eds), *Elites in France: Origins, Reproduction and Power* (London, Frances Pinter, 1981).

Kaiser, K. and Morgan, R. (eds), *Britain and West Germany: Changing Societies and the Future of Foreign Policy* (London, Oxford University Press for Royal Institute of International Affairs, 1971).

Keezer, D.M., *A Unique Contribution to International Relations: the Story of Wilton Park* (London, etc., McGraw-Hill, 1973).

Lasserre, R., Neumann, W., Picht, R. (eds), *Deutschland—Frankreich. Bausteine zum Systemvergleich*, 2 vols. (Stuttgart, Deutsch-Französisches Institut and Robert Bosch Stiftung, 1980—81).

Manfrass, K. (ed.), *Paris—Bonn: Eine dauerhafte Bindung schwieriger Partner. Beiträge zum deutsche-französischen Verhältnis in Kultur, Wirtschaft und Politik seit 1949* (Sigmaringen, Jan Thorbecke Verlag, 1984).

Morgan, R., *West European Politics since 1945: the shaping of the European Community* (London, Batsford, 1973).

Morgan, R. and Silvestri, S. (eds), *Moderates and Conservatives in Western Europe: Political Parties, the European Community and the Atlantic Alliance*, European Centre for Political Studies (London, Heinemann Educational Books for PSI, 1982).

Newman, M., *Socialism and European Unity: the Dilemma of the Left in Britain and France* (London, Junction Books, 1983).

Picht, R. (ed.), *Das Bündnis im Bündnis. Deutsch-Französische Beziehungen im internationalen Spannungsfeld* (Berlin, Severin & Siedler, 1982).

Picht, R. (ed.), *Deutschland—Frankreich—Europa. Bilanz einer schwierigen Partnerschaft* (Munich, Piper, 1978).

Picht, R. (ed.), *Kulturpolitik für Europa* (Bonn, Europa Union Verlag, 1977).

Poidevin, R. and Bariéty, J., *Frankreich und Deutschland: die Geschichte ihrer Beziehungen 1815—1975* (Munich, Beck, 1982).

Pompidou, G., *Pour Rétablir une Vérité* (Paris, Flammarion, 1982).
Putnam, R.D., *The Comparative Study of Political Elites* (Englewood Cliffs, N.J., Prentice-Hall, 1976).
Richardson, J. (ed.), *Policy Styles in Western Europe* (London, Allen & Unwin, 1982).
Ridley, F.F. (ed.), *Government and Administration in Western Europe* (Oxford, Martin Robertson, 1979).
Schmid, C., *Erinnerungen* (Bern, Munich, Vienna, Scherz Verlag, 1979).
Schmid, C. and Lapie, P.-O., *Die deutsch-französische Zusammenarbeit* (Bonn, Presse-und Informationsamt der Bundesregierung, 1973).
Schwarz, H.-P. (ed.), *Handbuch der deutschen Aussenpolitik* (Munich, Piper, 1975).
Volle, A., *Deutsch-britische Beziehungen 1945–1975* (Doctoral thesis, Bonn, Rheinische Friedrich-Wilhelms-Universität, 1976).
Volle, A., *Deutsch-britische Beziehungen. Geschichte und Gegenwart*, Politik kurz und aktuel no.43 (Berlin, Landeszentrale für politische Bildungsarbeit, 1985).
Waites, N. (ed.), *Troubled Neighbours: Franco-British Relations in the Twentieth Century* (London, Weidenfeld and Nicolson, 1971).
Watt, D.C., *Britain Looks to Germany* (London, Wolff, 1965).

Cultural, media and public opinion issues

Blumler, J.G. (ed.), *Communicating to Voters* (London, Beverly Hills and New Delhi, Sage, 1983).
Böttcher, W., *Deutschland aus britischer Sicht 1960–72* (Wiesbaden, Humanitas, 1972).
Boyer, B.M., *L'étude scientifique des stéréotypes nationaux dans les rapports franco-allemands* (Paris, Université de Paris I, 1972).
Buchanan, W. and Cantril, H., *How Nations See Each Other* (Urbana, Unesco, University of Illinois Press, 1953).
Central Policy Review Staff, *Review of Overseas Representation* (London, HMSO, 1977).
Dalton, R.J. and Duval, R., *The Political Environment and Foreign Policy Opinions: British Attitudes toward European Integration, 1972–79* (Tallahassee, Florida State University, and Morgantown, West Virginia University, February 1984).
'Dialogues franco-allemands', *Dialogues de France-Culture*, no.4 (Paris, France-Culture/Goethe Institut, 1976).
'Dialogues franco-britanniques', *Dialogues de France-Culture*, no.5 (Paris, Editions Menges, 1978).
Donaldson, F., *The British Council. The First Fifty Years* (London, Cape, 1984).
Farquharson, J.E. and Holt, S.C., *Europe from Below* (London, Allen & Unwin, 1975).
Gallup, G.H., *The Gallup International Public Opinion Polls: Great Britain, 1937–75*, 2 vols. (Westport, Ct., Greenwood Press, 1976).

Gallup Poll, *Attitudes to European Countries* (London, Social Surveys (Gallup Poll) Ltd., August 1983).

Grunert, T., *Langzeitwirkungen von Städte-Partnerschaften* (Kehl am Rhein/Strasbourg, Engel Verlag, 1981).

Halloran, J.O., Gray, P. and West, G., *Mass Media, Sport and International Understanding* (Centre for Mass Communication Research, University of Leicester, 1981).

Information et Communication. Les média et les relations franco-allemandes (Special number of *Documents*, Paris, December 1979).

Inglehart, R. and Rabier, J.-R., 'Trust between Nations: Primordial Ties, Societal Learning and Economic Development' (paper presented at XIIth World Congress of Political Science, Rio de Janeiro, IPSA, August 1982).

Jervis, R., *Perception and Misperception in International Politics* (Princeton, N.J., Princeton University Press, 1976).

Ménudier, H., *Das Deutschlandbild der Franzosen in den 70er Jahren* (Bonn, Europa Union Verlag, 1981).

Ministère des relations extérieures, Direction-Générale des Relations Culturelles, Scientifiques et Techniques, *Le projet culturel extérieur de la France* (Paris, La Documentation Française, 1983).

Myerscough, J., *Funding the Arts in Europe*, Studies in European Politics, no.8 (London, Policy Studies Institute, 1984).

Noelle-Neumann, E. (ed.)., *The Germans. Public Opinion Polls, 1967–80* (Westport Ct./London, Institut für Demoskopie Allensbach, Greenwood Press, 1981).

Office franco-allemand pour la Jeunesse/Deutsch-Französisches Jugendwerk, *Directives (Richtlinien)* (Paris/Bureau Permanent, Bad Honnef, Generalsekretariat, 1984).

Prix Jeunesse Foundation, *Young TV Viewers and their Images of Foreigners* (including summary by Halloran, J.D. and Nightingale, V.), (Munich, Stiftung Prix Jeunesse International, 1982).

Robert Bosch Stiftung/Deutsch-Französisches Institut, *Deutsch-Französische Kulturbeziehungen. Bilanz und Vorschläge* (Stuttgart/Ludwigsburg, R. Bosch/Deutsch-Französisches Institut, 1981).

Shepherd, R.J., *Public Opinion and European Integration* (Farnborough and Lexington, Mass., Saxon House/Lexington Books, 1975).

SOFRES, *L'image de l'Allemagne Fédérale*, SOFRES (La Société française d'études et de sondages), Montrouge, February 1983.

SOFRES, *L'image comparée de la France et de l'Allemagne de l'Ouest*, Montrouge, May 1983.

SOFRES, *L'opinion française et l'Allemagne entre 1973 et 1979*, Montrouge, February 1979.

Tiemann, D., *Frankreich- und Deutschlandbilder im Widerstreit. Urteile französischer und deutscher Schüler über die Nachbarn am Rhein* (Bonn, Europa Union Verlag, 1982).

Trouillet, B., *Das deutsch-französische Verhältnis im Spiegel von Kultur und Sprache* (Weinheim, Beltz Verlag, 1981).

Economic and industrial aspects

Boltho, A. (ed.), *The European Economy: Growth and Crisis* (Oxford, Oxford University Press, 1982), chapters on West Germany by K.H. Hennings, France by C. Sautter, and the UK by M. Surrey.

Borrus, M., *Responses to the Japanese Challenge in High Technology: Innovation, Maturity and US-Japanese Competition in Microelectronics* (BRIE, 1983).

Commission of the European Communities, *European Economy*, no.18, (Brussels, Commission of the EC, November 1983).

Commission of the European Communities, *Television without Frontiers*, Green Paper on the Establishment of the Common Market for Broadcasting, especially by Satellite and Cable (Brussels, Commission of the EEC, 300 Final, 1984).

Dalmas, P., *Le Cow-Boy et le Samourai: Réflexions sur la Compétition Nippo-Américaine dans les Hautes Technologies* (Paris, Ministère des Relations Extérieures. Centre d'analyse et de prévision, January 1984).

Hagrup, K., *The Aerospace-Industry of Western Europe* (Stockholm, 1980).

Hamel, G., *Renversement des Alliances: l'Histoire de l'Unidata* (Paris).

Horn, E.-J., *Management of Industrial Change in Germany*, Sussex European Papers no.13 (Brighton, Sussex European Research Centre, 1982).

Keizer, B., *Le Modèle Economique Allemand: Mythes et Réalitiés* (Paris, La Documentation Française, 1979).

Layton, C., *European Advanced Technology* (London, Allen & Unwin for PEP, 1968).

Messerlin, P., *Managing Industrial Change in France*, mimeo (Brighton, Sussex European Research Centre, 1983).

Organisation for Economic Cooperation and Development, *Trade in High-Technology Products/The Semi-conductor Industry: Industrial Structure and Government Policies* (Paris, OECD, 1984).

Organisation for Economic Cooperation and Development, *Trade in High-Technology Products/The Space Products Industry: Markets, Industrial Structure and Government Policies* (Paris, OECD, 1984).

Olson, M., *The Rise and Decline of Nations* (London, Yale University Press, 1982).

Sawers, D., *The technical development of modern aviation* (London, Routledge & Kegan Paul, 1968).

Schatz, K.-W. and Wolter, F., *International Trade, Employment and Structural Adjustment: the Case Study of the Federal Republic of Germany*, World Employment Programme Research Working Papers (Geneva, International Labour Office, 1982).

Servan-Schreiber, J.J., *Le Défi Americain* (Paris, Denoel, 1967).

Sharp, M., Shepherd, G. and Marsden, D., *Structural Adjustment in the United Kingdom Manufacturing Industry*, World Employment Programme Research Working Papers (Geneva, International Labour Office, 1983).

Shonfield, A., *Modern Capitalism: the Changing Balance of Public and Private Power*, (London, University Press for Royal Institute of International Affairs, 1965).

van Tulder, B. and Junne, G., *European Multinationals in the Telecommunications Industry* (University of Amsterdam, June 1984).

US Department of Commerce, *Assessment of US Competitiveness in High Technology Industries* (Washington DC, US Department of Commerce, February 1983).

Verner, Lipfert, Bernhard and McPherson, *Effect of Government Targeting on World Semiconductor Competition: The Case History of Japanese Industrial Strategy and its Costs for America* (Semiconductor Industry Association).

Foreign and defence policies and the European Community

Allen, D. *et al.*, *European Political Co-operation: Towards a Foreign Policy for Western Europe* (London, Butterworth, 1983).

Capitanchik, D. and Eichenberg, R.C., *Defence and Public Opinion* (London, Routledge & Kegan Paul for Royal Institute of International Affairs, 1983).

Cohen, S. and Smouts, M.-C. (eds), *La Politique Extérieure de Valéry Giscard d'Estaing* (Paris, Fondation Nationale des Sciences Politiques, 1985).

Cohen, S.S. and Gourevitch, P.A., *France in the Troubled World Economy* (London, Butterworth, 1982).

Flynn, G. *et al.*, *The Internal Fabric of Western Security* (London, Croom Helm for Atlantic Institute, 1981).

Gerbet, P., *La construction de l'Europe* (Paris, Notre siècle, 1983).

Grosser, A., *Affaires Extérieures: La politique de la France 1944–84* (Paris, Flammarion, 1984).

Hanrieder, W.F. and Auton, G.P., *The Foreign Policies of West Germany, France and Britain* (Englewood Cliffs, N.J., Prentice Hall, 1980).

Hill, C. (ed.), *National Foreign Policies and European Political Co-operation* (London, Allen & Unwin for Royal Institute of International Affairs, 1983).

Hrbek, R. and Wessels, W., *Die Interessen der Bundesrepublik Deutschland in EG and EPZ* (Bonn, Europa Union Verlag, 1984).

Hu, Y.-S., *Europe under Stress: Convergence and Divergence in the European Community* (London, Butterworth for the Royal Institute of International Affairs, 1981).

Kitzinger, U., *Diplomacy and Persuasion: How Britain joined the Common Market* (London, Thames and Hudson, 1973).

Kolodziej, E.A., *French International Policy under de Gaulle* (Ithaca, N.Y., Cornell University Press, 1974).

Kruse, D.C., *Monetary Integration in Western Europe: EMU, EMS and Beyond* (London, Butterworth, 1980).

Ludlow, P., *The Making of the European Monetary System* (London, Butterworth, 1982).

May, B., *Kosten und Nutzen der deutschen EG-Mitgliedschaft* (Bonn, Europa Union Verlag, 1982).

Merlini, C. (ed.), *Economic Summits and Western Decision-Making* (London, Croom Helm for European Institute of Public Administration, 1984).

Pickles, D., *The Uneasy Entente: French Foreign Policy and Franco-British Misunderstandings* (London, Oxford University Press for Royal Institute of International Affairs, 1966).

Putnam, R. and Bayne, N., *Hanging Together: the 7 Power Summits* (London, Heinemann Educational Books for Royal Institute of International Affairs, 1984).

Rideau, J. *et al.*, *La France et les Communautés Européennes* (Paris, Librairie de droit et de jurisprudence, 1975).

Ruehl, L., *La Politique Militaire de la Cinquième République* (Paris, Fondation Nationale des Sciences Politiques, 1976).

de Schouteete, P., *La Coopération Politique Européene* (Brussels, Labor, 1980).

Simonian, H., *The Privileged Partnership: Franco-German Relations in the European Community 1969—84* (Oxford, Clarendon Press, 1985).

Story, J., 'Convergence at the Core. The Franco-German Relationship and its Implication for the Community' in M. Hodges and W. Wallace (eds), *Economic Divergence in the European Community* (London, Allen & Unwin for Royal Institute of International Affairs, 1981).

Taylor, T., *European Defence Cooperation* (London, Routledge & Kegan Paul for Royal Institute of International Affairs, 1984).

Tsoukalis, L., *The Politics and Economics of European Monetary Integration* (London, Allen & Unwin, 1971).

Wallace, H. *et al.*, *Policy-Making in the European Community* (Chichester and New York, Wiley, 1983).

Wallace, W., *The Foreign Policy Process in Britain* (London, Allen & Unwin for Royal Institute of International Affairs, 1975).

Wallace, W., 'Independence and Economic Interest: the Ambiguities of Foreign Policy' in P. Cerny and M. Schain (eds), *French Politics and Public Policy* (London, Methuen, 1980).

Wallace, W. (ed.), *Britain in Europe*, NIESR/PSI/RIIA Joint Studies in Public Policy (London, Heinemann Educational Books, 1980).

Wallace, W., *Britain's Bilateral Links Within Western Europe* (London, Routledge & Kegan Paul for Royal Institute of International Affairs, 1984).

Willis, F.R., *France, Germany and the New Europe, 1945–67*, 2nd ed. (London, Oxford University Press, 1968).

Ziebura, G., *Die deutsch-französischen Beziehungen seit 1945. Mythen und Realitäten* (Pfullingen, Neske, 1970).

Index